BREAKING THE SILENCE

**The secret mission of Eduard Schulte,
who brought the world news of
the Final Solution**

BREAKING THE SILENCE

The secret mission of Eduard Schulte,
who brought the world news of
the Final Solution

WALTER LAQUEUR &
RICHARD BREITMAN

THE BODLEY HEAD
LONDON

British Library Cataloguing
in Publication Data
Laqueur, Walter
Breaking the silence: the secret mission
of Eduard Schulte, who brought the world
news of the Final Solution.
1. Schulte, Eduard 2. World War, 1939–1945
—Secret service—Biography
I. Title II. Breitman, Richard
940.54'86'430924   D810.58.S3/

ISBN 0–370–31013–6

Printed in Great Britain for
The Bodley Head Ltd.
32 Bedford Square, London WC1B 3EL
by Redwood Burn Ltd, Trowbridge, Wilts
First published in Great Britain 1986

Contents

List of illustrations

Between pages 148 and 149

1. Eduard Schulte around 1930.
2. Giesche's zinc and lead facilities at Beuthen,
   on the German side of the German–Polish border.
3. A main entrance to the Auschwitz camp.
   The sign reads: 'Labour makes one free'.
4. Heinrich Himmler (right), head of the SS, with
   an I. G. Farben official at Auschwitz, July 18, 1942.
5. Wilhelm Canaris, head of the Abwehr.
6. General Hans Oster, another leader of
   anti-Nazi resistance.
7. Dr. Eduard Waetjen, whose phone call
   saved Schulte's life.
8. Hans Bernd Gisevius, who helped Schulte escape.
9. Allen Dulles, U.S. Intelligence chief in
   Switzerland, later head of the CIA.
10. Certificate of appreciation from the British
    Government, signed by Field Marshal Montgomery.

The authors are grateful to the following for permission to
reproduce the photographs:
Ruprecht Schulte for No. 1; Wiener Library for Nos. 4, 5 and 6;
Dr. Eduard Waetjen for No. 7; AP/Wide World Photos for No. 8;
Comet Photo Agency, Zurich for No. 9; Washington National
Record Center for No. 10.

Introduction

THE COMPANY CAR draws up outside the entrance to the Breslau central railway station. It is a hot, sunny midsummer day in 1942: July 29, to be precise (and this day deserves to be precisely recorded).

The chauffeur holds open the door while Dr. Eduard Schulte gets out of the car, a little awkwardly. He starts walking to the station entrance—a large man, with a commanding, forceful air, in spite of a pronounced limp. Carrying Dr. Schulte's luggage, the chauffeur accompanies him into the station.

The place is full of soldiers arriving for home leave or returning to the front, with civilians of all ages crowding into the trains. Schulte asks for a ticket to Zurich, and the clerk eyes him with curiosity. The clerk's reaction is understandable: the war is now in its third year, and while a great many people are buying tickets from this part of eastern Germany to Berlin or even Munich, the purchase of a ticket to neutral Switzerland has become a rare event.

With his luggage stored safely on the rack, Schulte takes his seat. He waits for the train to depart; the expression on his face reveals nothing of his thoughts. Perhaps he is reflecting on the turn of events that has brought him to make this journey, and wondering what they are thinking about him back at the office.

This latest trip to Switzerland has come without warning to his colleagues and employees, even to Fräulein Jerchel, his secretary of many years. But no one is particularly surprised, because Schulte is known for sometimes taking a trip on impulse. Perhaps, as someone in the office has suggested, a sudden complication has arisen in the negotiations with the Swiss companies with whom he is dealing. Or maybe he is going through another of those restless moods of his, when he will use any pretext to get away. Be that as it may, he is keeping the reason for his journey very much to himself.

This time, in truth, Eduard Schulte has been compelled to travel not by business nor by the demands of an impulsive nature, but by a startling, indeed horrifying, piece of information that came to his attention only twenty-four hours earlier. As a result, he has decided to undertake a rescue mission unprecedented in history—the rescue not of one person or a family but of millions of people.

· · ·

For Eduard Schulte, chief executive officer of Giesche, one of Germany's leading mining firms, July 17, 1942, started much like any other working day; he began it at his desk in the Breslau office studying the newspapers. He looked briefly at the reports from the war fronts, which said that there was fighting at El Alamein and that German forward units had reached the Donets river in Russia; and he read that the United States had broken off relations with Finland. He was about to call his secretary when Otto Fitzner, the director of production, entered. Lowering his voice, Fitzner said that a very important visitor was expected later that day. "Who is it?" Schulte asked. "Himmler." Schulte was startled and apprehensive until Fitzner assured him that the leader of the SS and chief of all German police forces had no intention of inspecting the Giesche works. He had some important business in the vicinity, apparently in Auschwitz. Fitzner could not tell Schulte more at the moment.

Schulte had no reason to disbelieve Fitzner. His deputy had joined the Nazi Party before it had become fashionable to do so, and was on close personal terms with many of its leaders. Fitzner was always the first to get news of this kind. He even knew Heinrich Himmler, one of the three or four most powerful men in Germany at the time, and certainly the most feared.

Himmler looked like a caricature of a secondary-school teacher, a frail man (and a hypochondriac), whose outward appearance was as remote from the Nordic ideal of manly beauty as that of Goebbels or Hitler. He was not a flamboyant war hero like Göring, not a brilliant and powerful orator like Goebbels, nor an organizer of genius. He was a man seemingly without qualities. But this insignificant creature was one of the very few people implicitly trusted by Hitler, to whom he was "the most faithful of the faithful." Hitler made him head of the SS, the Nazi elite organization, which only the best physical specimens of German youth and those most devoted to Nazi doctrine were permitted to join. He eventually became minister of the interior and was, among many other things, in charge of the Gestapo and of all concentration camps. He was the ultimate arbiter of life and death in Nazi Germany.

Himmler, it was known, did not like to be away from his desk and home for long periods. What took him to Auschwitz, a little town that had been Polish prior to 1939 and Austrian before the First World War? It had no industrial importance, nor was it distinguished in any other way. An important trading center in the early Middle Ages, it had somehow been bypassed by the great industrial revolution. Auschwitz had stagnated and become a backwater. The fishermen continued to cast their nets in the small lakes around Auschwitz as they had done since time immemorial, but mining and heavy industry were located elsewhere. There was a concentration camp in Auschwitz, consisting mainly of old Austrian army barracks, but even this camp was not particularly distinguished. There were dozens of such camps in Greater Germany, and until 1942 some were considerably bigger. Himmler, furthermore, had never shown particular interest in inspecting them. In fact, he regarded this as the least pleasant part of his duties, and usually avoided it.

Schulte's curiosity grew when he was told the following day that Himmler's was not a short inspection tour of an hour or two; the head of the SS was staying on. The visit, as Schulte saw it, did not make sense.

News in the Upper Silesian mining region traveled fast. On the evening of July 17 Schulte already knew a little more about the visit, for on that evening, Himmler attended a dinner party given by Bracht, the Nazi Gauleiter, or party chief, of Upper Silesia. After dinner in Auschwitz the party moved on to the Gauleiter's villa in a forest near Kattowitz. The villa happened to belong to the company of which Schulte was general manager.

The spacious and modern villa had been built by Giesche for the use of its American directors (as the result of a complex financing scheme in the 1920s, Giesche's Polish operations were under American management). It was equipped with such luxuries as a golf course and a swimming pool, almost unheard of at the time anywhere in Europe, let alone in that backward corner of Polish Silesia. The villa had been loaned to the Gauleiter for Giesche's own protection, for after the annexation by Germany of Polish Upper Silesia in 1939, there was a constant threat that the Giesche holdings in occupied Poland would be taken over by one of the big German state conglomerates, such as the Hermann Göring Werke. The Giesche directors tried to think of various ways to avert this, and they bought the good will of Bracht by putting this wonderful villa at his disposal. The Gauleiter had received the gift with gratitude mixed with suspicion. Dr. Albrecht Jung, legal adviser of Giesche, stipulated that Bracht would receive the villa for the period of his incumbency.

"Do you think I shall get the sack?" asked the distrustful Bracht, a renegade member of the Catholic Center Party who had become a fanatical Nazi.

Jung did some rapid thinking and replied: "Surely one of these days Herr Gauleiter will be promoted to an even more important position."

On July 17 a transport of Jews arrived in Auschwitz (from Holland), and Himmler witnessed the gassing of 449 persons in Bunker 2, his first such experience. He then visited the experimental plant and laboratory and inspected the building of a dam. That evening Himmler had dinner in Auschwitz and later dropped into Bracht's villa in Gieschewald. Some of the details of Himmler's inspection tour were not discussed in front of the ladies at the villa. Himmler, against his habit, had some red wine and smoked a cigar.

The Auschwitz camps were almost hermetically sealed off from the outside world. By 1943 a curious German railway official was reported to have said that Auschwitz surely must have become one of the biggest cities in Europe: so many people entered it, and no one ever left! But in July 1942, the trains were just beginning to roll. Still, even then it was clear that something out of the ordinary was going on; the head of the German police had obviously come for a purpose.

The management of Giesche was interested in Auschwitz and not just because zinc was mined there. It was deeply suspicious of the intentions of the SS, whose appetite for seizing some of the land belonging to Giesche was second only to that of the Hermann Göring Werke. Some of this land was wanted for Himmler's agricultural experiments, other parts for con-

centration camps or yet other purposes unknown at the time.
Himmler had been in Auschwitz once before, on March 1,
1941, for a shorter visit, also accompanied by Gauleiter Bracht
and the local senior police chiefs. On that previous visit he had
given orders to expand the camp so that it could accommodate
thirty thousand inmates instead of the few thousands—mainly
Poles—there at the time. He also wanted a second, much bigger camp to be built—according to rumor—for prisoners
of war. And lastly, buildings were to be put up for
I. G. Farben, the big chemical trust. In the year that had
passed since his visit there had been much construction.
Then new orders had been given to build even larger installations.

Within a week and a half after Himmler's second visit to
Auschwitz, Schulte became aware of the purpose of all this activity. He found out that an important decision had been made
by Hitler and was about to be executed. Schulte, unlike his
deputy Fitzner, was not a Nazi. In fact, unknown to all but
those closest to him, he was consumed by a passionate hatred of
Nazism. He was utterly convinced that the Nazis would bring
about the ruin of Germany. He thought the Nazi leadership capable of committing any conceivable crime or folly. But the secret Nazi plans for Auschwitz and other camps that became
known to a few people during the last week of July were so
horrendous that even Schulte, who in his circle of close friends
would refer to Hitler as "that madman," hesitated for a moment. Surely, they would not dare . . .

The news Schulte learned shed new and ghastly light on
the true fate of the Jews. He had listened, like everyone else, to
the speeches in which Hitler had promised that he would eliminate European Jewry. But the term "elimination" could be interpreted in various ways. It could mean, for instance,
resettling them in Madagascar, as some had proposed. Almost
no one, not even a committed anti-Nazi like Schulte, believed
that "elimination" should be understood literally.

· · ·

No one had seen a written order. Instructions were passed on
by word of mouth on the basis of the "need-to-know" principle,
which now, more than forty years later, makes it difficult to establish with absolute certainty who learned what from whom
and at what date. All we do know for certain is that among
those who learned the secret one exceptionally courageous man

took the next train to Zurich to warn the Jews and the rest of the world that measures must be taken to prevent the mass murder. Why did Eduard Schulte act as he did, risking his life, while all others kept silent?

CHAPTER ONE

Düsseldorf and Breslau

The child is father of the man: from an early age, Eduard Schulte displayed impulsiveness, some⁺imes verging on rashness—but also the courage and will to cope with the consequences of that side of his nature. (More often than not, his impulsiveness would issue in acts of generosity.) A traumatic experience that he underwent at the age of eighteen epitomizes this truth about him.

In 1909, upon his graduation from school in Düsseldorf, Schulte decided to train for a position in industry. He was apprenticed to a company specializing in geological drilling for industrial purposes; the company was located in one of the suburbs. One day, working in the office, he saw through the window a number of workmen trying without success to push a heavily loaded railway car into a siding. Eduard, a strong young man, and always willing to lend a hand, jumped to help them. He slipped in a water puddle that he had not seen; his left leg got caught under one of the heavy wheels and was crushed.

He was rushed to the nearest hospital, but for days it was not clear whether he would live. His left foot was amputated, but then the bone was infected and there had to be further operations. Eventually his entire leg was amputated. He pulled through only owing to his iron constitution. But the psychological shock must have been terrible. A young man, active in many sports, a passionate hunter about to join one of the elite regiments, such as the 11th Hussars (the "dancing hussars"), like most of his contemporaries, had become a cripple overnight. There were the enormous handicaps that would face him in life—it would be a long time until an artificial leg could be fitted. There was also the social stigma attached to being crippled. Some, no doubt, would have become withdrawn facing such dismal prospects. Eduard Schulte was made of sterner stuff: he decided to ignore his infirmity.

· · ·

Napoleon said about Düsseldorf "C'est petit Paris," but when Eduard Reinhold Karl Schulte was born there on January 4, 1891, any resemblance to Paris was purely accidental. Düsseldorf had grown by leaps and bounds during the second half of the century. It was the seat of many administrative offices, state, provincial, and private, but it was still better known for its churches, its picture galleries, and its beer than for its industry. It was a comfortable city, neither too big nor too small, with many parks and greenery, and fine views to Cologne from the roofs of the higher buildings.

The Schultes, an old Westphalian family, had originally come from a small town on the Ruhr called Wetter, still today one of the nicer places in that industrial region. Other Schultes had come from Wengern, also on the Ruhr. Their first ancestor about whom details are known was called Detmar and lived in the seventeenth century. Of his sons and grandsons, some became farmers, others went into mining, and some turned to trade.

The grandfather of the hero of this story, also named Eduard Schulte, was born in 1817 and died in 1890. He had originally studied medicine, but his father died before he could graduate, and since he was the firstborn he had to provide for

the family. He went into the book business, training with Baedeker, the famous guidebook publishers, then located in Essen,
where they still maintain a very good bookshop. Subsequently
Eduard established a publishing house called Buddaeus in
Düsseldorf, specializing in art books. He also founded an art
gallery in the Alleestrasse, now Heinrich Heine Allee.

By the last decade of the nineteenth century, the Schulte
picture gallery had become one of the city's major attractions.
Baedeker of 1892 (the year after the protagonist of our story
was born) devoted several lines to it. The gallery specialized in
pictures by the local school of painters, founded by Peter Cornelius, which mostly dealt with religious subjects and landscapes. But it always had a good selection of older German
masters, and in later years, branches of the gallery were opened
in Cologne and in Berlin, where it acquired the Palais
Raedler—Unter den Linden 75—one of the best addresses in
town. It expanded and prospered; the emperor and members of
the imperial family were among its clients.

The founder of the gallery had a son who was also named
Eduard Schulte (1856–1937). He married Erna Berger, ten
years his junior, the daughter of an architect. The family was
by then well-off, partly as the result of marriage. The marriage
contract between Eduard II and Erna, signed in 1887 in
Kreuznach (where the Bergers had a small private bank), was a
lengthy document showing that their families were people of
substance. The Schultes were passionate hunters, a sport limited at the time mainly to the aristocracy, the upper middle
class, and poachers. They kept a pack of setters and pointers. A
family chronicle also reports a proclivity for collecting gold
watches.

The younger Eduard Schulte studied mining technology
but preferred the freedom of a consultant to a permanent job in
government or industry. This involved much travel, sometimes
to faraway countries. Eduard Schulte II spent as much time on
his hobbies as on his professional work. He was a collector of
weapons and a serious amateur photographer who developed
and enlarged his own snapshots. He was a do-it-yourself man,
manufacturing not only the bullets for his hunting rifles but
also his own hair cream of white and yellow petroleum jelly.

He was a good-natured man with a wide circle of friends,
but without much energy or ambition. He loved his children,
but took no great interest in their education. This was the responsibility of his wife, a striking woman with beautiful hair,

long enough to sit on, clever, widely read, full of initiative, and, by and large, the stronger character. Mama (the stress was on the second *a*) was tough and even domineering, and kept the unquestioned respect of the children all her life. There were four of them—Erna, the oldest; Reinhold, a boy who died in infancy; and Eduard and Oskar.

Eduard Schulte II had inherited the paternal home at Klosterstrasse 18. His two brothers took over the art gallery. The house was a stately home with a big gate that carriages could enter when the Schultes were entertaining. There was a smaller door for daily use. Eduard Schulte III shared a room on the first floor with his younger brother, Oskar. From the boys' point of view the location was ideal; their school, the city *Gymnasium* (high school), was the building opposite. They would wait until the school bell rang for classes, sprint across the street, and still arrive in time.

To run a house of this size, the Schultes, as was customary in those days in such circles, employed several servants, a female cook, a male servant, and also Lottchen, a lady who took the children out for walks when they were small. There was a big garden and hence the need for a gardener; the boys loved the fountain and the plants in the basin. In one corner of the garden the Schultes kept sundry gymnastic apparatus. Once a week Herr Wölk would come, a former sergeant major who gave private lessons to the sons and daughters of those who could afford it. Young Eduard excelled at the horizontal bars and the high jump.

The father belonged to an exclusive club and would have a glass of wine there with friends before dinner. Once a week the Schultes would attend the theater (which under Louise Dumont was one of the best in Germany at the time) or go out for dinner. They would spend the school holidays almost invariably in the Black Forest, never outside Germany. On warm Sunday afternoons the family would walk in the Hofgarten, Düsseldorf's impressive big park, or cross the Rhine and have a "*Platz*" (a raisin cake) in one of the many coffeehouses of Oberkastel. If it was an especially fine day, they would take the steamer and go down to Kaiserswerth, a much beloved destination for excursions.

The Schultes' passion for hunting has been mentioned. The family owned extensive grounds just outside the city in the direction of Oberhausen. A forester kept the grounds in good order, and also the substantial hunting lodge, which looked more like a small castle. It could accommodate fifteen or even twenty people in winter. Hunting was a way of life. Young Eduard learned this way from his father, who took hunting very seriously. The elder Schulte broke off relations with his best friend after the unfortunate man accidentally killed a doe.

The Schultes were good Protestants, but not overzealous. They disliked excessive religious observance. The family would gather on Christmas Eve in Uncle Hermann's big home (Hermann was one of the brothers who owned the gallery). Festivities started in the afternoon with oysters and champagne; young Eduard, who became something of a gourmet in later life, did not then appreciate such delicacies.

Religion was not discussed at home, certainly not in front of the children; nor was politics. Like most of their friends, the Schultes were conservative, and voted for the right-wing National People's Party after 1918. But theirs was an enlightened and tolerant conservatism.* They subscribed to the *Frankfurter Zeitung*, the leading liberal daily newspaper, if only because its financial columns were superior to those of other newspapers. Their friends in town were lawyers, bankers, physicians, and, above all, painters. Their next-door neighbor was Andreas Achenbach (1815–1910), one of the most celebrated local artists; when he drove out in his carriage the commotion would affect the whole neighborhood—it was almost a royal event. The painters were the uncrowned kings of Düsseldorf, and the Schultes, thanks to their business connections, had close social ties with them.

There were no startling or dramatic events to report from Eduard III's youth in a self-contained, affluent, and very well regulated household. There was no kindergarten, as in our day. Little children of the middle and upper classes spent most of their time in large upstairs nurseries, neither trained nor entertained. In the Schulte household the nursery furniture was old and massive, the toys indestructible: they included a rocking horse and, above all, a large collection of clockwork trains, very well made, with enameled dark-green surfaces on the locomotives and brass trim. Thirty-five years later Eduard Schulte's sons were to inherit some of these toys.

---

* They instinctively rejected Nazism in later years and broke off relations with Oskar Berger, one of Erna's relatives, who gave financial support to Hitler. Such behavior was quite remarkable in a family in which politics played no central role.

There was sincere affection in the family, but its expression
was strictly regulated. Behavior was low-key; great emphasis
was put on saying and doing the right thing. To make an exhibition of oneself or to commit a social *faux pas* was a cardinal
sin. Eduard Schulte's motto in later life became "*Anstand und
Würde*" (Decency and Dignity), and this had a great deal to do
with values inculcated in his early years. But it is also true that
the great effort which went into keeping the quiet, imperturb-
able façade, the fear of deviating from decorum and established norms of behavior, caused much anxiety and stress. His
sister was four years older, his brother four years younger, and
these differences in age did not make for great intimacy. But
there was still much affection in the family, especially between
the two brothers.

We know that Eduard read the usual books, among them
Robinson Crusoe and James Fenimore Cooper's *The Deerslayer*. He
was especially fond of a handsome edition of Theodore Roosevelt's African safari stories with large glossy pictures. But he
did not acquire his basic values mainly from books. Moral im-
peratives were part of the general ethos of the family, based on
a mixture of enlightened Protestantism and a classic-humanis-
tic tradition. Eduard was a keen observer of human nature
from an early age, and his opinions, once formed, were deep-
seated.

A severe and joyless childhood then, seething with suppressed conflicts? This was not how Eduard Schulte would remember it in later years. On the contrary, he considered that
his childhood had been very happy. A photograph of Eduard
aged twelve or thirteen shows an earnest, good-looking young
man who knows what he wants, lively, intelligent, unsmiling,
perhaps slightly skeptical: he is wearing gaiters; knee breeches,
or knickerbockers; and the cap obligatory for schoolboys in
those days.

Eduard went for three years to elementary school and then
to a *Gymnasium*, a German institution for which there is no
equivalent in the English-speaking world. A *Gymnasium* has
nothing in common with the sports grounds in ancient Greece
where young people engaged in various forms of physical culture. Throughout the nineteenth century, *Gymnasiums* were the
only German schools whose graduates could go on to a university. Latin was studied at ten, Greek a few years later. In young
Eduard's case, interest in the culture of ancient Rome and
Greece was not pronounced; he read Tacitus, Ovid, and even

Homer in the original, yet we find no reference to these classical authors in his later life. The curriculum of the German schools had lost touch with the real world, and it was only during the years of Schulte's youth that reforms were introduced such as the granting of (almost) equal status to modern languages and science. Eduard still belonged to the generation that could quote the beginning of the *Odyssey* by heart but did not have any proficiency in French and English. Study was a serious business: the Düsseldorf municipal *Gymnasium* that Eduard attended had a great reputation for academic standards, *esprit de corps*, and discipline. Together with the Graue Kloster (Gray Monastery) in Berlin it was thought to be among the very best in Germany.

Eduard Schulte's marks were excellent in all subjects. Years later his younger brother, much to his dismay, would be told by his teachers to take Eduard as an example. Early on Eduard showed signs of being an "achiever," oriented toward tangible results. He had the ability to dissect a problem with lightning speed, almost intuitively, and to express the essentials, verbally or on paper, with great clarity. And as he grew up he did this in such an authoritative way that his colleagues and even his superiors readily accepted his leadership.

Young Schulte needed achievement and acclaim, but he was an eminently practical young man. He did not enjoy the limelight; personal confrontation was not a game; competition not an end in itself but always subordinated to some purpose. The great realist, however, was also in his way a dreamer. He could imagine himself, as he grew up, the winner in a tricky business transaction, the diplomat getting his way in a crisis. Eduard Schulte was that rare exception, the boy who always knew what he wanted to achieve in life, who never wavered in his convictions, and who regarded everything that did not bring him nearer his target as a waste of time. He wanted to be a pioneer, a captain of industry, and to acquire wealth.

These were not unnatural ambitions, for Eduard Schulte's youth coincided with the vigorous, at times hectic, development of his native city and the region in which it stood. During the decade before and after the turn of the century, Düsseldorf developed more quickly than at any time before. True, the old city was still there with its quiet thoroughfares, its many inns, and its special kind of cheese (called *Halve Hahn*—half a chicken). The natives were still celebrating Carnival for three days, shouting "*Alaaf!*" at the top of their voices, masquerading in fancy dress, and drinking more than was good for them. The children participated in the St. Martin's Day procession in November, following the knight on a white horse riding through the old city to the town hall. To earn a few pfennigs, street urchins demonstrated their proficiency in cartwheeling—another hallowed local custom.

But a new Düsseldorf was rapidly emerging. The changes could be seen every year, almost every month. The year Eduard was born, Düsseldorf got its new central railway station. When he was eight years old the Oberkastel bridge was completed; up to that date the parts of the city on the left side of the Rhine could be reached only by ferry. In the same year Wilhelm Marx was first elected mayor of the city, and under his leadership it expanded in every direction. In the year 1900 Düsseldorf boasted a quarter of a million inhabitants. In 1902 a big industrial exhibition was opened. It was attended by the emperor (who did not like the city) and five million visitors. No German town had ever hosted a show of such magnitude. When Eduard was eighteen a Zeppelin made its first appearance over the city and the first major department store (Tiets, now Kaufhof) was founded. By 1913 Düsseldorf had an airport of sorts. These and other new developments were bound to kindle the imagination of a young man of vision and initiative.

School was one of the focal points of a young German at that time; the other was the family and one's circle of friends. Much has been made in later years of the terrible oppressiveness of this period in German life, of the tyranny of teachers and parents alike, the utter lack of freedom, of any possibility of self-expression, of being oneself. It is true that some very sensitive young people did suffer, complaining about suffocation. Some of the more misguided souls were to welcome the outbreak of the First World War as a liberation. But in truth, the order and discipline were more a matter of form than of substance. If young people observed certain conventions, they were pretty well left alone.

Young Eduard Schulte, as far as can be established, was hardly ever depressed or bored. The days were not long enough for the things he wanted to do. He played a great deal of tennis, and in winter the Schulte boys had table-tennis tournaments in their house. His closest friend was a young man named Poensgen, the son of a local doctor; he also went quite frequently to the home of a Jewish classmate named Herbert Simons, the son of a banker. It was in the Simons home that Eduard first learned that Jews, at least some of them, kept certain religious dietary laws, a subject that fascinated him. Together the two friends would explore Düsseldorf and its environs on their bicycles and observe the many changes taking place in the city.

Louischen should not be forgotten; she was his first love, about whom, unfortunately, we know very little. He met her at a *Tanzstunde* (dancing lesson), the obligatory social grace that once played such a crucial role in the life of young Germans. Louise's father had a country estate in the neighborhood. The Schultes liked her and would have welcomed her as a daughter-in-law. But Eduard had no wish to contemplate settling down at a time when he had not even started to make his mark in the world.

Eduard's partial disablement as a result of the accident to his leg in no way lessened his determination to get on. He became a trainee in the Darmstädter, one of Germany's leading banks; he quickly mastered the essentials of banking and showed great flair for the stock market. He seemed to know instinctively which shares would go up in value and began to offer unsolicited advice to his father, criticizing him for investing too cautiously. The father resented the son's recommendations and refused to accept them. He would have fared better had he listened: in 1919, at the worst possible time, the parental home in the Klosterstrasse had to be sold, and the parents moved to a house in the country.

Eduard soon realized that he needed a law degree; everyone who was someone was "Herr Doktor." But quite typically he did not want to waste a number of years studying theoretical subjects that were of no interest to him. He enrolled for two semesters at Cologne and Bonn universities, but seems to have attended only a few lectures. He took on a private tutor named Bechstein, who would impart to him after working hours the very minimum of knowledge expected from a graduate. Then he registered for one semester at Erlangen, a university known at the time for turning out graduates quickly and without putting too many obstacles in their way. In December 1912, at the age of twenty-one, he acquired the title of Juris Doctor with a dissertation on a rather obscure aspect of stock-exchange law that had to do with stamp duties on the purchase and sale of shares.

One more episode from this period must be mentioned. In 1909, having graduated from school but before entering a university, Schulte went to London for a couple of months, staying with acquaintances of his family. We know little about what he did in England other than that he acquired some rudiments of a language he never came to know very well. But it is a matter of record that one fine summer Sunday morning he went to Kensington Gardens and, at the Round Pond, met a young lady, a strawberry blonde, several years older than himself, also a visitor from Germany. A conversation ensued, and it appeared that Clara was taking courses at the University of London. Her special interest was a writer of whom Eduard (and indeed few other Germans) had never heard, Charlotte Brontë. They did not meet again in London and the incident would not have been worth mentioning but for the fact that, eight years later, in 1917, Eduard Schulte married the very same lady, Clara Ebert, from Bütow in Pomerania.

In the spring of 1913 Schulte left home and moved on to Berlin, where he became a junior employee of the Berlin Handelsgesellschaft, one of the biggest banks in the land. Among his peers were some of the people who were later to play an important part in his professional career and, in some instances also, in his private life. The Handelsgesellschaft had been founded in the middle of the nineteenth century but became a bank of major importance only under Carl Fürstenberg, a Jew who was Germany's most outstanding banker in the pre-1914 period. Fürstenberg co-operated closely with the mining industry, and he was a pioneer in the field of business relations with United States companies. The importance of the *Amerika Geschäft* (business with America) seems to have impressed Eduard Schulte early on and may account for his great interest in business relations with America in later years. Thus even after the Second World War had broken out, Schulte tried to enlist the help of Otto Jeidels, a former director of the Handelsgesellschaft and a contemporary of his, for pursuing negotiations with American firms. Jeidels, a Jew, had left Germany after Hitler took power, and joined Lazard Frères in New York.

For a while Eduard shared rooms with his brother Oskar in Berlin. He also saw much of his cousin Hermann Schulte, who was to inherit the picture gallery. Then in 1916, his services were requested by the office of supply in the Prussian War Ministry. This office had been established by Walther Rathenau, later foreign minister in the Weimar Republic, who was murdered in 1922 by terrorists of the extreme right. With raw materials in short supply, Schulte found himself concerned with the production of animal and vegetable oils and fats in a department of great significance for the war economy. He showed outstanding qualities of leadership and within a few months, though only in his twenties, he became head of the office responsible for the production and sale of soap in Germany. He held this position until well after the war, for the system of rationing and allocations continued beyond the armistice in November 1918.

Eduard established useful contacts with Germany's leading manufacturers of fats and oils, and it was not by accident that he entered this industry in 1921, first in Berlin, where his sons Wolfgang and Ruprecht were born in 1919 and 1920 respectively, and then at the early age of thirty as general manager of Sunlicht soap in Mannheim. Sunlicht was a German subsidiary of Sunlight, founded in 1889, and a leader in its field. Its Mannheim plant was of substantial size.

The family had a spacious house in a cul-de-sac off the Rheinauer Chaussee. It was ideal for growing boys, with its large garden full of cherry trees and wall fruit. On Sundays, they would go for a walk or Eduard would take the boys boating on the Rhine. Bringing up the children was largely in the hands of "Aunt Edith," a friend of Clara's—until Eduard turned against Edith. Eduard was an effective manager, but already in his Mannheim days he began to show signs of the restlessness that would become so pronounced in later years. Over and above the necessary business trips to the head office in Berlin or to Hamburg, he would convince himself of the need for at least one other trip a week, and the reason was not, as might be supposed, an urge to escape from home. He was a man of action, and if there was no action, he got bored. After three years, Sunlicht was taken over by Lever Brothers, which brought in its own manager. And so, shortly after the end of the great inflation in which his parents lost their estate, Eduard Schulte found himself unemployed.

He was offered a high position in the Bavarian civil service, but the salary was only a fraction of what he had been paid in Mannheim and the prospects for further advancement were poor. Schulte did not remain unemployed for long. One day in a Berlin street, he met an old friend of the family who told him that Giesche, a big eastern German corporation, and the leading nonferrous metal producer, was looking for a general manager. Schulte knew nothing about nonferrous metals, but he did not lack self-confidence. He wrote a letter of application,

lobbied a bit, was invited for a series of interviews, made a favorable impression, and within a few months found himself,
not quite thirty-five years of age, at the head of one of Germany's oldest, biggest, and most conservative corporations.
Giesche was in fact so old that its official history, published in
1904, needed three volumes to cover the bare essentials.

The story of Georg von Giesche's Heirs—this was its official
name—will occupy us later on. Suffice it here to quote from a
report published in *The New York Times* in 1926, the year after
Schulte joined Giesche, that it was "one of the oldest industrial
undertakings in the world and one of the most valuable in Europe." Before the First World War its value was estimated at
more than $100 million. Following the war it was split into two
parts, one in Poland, the other in Germany. Giesche engaged in
the mining, smelting, and refining of zinc. and, to a much lesser
extent, coal, lead, and copper. But it also manufactured various
chemicals, dyes, viscose—an early synthetic substance—and it
maintained basalt quarries, produced bricks and pottery, and
owned land and a fleet of river barges.

The headquarters of Polish Giesche was in Katowice (Kattowitz to the Germans), whereas German Giesche's head office
was in Breslau, where it had been located since the days of the
Holy Roman Empire. It was there, at Schweidnitzer Stadtgra-
ben 26, that Eduard Schulte would work for the next eighteen
years, indeed to the day that he took asylum in Switzerland.

Breslau (today located in Poland and called Wroclaw) is in
the Oder valley. It was the biggest (620,000 inhabitants) and
the most important city of eastern Germany and, its admirers
would add, also the most beautiful. It had a university, several
theaters, daily newspapers, big parks, an airport, railway stations, and a zoo. Among the tourist attractions were the city's
magnificent baroque buildings as well as its monumental modern structures, such as the Jahrhunderthalle (1913) with the
largest cupola and the biggest organ in the world. Concerned
no doubt that he might be in danger of neglecting the many
opportunities Breslau had to offer, Schulte's friends would
point out to him that it provided a very active social life and,
generally speaking, a most *gemütlich* atmosphere. If he was a
philosopher he could join the Kant or Schopenhauer societies,
as a Mason he would find any number of lodges, and as a
gourmet he could enjoy *Breslauer Korn* (a kind of *Schnaps*) or
Schlesisches Himmelreich, a dish consisting mainly of baked fruit.

In actual fact, Breslau did not differ that much from other

cities in East-Central Europe. The streets in the older parts of the town (it had been a bishopric since about the year 1000) were rather narrow, the façades of the houses resembled one another, as did the somber dark-gray blocks of flats of the working-class quarters. There were large factories and markets. In brief, it was a city of work, not of *savoir-vivre*. High society was not much in evidence; there were no royal merchants as in Hamburg, and Breslau had fewer artists than Munich. The university had been established fairly recently, and the city had not produced any important politician with the exception of Ferdinand Lassalle, who happened to be a Jew and a Socialist. (When the Nazis came to power they changed the name of Lassalle Square back to Karlsplatz.) There were some fine actors and musicians, but they usually went off to Berlin as soon as they had made their mark. There had been some outstanding writers and poets, but that was after the Thirty Years' War, centuries ago.

Yet despite the ugliness, the relative poverty—eastern Germany had always lagged behind the west—and the lack of fresh air, Breslau was on the whole an optimistic city, at least before the First World War. Progress was in evidence; technical advances were made almost every year. But when the war was over, the province of Posen and parts of Upper Silesia had to be ceded to Poland, and Breslau lost much of its hinterland. There was a feeling of stagnation, of narrowed horizons and limited prospects, though economic progress continued on a modest scale despite inflation and the world economic crisis. But there was the danger that Breslau, once an important center, had become a dead end.

This then was the city in which Eduard Schulte made his home in the middle 1920s, so very different from Düsseldorf, Mannheim, and Berlin. There were reasons for doubting whether a son of the Rhineland would easily adapt to his new environment. But Schulte was an extrovert who readily adjusted to new conditions. He took quickly to his new responsibilities.

When he looked out of the window of his office he saw the city promenade, which had been built alongside the city moat; Breslau had once been a fortress, but on Napoleon's orders the walls and towers had been torn down. The town gardeners had made this their masterpiece. In the moat ducks could be seen, and also white and black swans. In the winter the ice skaters took over, in the summer there were open air concerts with an early version of *son et lumière* and occasional fireworks. A wealthy merchant had donated money for building a magnificent atrium and observation tower just opposite the Giesche office. For a fleeting moment one could imagine oneself in Florence. In brief, the view from the window of the youngest top manager of any major German corporation was not at all bad.

One entered the Giesche building through a big gate which led to the administrative offices headed by Herr von Bülow. Also on street level were the legal offices (presided over by Dr. Jung), the archives, and the library. On the first floor through a frosted glass door one entered Schulte's office. The room had high ceilings and big windows. The atmosphere was strictly businesslike: there were few pictures but a great many drawings and photographs of mines and factories.

In the upper floors there were guest rooms where the Schulte family lived for a while. But the two boys were more intrigued by the carpentry shop in the back yard than by the dignified, staid business offices in front where, it seemed, nothing much of interest ever happened.

The family moved to Ahornallee 28 in Kleinburg, the wealthy southern suburb. The building had been bought by the corporation. There was a broad staircase and some ten rooms on several floors, a winter garden, a wine cellar, and a substantial outside garden. The doors were heavy, the corridors dark. In the entrance hall there was an enormous vase of Far Eastern provenance. Schulte got very angry when guests used it as an ashtray. There was yet another garage and an apartment for the chauffeur. The rooms were painted white or off-white; the decor had been designed to Clara's instructions. Eduard Schulte was a passionate hunter, but on his wife's firm orders the antlers were banished to the upper rooms, out of sight.

The house was well located; a few minutes away was the *Südpark* (today *Park Poludnia*), the finest in town for restful walks. Even nearer was the Kleinburg school attended by Wolfgang and Ruprecht, and the Black-Yellow tennis club.

Eduard Schulte was now at the beginning of a brilliant career. Well over six feet tall, he kept himself erect, moving quickly despite his disability. He was a lively and energetic man, full of ideas, the kind of individual who would not easily give up even in adversity. He had presence, that quality which is so difficult to define and even more difficult to explain. It was said that when he entered a room full of people he would immediately attract attention. There was the feeling of *voilà un homme*. His most pronounced facial features were his bushy eyebrows. He was a little vain, and when the first signs of baldness appeared, he had his head shaved to a crew cut, which did not really add to his appearance; much later his second wife succeeded in persuading him to revert to a more conventional hair style. He tried to keep fit and had a punching ball in his bedroom in Breslau. He practiced weight lifting not only at home but even when staying in his Berlin hotel suite. He was more interested in the physical than the intellectual education of the boys; they were paid a few pfennings for each short arm stretch on a horizontal bar. He was fussy about dental hygiene but on the whole ignored minor illnesses. He dressed well but not conspicuously. He brought back material (usually dark blue) for suits and coats from his travels to London and also an occasional Homburg and Borsalino. But he did not believe in formal dress, such as morning coats, smoking jackets, and tails; these seemed to him out of date. He also loathed the hand-kissing still prevalent at the time among the lower eastern German gentry. He was an orderly man but not pedantic, quite fearless, basically impatient but able to restrain himself if need be, a man of strong likes and dislikes but quite capable of dissimulating his feelings.

His attitude toward money was that of the Rhineland's upper middle class; one had money but did not boast about it. One lived well but not ostentatiously. One ought to be a member of the best clubs in Breslau and Berlin, but one never wasted money.

Schulte lost a great deal of money in the Wall Street crash of 1929. Having been in America the year before, he had unfortunately invested in American shares. The bad news reached him while he was hunting on his estate in Pomerania and he took it in his stride. He was making a great deal of money in those years. Not only did he have a very substantial salary; there were also large bonuses whenever he succeeded in concluding advantageous business deals.

In a reasonably good year Schulte made 200,000 marks, $50,000 according to the exchange rate then, which would be close to half a million dollars today. The money he saved he usually invested wisely.

He was a quick-witted man, though with limited cultural interests. He preferred hunting to reading or attending concerts and exhibitions. The Schultes' first radio set was bought only in 1928. Clara had argued, not without justice, that the children would spend most of their time outdoors if the Schultes did not make this concession to modern times. Schulte put the wireless set well out of the way on the windowsill of his room. In later years, when foreign stations became an important source of information, he would change his attitude toward the radio.

Having a country estate was part of one's station in society. The Schultes had a weekend house some forty miles south of Breslau. But in Pomerania, not far from where Clara Schulte grew up, Schulte bought a large estate that consisted mainly of open ground, forest, and some meadows, where potatoes and rye were cultivated. Called Gisolke, Schulte later expanded it by acquiring an estate called Klein Voldikov. It was a good place for hunting and inviting business associates for a long weekend. Schulte became very attached to this place and also to Herr Kaat, tenant of the agricultural portion of the estate who had once saved Schulte's life: while deer stalking, the industrialist had fallen into a bog and would have drowned but for Kaat's prompt action.

Schulte enjoyed his food, but did not smoke, and drank no hard liquor. He had an occasional glass of wine, but the bottles in the cellar were mainly for his guests. The cases of Scotch and bourbon left in his room at the Waldorf in New York by his American business associates were wasted. On the other hand, he would take the members of the Giesche executive, after a long and exhausting meeting (and Schulte was known for making business meetings long and exhausting), to a popular nearby inn where they had beer and considerable quantities of sausage.

It would be wrong to say that Eduard Schulte was not a good family man. But work was more important to him than family, and since his working day was roughly sixteen hours, he did not see his parents or his brother and sister very often after the move to Breslau. He took an interest in the education of his children only as they were growing up. He would not join his wife and children on summer or winter excursions to the Giant Mountains; by the second day the boredom would have been intolerable. But then Clara was very much living her own life, and it is doubtful whether she would have liked a husband who took too close an interest in what she was doing.

Clara's father had been a grain dealer, and while the

Schultes were financially and socially on a higher level than the
Eberts, she felt herself intellectually the equal of her husband,
if not superior to him. She had studied at Greifswald, the Sorbonne, and in London, at a time when such studies by young
girls were a rarity. She was an early, though not an extreme,
feminist. One of her heroines was Madame Curie; Clara had
attended her lectures in Paris, even though not particularly interested in radium and radiology. She cared mainly for literature, history, and the history of art. She had a little salon in
Breslau, which consisted mostly of ladies with intellectual interests and ambitions. Sometimes their husbands would also
appear on those midweek afternoons or evenings, and there was
occasionally a university professor present. Eduard seldom attended these gatherings.

Clara had taught at a Berlin girls' school during the First
World War, and she kept in touch with some of her former fellow teachers, as well as with contemporaries from her university days. Over the years, she published three books. One was a
historical novel (*The House on the Ring*) concerning the beginnings of two leading Breslau companies—Giesche and Korn,
the publishers. Another (*The Knight with the Dragon*) was also
historical in character; its hero was Nettelbeck, the mayor of
Kolberg (a city in Clara's native Pomerania), who had de-
fended the city in the Napoleonic Wars against all odds, and at
a time when the spirit of defeatism was rampant. These two
books were not distinguished works of literature, though the
former went into a second edition, nor do they tell us much
about their author. The third book offers such a glimpse. *Charlotte Brontë, Genius in the Shadow* was a literary biography in the
form of a novel: Clara Schulte quite obviously felt a great deal
of sympathy for her heroine, the clergyman's daughter trying
to succeed in a man's world. There was a fair amount of identification, but whether conscious or unconscious it is not possible
to say. Clara was not as painfully shy as Charlotte Brontë, nor
was she as gifted. But as an active, educated woman, she must
have undergone similar torments. This is the one work of hers
that is not mainly cerebral but was written from the heart.
Clara, like Charlotte, was happiest when she was working on a
book. She mistakenly thought that Charlotte Brontë had been
largely forgotten in her native country and that she was helping to rediscover her.

Clara was noted for her handsome figure and fine features.
She was not very feminine in her behavior. Both husband and

wife gave the impression of being reserved, even unfeeling and cold to those who did not know them well. Nothing could have been further from the truth. Clara was a very sensitive woman, too sensitive perhaps for her own good. She loved her sons— Wolfgang, the elder son, was her favorite—and she was unhappy when they were out of the home. But she did not want to be bothered by the practical details of bringing up children. This was left to her friend, "Aunt" Edith Marquardt. In the late 1920s, Clara again became pregnant, but she did not want a third child, and so had an abortion. Eduard had very much wanted the child and was furious when he heard what had happened. Edith Marquardt, whom he suspected of somehow having played a role in the decision, had to leave.

Clara was closer to her husband than might have appeared. They had few secrets from each other; he did not, in any case, succeed in keeping many secrets from her. And on some critical occasions when he was in danger, she intervened with some effect. For an hour or two on Sunday mornings they would discuss the events of the last week or the plans for the next. Often on a Sunday afternoon Eduard would get restless, complain about boredom, pack his bags, and take a train to Berlin or some other place.

If Clara's reticence was deceptive, so was Eduard's coolness. He had been brought up in the belief that it was wrong to show emotion. He was brilliant in handling people but had few, if any, close friends. He was not a practicing Christian; when Clara took the boys to the Johannes Church on Christmas Eve, he would stay home and prepare the Christmas tree and the presents. He was a generous father: the boys were permitted to give him a "wish list" on major occasions such as birthdays or Christmas—but this had to be four weeks in advance—and he was very good at finding the most recondite objects. Sometimes his ideas were a little unusual. When the boys were still quite small he brought home, to Clara's horror, two young foxes from a hunting expedition for which a special box had to be built. The boys were more impressed by the records he brought from New York in 1929. Schulte had no hobbies other than hunting. He played croquet sometimes, but preferred to go for a walk on the few occasions when he had some free time.

Eduard Schulte, in brief, liked to keep a private sphere into which others, including even his family, were not usually allowed to intrude. Many knew him, but no one intimately. He had a sense of humor, which tended sometimes toward sarcasm, even cynicism. Those who had dealings with him as a businessman describe him as constructive and innovative, a man whose mind always found a way out of even very difficult situations, an excellent judge of people, and a tactician of genius. He was not tense by nature, but the kind of man who gives ulcers to others. He had soon learned that hardness was of the essence for success in business, and while he did not suffer fools and bores gladly, he forced himself to be nice to them if they could be of use to him in his business dealings. In the years after 1933, the years of Nazi rule, the art of dissimulation would become a very important asset.

Schulte was a dynamic person and a born leader, accustomed to accept responsibilities in almost all areas of life. But this restless, boldly creative mind was also in some respects very conservative; his wife, only half jokingly, would sometimes tell him that he still lived in the 1890s and did not wish that certain things should ever change—social forms, personal appearances, the household management. He was all in favor of trying something new in his business or at home, but it was to be done upon his initiative and under his control. He did not like to be surprised.

In normal times metal prices, and above all the ups and (mostly) downs of the price of zinc on the London market, would have been of greater interest to Dr. Schulte than affairs of state, if only because in the one game he was a prominent player, in the other a mere spectator, one of many. Nothing is known about his political views prior to 1930. If Eduard Schulte had definite opinions one way or another, which is doubtful, he kept them very much to himself. His outlook was probably conventional; the owners of Giesche would not have put their trust in anyone but a man of such views: even a Catholic was suspicious in their eyes. Schulte was a patriot, he belonged to exclusive right-of-center clubs, he regretted Germany's defeat in the First World War and thought the Versailles Treaty unjust. Socially, in the clubs, while hunting, or at the meetings of the chamber of commerce, he would hardly ever meet men of the left, liberals, or intellectuals.

He did not share the anti-Semitism of many of his colleagues. He seems instead to have been critical of the over-representation of aristocrats in key government positions. In *von* Papen's government in 1932 (to give but one example) *von* Neurath was foreign minister, *Von* Gayl served as minister of the interior, Schwerin *von* Krosigk was minister of finance, *von*

Schleicher was defense minister, *von* Braun was in charge of food, Eltz *von* Rübenach was responsible for mail and communications. Even in the last governments of the empire there had not been such a concentration of *Herren von*. Was there perhaps in Schulte something of the liberal-democratic resentment of the Rhinelander against the Prussian *Krautjunker* (country squire)? If so he kept it generally to himself. Giesche was not the right place for airing anti-aristocratic views, for on the board of the company the aristocrats outnumbered the others by two to one.

But the main danger in Germany in the early 1930s did not come from the aristocracy and the conservatives. It was the seemingly irresistible rise of the Nazis, which was not only a revolt against the parties of the left, but a movement of protest against the center and the traditional right, against the whole parliamentary system. In Breslau, where the Schultes lived, 36 percent of the electorate had voted in 1924 for the parties of the right and 35 percent for the left (Social Democrats and Communists). In the elections of 1932 the left more or less kept its share, but the conservative right was virtually wiped out. Instead, the Nazis polled 43 percent of the total.

From 1930 on, as the economic crisis deepened, more and more Germans became convinced that the democratic system did not work and that a strong hand was needed to save the country from ruin. Schulte was not a passionate advocate of parliamentary democracy; few captains of industry believe in anything but an autocratic style of leadership. Nor was he a pacifist; he was pleased later when his two sons became army officers. But in contrast to many people of his environment, Schulte was aware from the beginning that a Nazi victory would bring about a relapse to barbarism and war, and that it would end in disaster.

There were plenty of warning signs even in the summer of 1932 when the Nazi terror in Silesia reached a new height: the Nazis were out to conquer the streets. Their enemies would not be allowed to arrange public meetings, or even to show their faces. There was the notorious Potempa case: Potempa was a village in Upper Silesia where a Polish worker, thought to be a Communist sympathizer, was trampled to death by storm troopers before the eyes of his family. This and similar murders were not accidental excesses, outrages committed in the heat of street battles. They had been ordered from above, and the Potempa case, one of many, became well known only because

Hitler published a statement openly associating himself with the murderers.

Few people in Schulte's circles welcomed incidents such as this, but there was the usual talk about omelets that could not be made without breaking eggs. In any case, Hitler was needed merely as a "drummer," to restore a little order, said some. Once he had done his duty he would be put under strict control by his conservative allies without whom he would be incapable of governing. The composition of the first Hitler government of January 30, 1933, seemed to justify these expectations: there were only two other Nazis in the list of ministers announced on that day, the minister of the interior and a minister without portfolio. The co-option of Hitler seemed complete.

Schulte did not share these delusions. He confided to a few trusted friends that the Nazis were gangsters; they would ruin Germany. Everything he witnessed only strengthened this belief. He could not, of course, talk quite so openly at Giesche, for some of his closest collaborators, such as his number two, Otto Fitzner, were fanatical Nazis. Even at home he had to restrain himself, and not only because the domestics might overhear an incautious remark. There were certain comments that could not be made in front of the children. In 1933 Eduard Schulte would have agreed with most of his countrymen that a new era in the history of Germany had dawned. But he did not think that it would last a thousand years, as Hitler had predicted, nor did he have any doubts how it would end.

CHAPTER TWO

Business and Politics

I n the late afternoon of February 20, 1933, a fleet of limou-
sines, big and very expensive, arrived at the official residence of Hermann Göring, the president of the Reichstag (the
lower house of Germany's parliament), in the very heart of
Berlin. The residence, a small palace, was mainly used for re-
ceptions. Alighting from the cars were Germany's leading businessmen. Among them were Gustav Krupp of the Krupp
steelworks; Albert Vögler, the director of United Steel; Fritz
Springorum, another of the steel kings; Georg von Schnitzler of
I. G. Farben; other top industrialists; and a cross section of the
German banking elite. Many had delved into parliamentary
politics before, but hardly ever as a group. Exactly one week
later the nearby Reichstag building was set afire in the dead of

night. The circumstances of the fire are not entirely clear to this day.

One of the twenty-five or so business titans at this meeting was Eduard Schulte. Like the others he had been invited by Göring, the famous World War flying ace and now the flamboyant leader of the Nazi faction in the German parliament, and Dr. Hjalmar Horace Greeley Schacht, Germany's best-known banker. The guests had been told that Hitler would like to meet them. Some had come because they sympathized with the new regime, others out of a feeling of duty or, like Schulte, out of curiosity.

One of those who had definitely not come out of curiosity was Schacht. Born in Germany's far north, he had the reputation of a financial wizard, the man who had led Germany out of the depths of galloping inflation to the economic miracle of the 1920s. He had been head of the state bank, the Reichsbank, from December 1923 to 1930 and was to play an important role in the Nazi era. He had no firm political convictions; after the First World War he had belonged to the slightly left-of-center German Democratic Party, but following meetings with Göring and Hitler in the winter of 1930–31 he had gained the impression that "Hitler was a man with whom one could co-operate," to use his own words from the Nuremberg trial after the Second World War. He had not joined the Nazi Party but regarded its rise as more or less inevitable. Nor did he think its ascendancy undesirable, because it would give Germany, as he saw it, some much-needed stability, a precondition for its recovery after the great economic crisis.

The meeting had been called to raise funds for the March elections. Strictly speaking, it was not even a partisan affair, for the money collected was to be used not just for the Nazis but also the right-wing Nationalist Party (the Deutschnationale) and even the national liberal group (Deutsche Volkspartei). But it was common knowledge that the Nazis badly needed funds whereas the other "national" parties had more money than they could spend. They lacked voting appeal rather than donations. The meeting was not to receive any publicity.

The visitors were made to wait some fifteen minutes for Göring and Hitler. Hitler shook everyone's hand and then subjected the gathering to one of his famous monologues, a rambling and violent speech briefly covering every possible topic—foreign and domestic policy, economic policy and the need for rearmament, the dangers of liberalism, Social Democracy, and, of course, Bolshevism. Germany needed a new spirit, he said, and incidentally also a new political system. Democracy would not do, because it led to anarchy and, in any case, it was not compatible with private enterprise. He criticized the right-wing German Nationalists, his partners in the coalition; they had no electoral appeal and had only impeded the rise of National Socialism. Marxists, which meant all those disagreeing with the Nazis, had to be smashed. He hinted that there would be an armed take-over if the national coalition did not gain the necessary majority. He said that he greatly preferred a smooth transition to the new order. And it was mistaken to argue, as some were doing, that victory had already been attained by the Nazis. Victory would not be assured unless the enemy was destroyed.

Krupp said some words of little consequence after Hitler had finished, whereupon the Führer, who, as a matter of principle, never talked money, rose and left the meeting. Göring, who spoke next, said that the coming elections would be the last for ten years, more likely for a hundred years. He also declared that it was only fair if the circles not directly involved in the political struggle, meaning the industrialists and the bankers, made substantial financial contributions. This was the sign for Schacht to take over: *Meine Herren, zur Kasse* [Gentlemen, take out your checkbooks]. It was a figure of speech, for all he expected were pledges. Later on Schacht would be more specific: he asked for three million marks, slightly less than a million dollars.

Schulte, like most of those present, kept silent during the meeting. He had been bitterly opposed to the Nazis before; now he realized that the new rulers of Germany were no better than gangsters, embarking on a policy of naked violence at home and abroad, which, sooner or later, he felt, would lead the country into a war. He had met Göring on a previous occasion—it was at the Berlin club, the Herrenklub—and he had not liked his bombast. But Göring was the nonplebeian front man of the Nazis for the German middle class and the establishment, a moderate compared with Hitler, whom Schulte had come to regard as a raving lunatic.

Schulte's invitation to the meeting was a measure of how far he had come in the more than seven years he had spent with Giesche. In the beginning the situation had not looked promising. Giesche was heavily in debt and unable to finance the modernization of its existing mines, let alone development of new ones. It had been very difficult to secure large loans in Germany in 1925. The company had haphazardly acquired new properties and subsidiaries in a desperate attempt to diversify. As a consequence it was facing serious trouble with its creditors.

In 1925 Schulte also confronted the Polish problem, immune to any conventional business remedy. Following the partition of Upper Silesia in 1922, the new border between Poland and Germany divided the Giesche holdings, cutting right through its Bleischarley mine. Eighty percent of Giesche's property was on the Polish side, including all its zinc refineries. A hostile Polish government began to take aim at Giesche and other German-owned firms, planning a huge increase in taxes that would have made Giesche's entire Polish operation impossible to run profitably. Yet Giesche could not abandon its Polish branch; it needed the ores and the refineries. What was left in Germany was worth, in the assessment of one outside expert, only about $15 million, compared with a prewar value for the entire company of roughly $100 million.

Schulte was not even certain of his own position. Giesche's Heirs was something of a cross between a family firm and a modern corporation; a broker would have said that its shares were very closely held. There was a board (*Repräsentanten-Kollegium*), a six-man body that had once run the firm and still held a great deal of influence. Schulte's predecessor, Mewes, was the first *Generaldirektor*, the first chief executive officer, from outside in the company's history. Although the position of *Generaldirektor* was the loftiest in the German corporate world, Mewes had served a very difficult three years and then resigned. Now Schulte's powers were vaguely defined and circumscribed. He had to consult the board on major decisions, and Giesche's debts were so pressing that drastic measures were needed right away.

The government of the state of Prussia, the largest state in Germany, had its own mining firm, Preussag, which was interested in some of Giesche's German property. The Prussian government reluctantly offered to extend a new loan to Giesche, provided that Preussag was given majority control of Giesche's major German mine. This loan would not have sufficed to cover existing debts, and Giesche would still have had the Polish problem on its hands. And in all likelihood, the terms would have meant the end of German Giesche as a major independent force in the mining industry. Mewes had begun negotiations with representatives of the American financier W. Averell Harriman, who either independently or as part of a consortium with the Anaconda Copper Mining Company, which was also interested in the Giesche holdings, could supply short- and long-term loans. But the Americans wanted adequate security, which was hard to arrange without giving them control of a good part of Giesche.

To solve two problems at one blow, Schulte decided to sell a majority interest in Giesche's Polish properties to the Americans, mainly because American investors were far more welcome in Poland than Germans. The Americans apparently raised this idea to meet German objections about an American take-over of an old German company, and Schulte grasped at it eagerly.

On November 4, 1925, the Giesche stockholders met in Breslau to consider the Prussian government's loan and the Anaconda-Harriman offer. The decision was politically sensitive, and newspaper reporters were barred from attending the meeting. But Averell Harriman himself, as well as Cornelius F. Kelley, president of Anaconda, made their pitch successfully. Although the board was divided, by a slim majority the stockholders of Giesche approved a deal by which Harriman obtained a six-month option to buy 51 percent of the Giesche Corporation of Poland and a portion of Giesche's German zinc production, and the German company received an immediate infusion of much-needed cash. That gave both sides enough time to investigate the complicated deal thoroughly and to sound out the various governments.

The Polish government eventually proved willing to waive its new taxes to encourage American investment in their country. But the climate in Berlin was extremely hostile at first. Prussian officials saw the deal as a virtual American take-over of the whole Giesche operation and an attempt by Anaconda to create a worldwide zinc monopoly. In addition, the German press was filled with articles about Giesche's lack of concern for national interests, a very sensitive subject ever since Germany had been forced to sign the hated Treaty of Versailles ending the First World War. Some Germans suspected that Anaconda, which controlled roughly 7 percent of worldwide zinc production, would force Giesche not to build any new zinc refineries in Germany.

A few weeks after Schulte took the helm of Giesche, *The New York Times* carried a front-page article entitled "Prussia to

Void Harriman-Anaconda Deal for Monopoly of German Zinc Production," which quoted extensively from the Prussian finance minister's critical speech before the Prussian parliament. The Prussian government insisted on appointing its own representative to the Giesche board as a way of preventing the company from acting against the national interest.

But not everyone in Berlin was unsympathetic. Reichsbank president Hjalmar Schacht was in favor of the deal, and it was during these protracted negotiations that Schulte first made Schacht's acquaintance. Since Harriman and Anaconda were not scared away by the negative publicity, Schulte did not get ruffled. He very much liked the famous American railway magnate and financier, but he quarreled from time to time with Harriman's deputies, such as the Berlin representative, Irving Rossi.

The Anaconda-Harriman offer made too much sense for Giesche to drop. Instead of lashing out bitterly against the critics of the deal, Schulte exploited their sensitivities to his advantage. In May 1926, even before the Anaconda-Harriman group exercised its option, Giesche concluded another agreement with the Prussian government. Prussia agreed to lend the company 15 million marks to construct a new zinc refinery in German territory and another 10 million marks for working capital, all at very low rates of interest. Giesche's agreement with Harriman and Anaconda was also modified so that the Americans had no equity in the German corporation and no guaranteed right to any German ore production. These changes mollified nationalist sensitivities and the deal went through.

Harriman and Company and Anaconda Copper formed the Silesian-American Corporation of Wilmington, Delaware, which became the formal owner of the Giesche Corporation of Poland. The Silesian Holding Company (65 percent owned by Anaconda, 35 percent by Harriman) held 51 percent of the Silesian-American stock; Giesche held the remaining 49 percent. Experienced Anaconda executives and employees now took over management of the Polish Giesche properties. They were confident that the introduction of better management and new American technology would quickly return the firm to profitability. The Anaconda-Harriman consortium believed it had acquired cheaply a company with extremely valuable assets, which made up for the political risks. They could not have anticipated how events in Germany in 1933 would multiply the political dangers.

Schulte was content to adopt a low profile in the Silesian-American Corporation and to let the Americans take charge in Poland. That was what the political situation there required, and there were certainly things that he and his staff could learn from the American managers in Katowice. There were other reasons for the two Giesche companies to work together. For the time being, German Giesche had no zinc refineries, while Polish Giesche had excess refining capacity, and transportation costs between the two companies were insignificant. Polish Giesche had a sizable production of coal to dispose of, whereas German Giesche had a coal sales business. Moreover, Anaconda held patents in the area of electrolytic zinc refining, the modern process for turning out high-grade zinc, which Schulte was most interested in for Giesche's planned new refinery to be constructed in Magdeburg.

But when Schulte invited Anaconda to participate in the new zinc refinery and asked for a license to use Anaconda's patented electrolytic refining process, the American company parried the request, for it would have created powerful competition for the Polish zinc refineries and made German Giesche more self-sufficient.

Inevitably, there were other sources of friction. In the end, both Giesche companies mapped out certain areas in which they would cooperate and other fields in which they would compete. The fact that they did not allow specific disagreements to disrupt their overall corporate relationship was a tribute to good business sense and the emotional maturity of Schulte and George Sage Brooks, Polish Giesche's American manager. And Schulte actually became quite friendly with Fred Gaethke, manager of Polish Giesche's Bleischarley mine and later vice-president of the company.

Although both Schulte's company and the Anaconda-dominated Polish Giesche expanded and made profits during the next two years, there were too many zinc mines turning out too much ore worldwide. An international zinc cartel made little progress in stabilizing prices, and then, in 1929, the world economic crisis caused a virtual collapse of demand for the metal. The price of zinc fell from 23–24 pounds sterling per ton to a low point of 8½ pounds in 1932. It was impossible for either Giesche to produce profitably at that level.

Despite the collapse of the zinc market, during 1932 Giesche's proposed Magdeburg zinc refinery won some prominent supporters within the national government. At the end of April, Wilhelm Groener, who was simultaneously defense minister and interior minister, notified Chancellor Heinrich Brüning that the proposed refinery was very much in the national interest. The army needed an adequate domestic supply of electrolytic zinc for the production of brass ammunition casings; at present, Groener wrote, all electrolytic zinc was imported and vulnerable in case of war. In addition, an electrolytic zinc refinery would also produce oleum as a by-product, a substance used in manufacturing explosives, and oleum too was in short supply in Germany. Zinc was transformed into brass, die-castings, battery casings, and coating for iron and steel objects to protect them against corrosion. Zinc was used in the production of ammunition, electrical and automobile equipment, and airplanes. Groener's forceful intervention for Giesche might have had the desired effect, except that he was forced to resign both his cabinet posts during May. Groener had issued a decree banning the Nazi SA and SS forces and thereby alienated the upper echelon of the military and President Hindenburg. Chancellor Brüning too lost the President's confidence and was forced to resign.

Brüning's successor, Franz von Papen, was also asked to approve government assistance to Giesche for the Magdeburg project. Again army officials came to Giesche's support, turning back protests by executives of I. G. Farben, Germany's giant chemical concern.

But the complicated negotiations among Giesche, the Prussian state mining firm, and the government dragged out into November. By then Franz von Papen's government was on its last legs. Germany's political system was falling apart, and Adolf Hitler was waiting for a chance to show that he could get Germany moving again.

Despite its name, Hitler's National Socialist German Workers' Party had actively solicited corporate support at least since 1927. Hitler's "socialism" simply meant little more than bringing all patriotic (and racially acceptable) elements of German society together to work to strengthen the country. Although the Nazis had little success at first in recruiting prominent businessmen, continuous battles with the trade unions during the Depression induced some businessmen to view the Nazis as a useful counterweight. There were even a few Nazi enthusiasts among the business community. However, after Hitler became chancellor on January 30, 1933, many more business leaders began to see the political and economic advantages offered by the new regime: government contracts to stimulate the economy, rearmament, no danger from parliament or the left, no more troublesome, independent unions.

The Nazi government had good reason to take an interest in Giesche's Magdeburg plant. The Führer felt strongly that Germany had to become self-sufficient in critical raw materials. He believed that the British blockade of Germany had been decisive during the First World War, and that this could happen again. He gave high priority to measures to reduce Germany's dependence upon imported raw materials, and zinc fell into that category. Germany consumed roughly 135,000 metric tons of zinc in 1933 and produced only about 51,000 tons. The balance came from Norway, France, Canada, and Australia, none of whom could be relied upon if war broke out. Rearmament clearly meant an increasing demand for zinc, particularly for the pure zinc produced by electrolysis.

In mid-1933 Reich Finance Minister Count Lutz Schwerin von Krosigk arranged for Giesche to obtain a long-term government construction loan of 15 million marks. A modern electrolytic refinery in Magdeburg, capable of producing zinc that was 99.975 percent pure, was completed in August 1934. It soon became Germany's largest producer of zinc and a major source of sulfuric acid and cadmium. In 1935 Giesche again turned a profit.

An outsider might well have concluded from this that the relationship between Giesche and the Nazi government was ideal. The expansion of zinc mining and refining served the new rulers' plans for rearmament. Schulte's staff gave guided tours of their facilities to the "brown-shirted bosses"—such tours could hardly be avoided.

But the company's annual report for 1933, issued in 1934, contained no florid expression of gratitude to the new Nazi leadership. Schulte made sure that the government loan was paid back as soon as possible—even though the company had to take out new loans from private sources. No major German company could isolate itself from the Nazi government, which assumed more and more economic authority during the mid-1930s. But an upturn in business did not blind Eduard Schulte to the true character of the new regime.

Many other Germans, however, had more positive feelings

during the early years of Nazi rule. A new hope and a new sense of purpose pervaded the country. Unemployment was largely eliminated; the factories and the mines reopened; Germany was about to become a major power as the draft was reintroduced and rearmament began. Critics of the new regime did not fare well; even some of its erstwhile leading supporters were murdered in the Night of the Long Knives, June 30, 1934. But this seemed to many Germans a cheap price to pay for the progress that had been achieved.

Berlin was never busier than in the summer of 1936, the year of the Olympic Games. The capital had been embellished for the many thousands of foreigners who were to be shown the achievements of the new Reich. Hitler and his party were at the height of their prestige. Few Germans were without jobs; great new superhighways were being built, and other public works were being carried out all over the country. If Germany was rearming, so was everyone else, and an army, after all, was part and parcel of a sovereign nation. In countless speeches Hitler stressed the new unity of the people, its strength, but also its desire for peace. He belonged to the generation that had witnessed the horrors of the First World War. It was unthinkable that he and his comrades wanted to unleash (as some of his enemies claimed) a new and even more horrible war! Hitler opened the Olympic Games ("I am calling the youth of the world") by advocating peaceful competition and a new spirit of harmony.

Most foreign visitors who went to Berlin that year returned deeply impressed not only by the prowess of German athletes but by the new mood permeating Germany, the new optimism, the faith in the future, so much in contrast to the defeatism and despair of only a few years back. Yes, there were concentration camps, and the Jews had been made second-class citizens. But this affected only a small minority. It all seemed worth it considering the tremendous achievements of the Nazis, which, they said, were only the first steps in the direction of an even more brilliant future. In ten years, Hitler had boasted, no one would be able to recognize Berlin.

There was a great deal of enthusiasm in Germany in 1936 for Hitler the peacemaker, and the wretched émigrés in Paris and Prague writing about deep internal rifts among the Nazis and the coming downfall of Hitlerism were hopelessly out of touch with German realities: or so it seemed to the gullible. The Reichstag election of 1936 was hardly free, but if there had been free elections, the Nazi Party would surely have gained an overwhelming victory.

Not long after Schulte became general manager of Giesche, he took a suite in Berlin which was to be permanently at his disposal and occasionally used by other senior staff of the company. The decision could easily be justified, for there was more and more business to be transacted with the government ministries and the big banks in the capital of the Reich. The foreign companies with which Schulte dealt also had their headquarters in Berlin. Schulte took relatively little interest in the details of production, which were in capable hands. Giesche's main difficulties during all these years were financial; Schulte's job as he saw it was to guarantee the financial survival of the company.

From 1936 the Coburger Hof (also called the Coburg) became the second headquarters of Giesche, and during the war years, it was the main headquarters. The Coburg, in the Georgenstrasse, was not one of Berlin's biggest hotels, like the Adlon, but it was certainly among the most exclusive. Formerly the town house of a duke, it was later divided—the building next to it likewise became a hotel, the Russischer Hof, and there was also a third, the Georgen Hof. The manager was an individual with a wild mane of hair but quite good-tempered who had previously run a hotel in Alexandria, Egypt. He kept a collection of Meissen of an erotic character that would be shown only to the very best guests. The food was not always of the highest standard; about the salmon Schulte's comment was (as his son would later recall) "*à la maison*, dry and bad." But the service was excellent, and Schulte felt comfortable. Service was on a different level than today. Regular guests neither had to unpack nor pack; all this was done by the servants, who would run errands and obtain anything humanly possible for the guests. The Coburg was located near the Friedrichstrasse railway station, in the busiest part of Berlin's longest thoroughfare. In the Friedrichstrasse one saw the densest traffic in town; the stream of people on the pavements never ceased. High finance was there, major office buildings, the great newspapers as well as many of the big restaurants and coffeehouses. And when the customers and the office workers had gone home, new crowds would arrive on the scene, those frequenting the variety theaters, such as the Wintergarten opposite the station, the Admiralspalast, or a dozen others.

Eduard Schulte made his rounds in the capital. He was a

frequent visitor in the leading banks. Otto Fischer of the
Reichskreditgesellschaft was a friend and a board member of
Giesche. Schulte would see Schacht, in 1936 minister of economics, but about to be dismissed. With his cousin Hermann,
the owner of the picture gallery, he would breakfast at
Horcher, or have supper at Kempinski. Hermann would also
take him to meetings of the Herrenklub (or Deutscher Klub, as
it was now called), home of a group of conservative politicians,
bankers, and senior military people who had once been quite
influential. (It was at the Herrenklub that Schulte met Göring.)
These conservatives would cautiously moan, regretting the loss
of their political influence; some would point out guardedly
that the resurgence of the economy would have happened in
any case, because Hitler had come to power at the end of a re-
cession. Some went even further and stressed that the revival
was not on a solid basis, that the basic economic problems had
not been solved. Schulte knew all this. At Giesche the turning
point had come in mid-1932, not after Hitler's rise to power.
But he was struck by the fact that no one seemed to go much
further in criticizing the regime. Many found fault with certain
aspects of Nazism, but by and large they saw no alternative.
And the military seemed enthusiastic, for at long last they were
getting a strong army, navy, and air force.

For the opponents of Nazism, 1936 was not a good year.
Hitler's domestic and foreign policy could be seen as moderate
and sensible. He had saved Germany from ruin and was leading it toward a better future: he was a Roosevelt, German-style,
according to some foreign observers, and his program something like the New Deal. When Schulte uttered criticism, even
among close friends, he would face incomprehension and even
horror. One ought to wait, he was told; in all likelihood the regime would mellow in the course of time. One should not take
Mein Kampf and the extreme rhetoric too seriously. And so
Schulte also waited, without illusions. He watched his sons
growing up, enjoyed the stays on his estate, concluded some
new business deals. But he was one of those who were not at all
optimistic about the future of Germany. There were not many
of them in 1936.

Why did Eduard Schulte come to dislike Nazism so intensely? It is an obvious question, but not an easy one to answer. There was nothing in his earlier life that somehow
predestined him to become a sworn enemy of the Nazis. He was
not a leftist or a radical democrat, or a member of any religious

group persecuted by the Nazis, or a Freemason or a right-wing monarchist. He was not Jewish. What bothered him above all was that Nazism made him do things he loathed.

One Sunday evening late in 1934 he saw his sons returning home in their uniforms from a march organized by the Hitler Youth. He knew it was harmless enough. They had spent the day in some forest in the vicinity; there had been war games and a campfire, and not really much politics. But the uniforms and the red flag with the black swastika still annoyed him no end. He expressed his displeasure to Clara. She reminded him that in the *Gymnasium* everyone had to belong to the Hitler Youth unless he was a Jew or physically handicapped. If Schulte were to compel his sons not to join in with all their friends and classmates, it would mean trouble all along the line. He still thought it a bad idea and went on grumbling. The children, unable to form an independent judgment, would be indoctrinated with the "brown poison" (as he called it). Whereupon Clara said that he was making mountains out of molehills, and in any case, was it not true that Eduard too had had to strike a compromise with the new order? He had become a member of the German Hunters Union, a Nazi organization. Without this membership he would not have obtained a license to keep a shotgun and would not have been able to hunt on his own grounds. He was a member of the DAF, the German Labor Front, because without such membership no one in Germany was permitted to work or to be the head of an enterprise. And lastly, he was a member of the NSV, the Nazi Socialist Welfare Association. It meant no more than making small monthly contributions, which were allegedly used for the poor. If he had refused to join, there would have been a major scandal. The SS newspaper or some other Nazi organ would have come out with a headline such as "Anti-Social Elements at the Helm of a Leading Corporation." It would have been interpreted as an act of open defiance, and the consequences would have been incalculable. Most probably it would have been the end of his career.

And so Eduard Schulte had been forced to compromise not just once, but three times, which made him all the angrier. He was an independent man, not carried away by waves of mass hysteria, not willing to be made to join organizations that he abhorred. He disliked being given commands by leaders who had no claim to respect. He had known many people in high places, and with a few exceptions he had not been impressed.

Under the republic they had at least left him alone, but now he was to obey blindly.

But Eduard Schulte was not willing to obey blindly. He opposed the Nazis because his instincts, which were seldom wrong, told him that the Nazi propaganda, which so deeply impressed many of his contemporaries, was fraudulent. His instincts told him that when Hitler and Goebbels made their emotional speeches about the need for peace and their own deep personal attachment to the cause of peace, they were lying. They were lying when they conjured up the horrors of the First World War; how could any sane person advocate a repeat performance? They were lying when they claimed that they did not have a single territorial claim in Europe.

His instincts told him that the rearmament could have no other purpose but to make war. What he heard from his friends in high places about what Hitler had told the army chiefs only reinforced his conviction. He knew that the economic policy of the Third Reich did not make sense unless it was preparation for a war of expansion and conquest. Hjalmar Schacht was a foxy opportunist, a doubtful character who lacked sincerity and who had helped Hitler to seize power in 1933. But Schacht, whatever his liabilities, still had a certain professional integrity, and he confirmed Schulte's suspicions: Nazi policy was a gamble that would succeed only if the coming war were short and victorious.

It is easy to be wise after the event. In later years many Germans agreed that one could have seen the warning signs early on, perhaps as early as 1933 when the Nazis were burning the books and setting up the first concentration camps. But in the early years only a very few people such as Schulte did see the writing on the wall. Most accepted Nazi rationalizations of the steps toward war. Germany was leaving the League of Nations? The league had done nothing for Germany, and it had become a bit of a laughingstock anyway. Germany repudiated the Versailles Treaty of 1919? Everyone in Germany agreed (and so did more than a few Englishmen and Frenchmen) that it had been a cruel, unjust peace treaty that had caused untold damage not just to Germany but to the whole world. Hitler reintroduced the draft, but then every country in Europe had a sizable army. Why should Germany alone among the nations be denied this elementary right?

So it went on up to the *Anschluss*, the German take-over of Austria in March 1938. If the great majority of Austrians wanted to be part of a Greater Germany, no one had the right to oppose this desire. If more than three million Germans in Czechoslovakia found it intolerable to live under alien rule and also wanted to become part of the Reich, did not elementary justice demand that their wish be fulfilled?

Schulte kept his thoughts largely to himself. But he became absolutely convinced that his reading of the situation was right, that most of those around him were blind, and that Germany would start a war it would lose.

. . .

As the storm clouds began to gather in 1938, Schulte spent much of the year outside Germany, five months to be precise. The company board got restless; there was even some talk about firing him in view of his long absences, but Dr. Lothar Siemon, Giesche's trustee and director of administration, and a good friend of Schulte's, submitted an expert opinion according to which the constitution of the firm did not provide for the dismissal of the chief executive officer. Apparently the question had never arisen, nor had the necessity to take such action been envisaged. Schulte spent most of this period in Switzerland but also paid several visits to London, and those close to him knew the reason—the firm was once again on the verge of bank-ruptcy. While Giesche had enormous assets, it also had a peren-nial cash-flow problem.

The interest that German Giesche had to pay to the Sile-sian-American Corporation (SACO as the American-owned company was called) was high—some 8.5 percent. The German government stepped in and helped to a certain extent, for the loss of the nonferrous mines would have had grave conse-quences for German industry in general. But the government had no foreign currency holdings, and Schulte was told by Schwerin von Krosigk, the Reich finance minister, to try to find money abroad to service the company's debts.

Schulte did this by establishing a number of companies in Switzerland (e.g., Non-Ferrum and Erzag) mainly for the pur-pose of raising loans to pay back other loans (interest in Swit-zerland was lower at the time than in Germany). But the Swiss banking consortium wanted collateral, and it received it in the form of Giesche shares. Schulte also made a smaller deal with the London firm of Brandeis Goldschmidt, then the world's leading private copper sales company.

And so Schulte found himself in July 1938 on a quick visit

to London to talk to Julius Schloss, a heavyset man in his fifties whom he had known well in Berlin as a manager of the Montangesellschaft, one of the biggest international mineral sales companies. Schloss had been one of the leading figures in the German metal trade; after his emigration he had not found it too difficult to get a job in England, though not one of equal influence and standing.

They had an early dinner in Schloss's home on Fitzjohn's Avenue, a street leading up from Swiss Cottage into Hampstead Village. It was one of the old massive, red brick, not particularly handsome houses built well before the turn of the century. Schulte said that he was glad his friend had found, after the tribulations in Germany, a new comfortable home. "In some ways I envy you," Schulte said. "Envy me?" Schloss asked incredulously. He told his old friend that he would not feel happy in an unfamiliar environment. Neither of them was a youngster anymore, and Schulte wouldn't be happy without his estate. Schulte seemed disinclined to continue the conversation at the table, and as they had already had their coffee, Schloss suggested a walk to Hampstead Heath. It was one of those fine London summer evenings in which night would not fall for a long time after dinner.

There were crowds in the streets, mainly outside the pubs on both sides of Heath Street: young people, quite obviously enjoying themselves. Some were dancing on the pavement. How much longer will this go on? Schulte asked. Didn't Schloss consider that this could well be the last summer of peace? Schloss was unsure who would make war on Germany—certainly not Mr. Chamberlain.

Schulte said that he knew the Nazis. The Germans no more wanted war than anyone else. But Hitler and his gang would lead them into war, and they would follow like a herd of sheep. Austria was the first step; Czechoslovakia would follow, or Poland, or perhaps both. Eventually the Western powers would have to stop Hitler, whether they liked it or not. Schloss replied that Schulte surely exaggerated Hitler's ambitions—would he knowingly swallow more than he could digest? And what about the generals and the industrialists and the bankers—did they really want to go to war?

Schulte dismissed this observation. The businessmen would utter half-muted criticisms, and they would applaud when Hitler was successful.

Schloss noted that Germany did not have the raw materials to conduct a long war. What about zinc? "We produce almost all the zinc we need," Schulte said. "Copper is more a problem; our stock is less than half of what is needed." But Hitler was not thinking in these terms. He wanted a short war, and he thought he would seize all the raw materials needed within the first months of the war.

Schloss smiled. "You are a strange man. Here you have come to ask us to help you to get a loan and suggest business deals for many years ahead, and at the same time, you try to convince me that we shall have war next year or the year after."

Schulte said that even if there was a war, business transactions would continue as they had in the last war; the deal was between London and a Swiss company, not with Germany, and Switzerland, no doubt, would remain neutral.

Schloss was not convinced. "You need not answer my question of course, but have you ever contemplated emigration?"

Schulte said that he hated the Nazis and all they stood for. They would not become more moderate; on the contrary. So far they had deceived the world, hiding their ultimate aims. If he were a Jew, he would drop all his possessions and take the next train while the going was good. But he was German. What would he do in London or Paris or New York? His family and his friends and everything he had built were in Germany. And so he would stay with his people to the bitter end.

"To the bitter end?" Schloss interjected. "But Hitler is going from strength to strength. Who will be able to stop him?"

"No one in the short run," Schulte said, "but eventually the whole world will be lined up against Germany."

They got a beer with difficulty in Jack Straw's Castle, for there was a long line, and then they began to make the descent to Fitzjohn's Avenue. Schloss said that it was unrealistic to expect a loan of 600,000 pounds in present conditions. Schulte was not alone in his misgivings about the future; the banks were also nervous. "You'll be lucky if you now get one third that amount."

Mrs. Schloss opened the door when they returned. "Did you have a nice walk? I hope it wasn't too tiring, Mr. Schulte?"

"Oh, no," Schulte said. "It was very enjoyable, the heath and the fresh air and the young people enjoying themselves. Ah—to be twenty again." He thought for a moment and added, "If I were an insurance broker, I would be more careful in my statements. They will have to do the fighting in the coming war."

Schloss said, "Here we go again."

Soon after, the car came to take Schulte back to his hotel; he had an early train for Zurich the following day.

Schulte's pessimism was justified: a major pogrom took place in Germany a few months later, touched off by an assassination. Seventeen-year-old Herschl Grynszpan walked into the German Embassy in Paris on November 7, 1938, and shot the third secretary, Ernst vom Rath, as a protest against the brutal German deportation of thousands of Polish Jews, including Grynszpan's parents, who had been living in Germany. The Nazi leadership was about to gather at the Old Town Hall in Munich to celebrate the fifteenth anniversary of Hitler's unsuccessful Beer Hall Putsch. For Hitler, the shooting was another chapter in the international Jewish campaign to provoke Germany. Nazi Germany could not allow such effrontery to go unpunished. Some Nazi actions against Jews began as early as November 8, the next day. On November 9 Rath died from his wound. That evening Hitler had a long conversation with Propaganda Minister Joseph Goebbels. The Führer was overheard to say that the SA (Nazi storm troops) should be allowed to have a fling. Goebbels quickly took charge and began to organize the "spontaneous demonstrations." The police were instructed not to interfere.

During the next twenty-four hours approximately three hundred synagogues and seven thousand Jewish-owned businesses across Germany were destroyed. More than ninety Jews died in the violence, and thousands more were beaten or tortured. Many thousands were carried off to concentration camps.

On November 10 Schulte happened to be in Munich, where he ran into an old friend with whom he could talk openly. The friend remembers Schulte saying: "The bandits begin to unmask themselves. You never wanted to believe me. You always claimed that I saw everything too black. They don't even take the trouble to use alibis and fig leaves. The whole band of criminals has to be liquidated. That's the only possible way to lead German politics and Germany back to a normal course. But naturally, that's a job that the two of us cannot carry off alone."

CHAPTER THREE

Into Battle

Adolf Hitler played foreign policy like a compulsive gambler letting his winnings ride: every victory was the prelude to another toss of the dice at higher stakes. In the famous summit meeting with the British and the French leaders at Munich at the end of September 1938, Hitler had managed to carve off a major chunk of Czechoslovakia with the consent of Czechoslovakia's allies, and German troops would move in without firing a shot. The British and the French had issued an empty promise to guarantee the independence of the remainder of the country. Then in March 1939 Nazi envoys induced Slovakian politicians to declare the secession of Slovakia from Czechoslovakia, and two days later Hitler compelled the aged and browbeaten president of Czechoslovakia to agree to German occupation of Bohemia and Moravia. Afterward, Hitler told his secretaries: "This is the greatest day of my life. I shall be known as the greatest German in history." He flew to Prague and announced that Czechoslovakia had ceased to exist.

Less than a week later Ribbentrop, the German foreign minister, raised territorial demands with regard to Danzig and the Polish Corridor, and Germany forced Lithuania to cede the Baltic city of Memel. Responding to rumors about German designs on Poland, the British government announced that both Britain and France would support any Polish resistance to threats to its independence. Hitler instructed the German military to be prepared, and in April Germany canceled its 1934 nonaggression treaty with Poland.

Nazi expansion was to continue, but would Hitler be allowed to conquer Poland unhindered, or would a German attack on Poland lead to a general European war? In May the Führer explained to the chiefs of the armed services that an attack on Poland might lead to war with the West, in which case Germany would have to occupy Belgium and the Netherlands—partly to provide a base from which to attack Britain.

From various military contacts Schulte knew some of the Nazi plans in 1939. Even if the war was limited to Poland, there was bound to be trouble for Schulte's company, with its various German, Polish, and American components, and even more problems for Schulte personally. He would have to make some very tough decisions. Eduard Schulte was a man of principle who had reached certain conclusions about Germany's future on the basis of common sense. Whether Nazi Germany won military victories or not, the Germany he knew and loved would be destroyed, either from within or from without. The more lands Hitler conquered, the greater the devastation and the longer the ordeal. But in the end, Hitler would lose, for the man had no sense of limits.

Being a practical man, Schulte was bound to ask himself whether he could do anything to help avert disaster. Only one thing could prevent war—the removal of the Nazi regime. But economic improvement and diplomatic success had made the Führer popular, and the Gestapo had easily disposed of all opposition. At one stage Schulte seems to have hoped that the initiative for overthrowing Hitler might come from Germany's military leaders. The generals and colonels had, of course, welcomed the great buildup of Germany's armed forces. But they had resented the oath of unconditional obedience to Hitler in

1934. Many had been angered by the murder of General Kurt von Schleicher during the Night of the Long Knives in June 1934, and the contemptible, trumped-up charges against some of their most respected leaders in 1938. Most of them were not fools. They considered that Hitler's designs were overambitious and therefore bound to fail in the end. There was some half-hearted talk about conspiracy in 1938 by a group of senior officers, among them General Ludwig Beck. But the German military opposition to Hitler was undercut by Hitler's diplomatic success at Munich and the bloodless take-over of Czechoslovakia.

Over the years Schulte had met such leading generals as Beck, Brauchitsch, Fritsch, Manstein, Reichenau, and Rundstedt. He had worked closely with General Joachim von Stülpnagel, who had served on Giesche's board, and whose cousin was the Army's quartermaster general. He knew the officers in charge of weapons procurement and the war economy. A few were Nazi sympathizers, but most were pessimistic. Over time Schulte saw their weaknesses all too clearly. They had no forceful leader, they lacked political know-how, and they were hopeless as conspirators against a ruthless band of political gangsters. He could not see himself cooperating with this group.

Schulte could have tried to undermine the Nazi regime by delivering inferior zinc or sulfuric acid, but this was hardly a practical proposition. Too many people would have to know about such sabotage, and too little would be gained. There was a better way for him to do something against the Nazi regime—to warn and assist potential victims of Nazism.

Until 1939 Nazi Germany had harassed and persecuted Jews, stripping them of their citizenship and their dignity, robbing them of their property and most of their income, and isolating them from "respectable" Germans. But the Jews who remained in Germany were not generally thrown into concentration camps—the mass arrest of many thousands after *Kristallnacht* in 1938 was a special measure. Hitler, however, issued an ominous hint, in a speech to the Reichstag in January 1939, that the outbreak of war would produce even stronger measures:

> If international finance Jewry within Europe
> and abroad should succeed once again in
> plunging the peoples into a world war, then the

consequence will not be the Bolshevization of
the world and therewith the victory of Jewry,
but on the contrary, the destruction of the Jewish race in Europe.

Whatever Hitler planned, it would not be wise for Jews in Ger-
man-controlled territory to wait to find out. Yet in 1939 it was
next to impossible for central European Jews to obtain permission to enter other countries, where existing laws or hastily
constructed new regulatory barriers blocked their path.

Eduard Schulte did not worry much about official disap-
proval of German contacts with Jews, and there were Jews
whom Schulte had done business with who were in dire straits
by the late 1930s. Martin Mannheim, for example, was the
head of a small transportation company controlled by Giesche.
When the Nazi Party learned that Mannheim was Jewish, it
ordered Giesche executives to force him out. Schulte refused.
Nazi officials then put Mannheim's company on the list of Jewish firms, which meant that it could be seized without compensation. Mannheim insisted on resigning to prevent Giesche
from incurring an outright loss, but that left him without income. Schulte granted him a pension from Giesche's funds,
which continued until Mannheim managed to emigrate to
Shanghai, virtually the only place in the world that did not require an entrance visa of some sort. Upon Mannheim's departure, Schulte promised Mannheim that he would send the
pension payments to Shanghai as soon as he could figure out
how to do so. There were other cases where Schulte helped
Jews to leave the country with some money.

To assist Nazi victims was simply a question of decency for
Schulte. He felt that he had to do so, although he knew that
considerable risk was involved. He also knew that such actions
would not weaken the Nazi grip on Germany. If he really wanted
to hurt the Nazi regime, he would have to accept graver risks.

One of Schulte's Swiss business associates later told American authorities that, before the war, Schulte had . . .

> . . . advise [d] foreign bankers and writers . . . of
> the situation in Germany, of the dangers in-
> volved thereby for the freedom of the demo-
> cratic   countries,   and   whenever   and   to
> whomever he could do so not to permit any
> compromise with Hitler. . . . He has also, wher-
> ever he could, attempted to communicate his

advice to persons whom he thought to have
some influence in the United States.

.   .   .

But Schulte's warnings, as far as can be judged, fell on deaf
ears.

Once diplomacy ended and war began, there would be additional obstacles for Schulte to confront. Most German opponents of Hitler thought that they had the right to overthrow
the Nazi regime, but that they must not give aid and comfort
to Germany's enemies. Military victory would be victory for
the whole German people, and all Germans would suffer from
defeat. The very idea of passing a warning to the "enemy" ran
counter to all that was expected of a patriotic German. And
history has rarely been kind to traitors. Was a German patriot
condemned to keep silent once war broke out?

Schulte knew one German businessman who had decisively
cut the knot tying him to the Nazi regime. Gero von Gaevernitz, the son of one of Germany's best-known economic historians, continued to travel and do business in Germany. Yet he
made no secret of his hatred for the Nazi regime. The fact that
Gero was half-Jewish according to the Nazis' Nuremberg Laws
seems to have escaped the Gestapo, perhaps because he looked
like an archetypal Aryan—tall, blond, very good-looking. But
in any case, he had additional protection, for he had become an
American citizen.

Gero was deeply influenced by his father. Gaevernitz senior
was a leading German liberal, a Quaker, and a vegetarian. He
was also the prototype of the absentminded professor, but with
all his foibles, there was no one in Germany better informed
about world economic trends. Gero's mother came from a
wealthy, highly cultured, and well-connected Jewish family in
Mannheim named Hirsch. Like his father, Gero had become a
Quaker, and had spent time studying in Russia when few Germans were interested in the new Soviet regime. When he finished his academic work, he settled in New York and worked in
a local banking house (Morgan Livermore). Later he established a small investment trust company. Not long after 1933,
partly because of his disgust for the Nazi regime, he applied for
and obtained American citizenship.

Gero's sister Marga had married Edmund Stinnes, the son
of Germany's most famous industrialist in the early 1920s, who
owned a major piece of a mining concern headquartered in

Vienna. Edmund was a renegade from the conservative Stinnes family and was also a Quaker. In 1938 he and Marga left Germany and settled in Ascona, Switzerland, near the Italian border. Gaevernitz went to Europe frequently during the 1930s to see his parents and to help his brother-in-law on business matters.

Gaevernitz had excellent contacts in the German diplomatic corps, in banking and industrial circles in Berlin and Vienna, and even among the military. Like Schulte, he could gather information from some of the best sources in the country, inside and outside of government. And with his brother-in-law settled in Switzerland, Gaevernitz too had occasion to go back and forth from Germany to Switzerland (where he would move permanently after war broke out).

The Gaevernitz family had an estate not far from Breslau, and Schulte met Gaevernitz at the house of a mutual acquaintance sometime before the war. It took a while for Schulte to realize that while there was a streak of the dilettante, the romantic, and the adventurer in Gaevernitz, and while he liked to rub shoulders with the rich and powerful, he was both sincere and courageous. He never wavered in his belief that Hitler was a menace to all mankind. Once Schulte realized the depth of Gero's convictions, he knew he had found a kindred spirit.

Gaevernitz, though, had little difficulty reconciling his principles with his patriotism. Although he spent much time in Germany, he no longer made his home there; and, unlike Schulte, he had no sons in the country who would have to enter the German Army if war broke out. As he had transferred his business and his citizenship, so he transferred his patriotism and looked for a way to serve his adopted country. For Eduard Schulte, the conflict between moral principle and patriotism was more severe. Schulte had no wish to sit out the war quietly in Switzerland. By background and training, by language and culture, in his likes and dislikes, he was unalterably German. Gaevernitz was cosmopolitan; Schulte was not. There was no easy solution to his dilemma.

. . .

As war drew nearer in the summer of 1939, Schulte found himself on his way to a party: it was late one Saturday afternoon in August. Eduard Schulte did not like parties. With rare exceptions he found them boring and a waste of time. There were, however, certain obligations that could not be shirked, and so Schulte drove out of Breslau to attend the Paulys' annual summer fete, a dinner dance on their estate near Oels. Oels was located some twenty-five miles from Breslau, about halfway to the Polish border. The estate, which originally belonged to the king of Saxony, had been owned by Curt Pauly ever since his release from the Army—the cavalry to be precise—at the end of the First World War. Schulte had known Pauly for years. Politically they were close—both detested the Nazis—but they did not generally move in the same circles. Pauly had, however, agreed to employ Ruprecht Schulte, who wanted training as a farmer. Under the circumstances Schulte had to accept the invitation.

Schulte handed Pauly a bottle of whiskey that he had brought from his last trip to London. It was greatly appreciated, for it was virtually unobtainable in the shops. The Schultes were then welcomed by a sunburned Ruprecht, who appeared more muscular than before. Eduard noted that agriculture seemed to agree with Ruprecht; his own attitude toward it was ambivalent. He invested money in buying up farmland, but he would have found it intolerable to devote much of his time to farming.

Wolfgang, Schulte's elder son, could not attend, and Clara conveyed his regrets. He had been about to be released from the Army, and had even ordered civilian clothes and enrolled as a student of law. Then it had been announced that the summer maneuvers would last longer this year than ever before— they also took place nearer the Polish border than on past occasions. And so, instead of joining them at the party and then leaving on a long-planned trip to Switzerland and Italy before beginning law school, Wolfgang had been summoned to follow his regiment.

It was not a very big affair—dinner for thirty—but it lasted till well after midnight. Among the guests were neighbors of the Paulys, friends from Breslau, and some even from faraway Berlin. As at most parties the families split up after a while, and several distinct groups emerged—men, women, and the younger generation. The men, as so often, talked about the state of the world. Schulte stood in one corner of the big reception hall together with Pauly and Mrs. Pauly's cousin Woldemar von Schwerin, who for once had changed his uniform (he was an officer on the Army General Staff) for a dinner jacket.

Schulte had not seen either man for a while, and instead of volunteering his comments, which as a rule he would do freely only with those he knew really well, he solicited the opinions of the other two: what were the prospects for war? Pauly's answer came without hesitation. He had decided to send his only son, Egbert, aged thirteen, to friends of the family in Switzerland. Need he say more? He did not want his son to get a Nazi education. Pauly added that he was, as the others knew, a backwoodsman without well-informed contacts. But did one need special contacts to know that Hitler wanted war and that sooner or later—probably sooner—he would get it? Pauly had been an uncompromising enemy of the Weimar Republic, and he still thought that the Versailles Treaty, in which Germany had lost so much territory, was a crying injustice; but he had no confidence in the present leaders—they were both reckless and incompetent, a dangerous mixture.

Schulte had first heard of Pauly a decade earlier when Pauly had enjoyed some fame as a hothead leading farmers' demonstrations against taxes and farm foreclosures during the world Depression. Pauly had certainly come a long way since then; he had been a colorful and courageous man, but politically more than a little confused. But now he too had seen the light.

Both men then turned to the man in uniform. Woldemar von Schwerin, a bachelor about forty, came from a family that had given Prussia many generals. He served in the planning department of the General Staff. In fact, he was associated with *Fremde Heere West,* the department collecting military information about the French and the British military buildup. He hinted that he thought world war a foregone conclusion, even though no date had as yet been fixed for *Fall Weiss* (Case White)—the German attack against Poland.

Schwerin said that if war was over in a few weeks, it would probably end in a German victory. But if it lasted for several years, it could be 1914–18 all over again. Schulte asked about the quality of the senior military leadership. Schwerin answered that the generals were fairly competent, but that all important decisions were made by the Reich Chancellery (he refrained on purpose from mentioning Hitler's name). As for the quality of those in the Chancellery, he was not really in a position to judge. But the way he said it made it clear that he did not really think much of them.

Meanwhile, the younger guests had been rowing on the

nearby brook, while the ladies discussed the problems of running their homes in the face of various shortages. Clara, who was easily bored by talk of housekeeping, said she was very glad to be out in the country for the evening. It was so nice, warm but not too much so. Above all, it was so peaceful. Then, changing the subject, she said that she had recently read the best seller *Vom Winde verweht* (*Gone With the Wind*). In her opinion it was not a great book, but quite entertaining, an interesting description of the disappearance of a whole way of life. And she told the other ladies, who had not yet read this long book, about a scene that had particularly stuck in her memory— about the big party on the estate that was in progress when the announcement came that the Civil War had broken out.

Conversation came to an end when the hostess announced that dinner was ready. Afterward, the French doors leading to the dance floor were opened, someone brought the Gramophone in, and the young people began to dance to the tune of "Tiger Rag" and "The Lambeth Walk." The parents had their coffee and brandy or liqueur. For most of those who attended the party, it was their last formal affair for a long time.

Quite soon after the party, Ruprecht was out in the potato fields one morning when he saw squadron after squadron of Stukas and Junkers flying in the direction of the Polish border. He knew that the German attack had come. A few hours earlier, at 4:45 A.M. on September 1, German forces had opened fire all along the Polish-German border. Fifty-eight German divisions with thousands of tanks, armored cars, and heavy guns invaded Poland. Without a formal declaration of war, the Second World War began. Two days later Britain and France declared war on Germany.

Unlike Ruprecht, Eduard Schulte knew of the German invasion before it actually took place. Schulte may have obtained this information from Hans Werner von Tümpling, a prominent Berlin banker. Tümpling, a native of Breslau, had served as a cavalry major in the First World War. He had always been conservative politically; he had contacts with the Stahlhelm (Steel Helmet) veterans' organization and with men who had been close to Field Marshal and President von Hindenburg. But Tümpling was one of the anti-Nazi conservatives, an enemy of Hitler and the Nazi regime. Like Schulte, he was convinced that the Nazis would turn the whole world against Germany and produce a total disaster. Tümpling had close rel-

atives who were senior officers in the Army, and many of his
fellow officers of 1914–18 were colonels or generals in 1939.*

Schulte did not keep this valuable information to himself.
He had resolved the issue of principle versus patriotism, for he
immediately passed on the news of the invasion plan to various
Swiss bankers he knew.

Among Schulte's closest contacts in Switzerland was Alfred
Schaefer in Zurich. Schaefer, the son of a Swiss architect, had
studied law in Rome, Paris, Geneva, and Zurich. Three years
after entering the Union Bank of Switzerland he had become a
vice-president. By age thirty-four he was the chief executive officer of what was then the second-largest bank in the country.
He was a passionate horseman and an amateur student of history, but above all, like Schulte, an exceedingly capable businessman who thought in grand terms and was full of
innovative ideas.

In 1929 the Union Bank had given a large loan to Giesche.
A friendship developed between the two hardheaded chief executives of these companies, based on feelings of mutual respect, trust, and even some warmth—in a field in which there
is, on the whole, little room for such emotions. Forty years later,
Schaefer would recall with evident relish the proverbs frequently quoted by Schulte which epitomized his business philosophy, such as "While the organ is playing, the church service
is not over yet" or "*Den letzten beissen die Hunde*" (The hindmost
is bitten by the dogs), popular sayings of considerable wisdom,
the meaning of which was clear without detailed explanation.

It was not at all surprising that during the great world crisis
of 1938 Schulte and Schaefer began to discuss world affairs.
They spent some time in contact with each other: Swiss industry depended on the import not only of coal and iron but also
nonferrous metals, and there was at least one of these, namely
zinc, that Giesche could supply. Schulte, as often, made no se-

---

* Tümpling was arrested by the Gestapo soon after the July 20, 1944, coup
against Hitler. But he was one of the few who managed to talk his way out of
prison. Like Schulte, he had been almost obsessively security-minded. He was
seized on the basis of a denunciation, but his name was not found in any of
the documents seized by the Gestapo at the time. Tümpling told his captors
that someone had impersonated him, and that he would be only too happy to
help them find the real culprit. The Gestapo seems to have swallowed this
cock-and-bull story. He was put on the list of people to be under strict supervision, but he survived the war and lived for many years. His last position was
that of general manager of the Handelsgesellschaft—the leading German
bank in which Schulte had begun his business career in 1913.

cret of his contempt for the Führer and his concern for European civilization.

With the approach of war and Switzerland in danger of becoming one of Hitler's victims, Schaefer was persuaded to assist his country. After all, a leading Swiss banker met a great many visitors from Germany and could supply much information to Swiss military intelligence. But it is important to remember that Schaefer was only one of Schulte's Swiss contacts. Schulte also had close ties to the Basel branch of Swiss intelligence, which specialized in collecting news from Germany and was headed at the time by a lawyer named Häberli.

On August 27, 1939, Swiss military intelligence learned that Hitler had announced a new Y-day: the German armed forces were orde ed to attack Poland on September 1.* What no one except a ew Swiss bankers knew was that this information had come from Eduard Schulte. Despite Swiss neutrality, Swiss intelligence had close ties with the French, and so the information about the German attack quickly went to Paris and London.

Schulte's was of course not the only warning received in Paris and London. Given Hitler's record of aggression and the denunciations of Poland in the German press, any attentive newspaper reader was bound to reach the conclusion that war in Eastern Europe was quite likely. But if the outbreak of war seemed probable, it was not certain, and it was not known in the West that Hitler had actually fixed a date for the attack, postponed it, and set a new one.

Good intelligence, though, does not always make a difference. Britain and France stayed virtually immobile on the western front, and the German armed forces, which were concentrated in the east, crushed the Polish Army with great ease. By the time Russian troops invaded Poland from the east on September 17, the battle was already decided.

Despite Schulte's opposition to the war, there was no denying that the defeat of Poland brought advantages to Giesche almost immediately. On August 26 Polish military authorities had appointed special representatives to run Polish Giesche, under a secret law giving the government special powers in the event of war or the threat of war. The American executives

---

* The original Y-day was August 26, but after Mussolini's intervention and the signing of a British defense treaty with Poland, Hitler decided to postpone the invasion for a few days.

were forced to leave the country on August 28. Since Poland had taken over Polish Giesche from the Americans, German military authorities took it back as the Army ripped through Upper Silesia. The Giesche firm fell into the category of vital military plants (*W-Betriebe*), so there was no possibility of bringing back the American management, even though the United States was still neutral in the war: no foreigner was allowed to manage a *W-Betriebe*. Schulte's military connections now came in very handy. German military officials almost immediately (September 3) appointed Dr. Albrecht Jung as state commissioner for property in Upper Silesia with full power of management. Jung was considered better "qualified" for the appointment than Schulte, because Jung was a nominal party member (since May 1933); Schulte, of course, was not. But Jung, legal adviser to German Giesche, was completely loyal to Schulte. This meant that the two parts of Giesche were reunited under a single management, although for bookkeeping purposes they remained separate operations. Schulte quickly notified Anaconda executives that he would look out for American interests as much as he possibly could. His main difficulty would undoubtedly be maintaining payments on the loan from the Silesian-American Corporation, for the German government was not making foreign exchange available.

In October, control of Upper Silesia passed from the military to a civilian administration, headed by none other than Otto Fitzner, German Giesche's number two. Fitzner was a very different man from the proper and trustworthy Jung, but Schulte could still count on him to protect Giesche's interests.

Three years older than Schulte, Otto Fitzner had joined the firm in 1925. He was born in Laurahütte, in the part of Upper Silesia that became Polish in 1922. Like many German families that lived in border regions, the Fitzners were very conscious of their German identity. While a university student (at Breslau and Greifswald), Fitzner joined the young *völkische* movement, an ideological precursor of Nazism. He then married a Dutch woman related to Deterding, the mysterious founder of Royal Dutch-Shell, the firm that later became Shell Oil. The Fitzners named their sons after characters from Nordic sagas—Ruthard and Amer—outlandish names that no German had borne in many centuries.

Otto Fitzner had a good war record. He served first in the infantry and then in the air force. By the time the First World

War ended, he was head of Squadron 56, a highly decorated colonel. He participated in postwar battles against Polish insurgents in Upper Silesia. After the war he founded his own mining firm, which was acquired by Giesche in 1925. As part of the deal, Fitzner, with training in engineering and chemistry, became director of production at Giesche. He was hardworking, aggressive, and good-looking—a man of action, an optimist, and something of a daredevil.

His position at Giesche became entrenched after 1933 because of his political influence. Fitzner had joined the Nazi Party in 1931, and his ascent in the party was rapid. After becoming a senior commander in the SA, he switched over to the more fashionable SS and obtained a largely nominal appointment to Himmler's staff. The Nazis were short of politically reliable and technically competent people, and Fitzner admirably fit the bill. So he was appointed to a wide range of governmental and advisory posts. He became head of the metal industry branch within the Ministry of Economics, president of the Silesian economic commission, chairman of the Breslau chamber of commerce, and member of several other important committees. The Kaiser Wilhelm Institute (today the Max Planck Institute for the study of metallurgy) was developed largely owing to his initiative.

With all these commitments, he soon had little time to spare for Giesche, but he had no wish to give up his substantial salary. Schulte was not enthusiastic about the situation, but Fitzner indicated that it was in Schulte's best interest to be cooperative; if Schulte's attitude toward the Nazi leaders became known to the authorities, the consequences would be most unpleasant. This disagreement seems to have been resolved by Clara Schulte. She paid a visit to the Fitzner estate, and the result was that Fitzner continued to receive his salary and was of occasional assistance to the firm, securing exemptions from military service for its employees, alerting Schulte to what was going on among Nazi leaders. Through Fitzner, Eduard Schulte had an inside line on the Third Reich.

As the new chief administrator of the district of Kattowitz, Fitzner in October 1939 met with an SS official from Berlin named Adolf Eichmann, who had come to Kattowitz on secret business. His orders were to supervise the deportation of Kattowitz's Jews to Poland proper. The city was to be emptied of Jews, to become *judenrein*. Fitzner thus was privy to some of the most sensitive matters in the Third Reich even before his good friend Karl Hanke became governor and Nazi Party boss (Gauleiter) for Lower Silesia in 1941.

As Schulte continued to acquire extremely sensitive information, he worried increasingly about making good use of it. Ironically, it was a Polish acquaintance who gave Schulte the safe channel he needed to send his valuable information to the Allies. In the early 1930s Schulte had met a Pole by the name of Szczesny Chojnacki in Breslau. A hardworking man of great charm in his late thirties, Chojnacki was Polish vice-consul in the Silesian capital, but Schulte suspected that he also worked for the Polish Secret Service. His bearing was that of a military man, and he showed great interest in industries of military importance. Schulte noticed his aristocratic mannerisms and always referred to him as *von* Chojnacki. Schulte liked the young Pole. Although Schulte was no sentimental lover of anything Polish—few Germans were—both men recognized Hitler for what he was. It was an important common bond.

Chojnacki was later transferred from Breslau to Leipzig, one of the main bases of Polish intelligence in Nazi Germany. He then served in Frankfurt and Munich, becoming one of the top Polish intelligence experts on Germany. Polish intelligence was among the most competent in the world before the Second World War. The Poles knew how important an early-warning system was for their country, threatened as it was by powerful neighbors in the east and in the west. They had invested far more heavily in intelligence during the 1930s than the British and the Americans. In fact, a group of brilliant young Polish mathematicians reconstructed the German coding machine, Enigma, and broke some of the most secret German codes. Fortunately, the Poles passed along their information, and even models of Enigma, to the British and the French just before the war, for all the intelligence in the world could not prevent Germany and the Soviet Union from conquering Poland within a month.

Chojnacki was an ardent Polish patriot, and his service to his country did not end in September 1939. In its hour of defeat Poland needed him more than ever before. There was still a Polish government-in-exile, initially in France, then in England, and there were Polish diplomats and officials in all neutral countries. Chojnacki managed to make his way to Switzerland in September 1939 and put himself at the disposal of the Polish Legation in Bern. The Polish minister in Bern was not overjoyed to see him, for he foresaw that Polish intelligence activities in Switzerland would cause trouble with the Swiss government—it was difficult enough to persuade the Swiss not to withdraw recognition of the Polish government-in-exile. But Minister Komarnicki was soon replaced, and Chojnacki began work as assistant to the Polish military attaché—a lowly title. Swiss authorities tolerated him, as they tolerated the Czech Secret Service, on condition that he act unobtrusively and share with them information of common interest.

Chojnacki adopted a cover name, Jacek Lubiewa, and began to build up an intelligence network. He soon ran into Eduard Schulte in Zurich; the exact date of their meeting is unknown, but it was apparently late in September 1939. When Chojnacki asked Schulte about conditions in Germany, Schulte talked willingly, and the two decided to meet during Schulte's frequent visits to Switzerland. They also maintained contact through a Basel banker, whose identity is uncertain.

Schulte did not dream of asking for anything in return. He had all the money he needed, whereas Chojnacki had to operate on a very limited budget. With the information that Schulte and others provided, Chojnacki sent a steady stream of messages to the Second Bureau of the Polish General Staff in London. He used the diplomatic mail pouch, and also a secret radio transmitter, first at St. Ursanne, near the Swiss-French border, and then in the Swiss town of Locarno, in the house of the mayor. (Local authorities suffered great embarrassment when the set was eventually discovered.) The Second Bureau turned over all the information to the British government and a good deal to American officials in New York and Washington as well. Polish officials wanted not only to help defeat Nazi Germany, but also to safeguard Poland's future in the peace settlement. Chojnacki became Schulte's best link with the Allies during the war.

There is reason to believe that during 1939 and 1940 Schulte also continued to meet with Gero von Gaevernitz and gave him information. Just before Christmas 1939 Gaevernitz met with a German whom he described only as "still the leading man in one of the big German industries." This industrialist warned Gaevernitz that Germany would soon try to conquer the Netherlands and Belgium and to launch an attack on England from their shores—precisely the strategy we now know Hitler to have outlined to the armed services chiefs in May 1940. The British would be softened up first by continuous bombing and submarine raids. The industrialist feared

that the British munitions factories would be damaged, and
that the United States might not be ready to step into the
breach. He urged Gaevernitz to make the German plans known
to Washington, and Gaevernitz wrote up the information and
passed it on to American diplomatic contacts.

In March 1940 the same person again told Gaevernitz that
the United States would have to provide assistance to the Allies
without delay. He denounced American businessmen who
thought that the U.S. could live with a continent dominated by
Nazi Germany. A wait-and-see policy by the Americans, the industrialist explained, would lead to another Munich-type conference and the surrender of more territory to Germany. He
only hoped that

> either Hitler dies . . . [an assumption on which
> one cannot really build] or that the Allies man-
> age to hold out through the summer and the
> next winter . . . when the USA will be sending
> them war materials at full speed and strength,
> as he [the industrialist] believes definitely they
> cannot win without us [the USA].

Again and again, the informant warned Gaevernitz that there
was no compromise with the Nazis—they were gangsters and
Hitler was a madman. Misled by propaganda and confident
that Germany would win the war, the German people, regret-
tably, he said, would go along with the regime.

The industrialist was not on the mark in every particular.
He was certain that Germany would mount an attack on Great
Britain soon, whereas Hitler might continue to spare France in
the expectation that, if Britain were defeated, France would
quickly make peace. Actually, Hitler had decided to reverse the
order. Some information seemed so outlandish that Gaevernitz
left it out of his initial report, because it might detract from
credibility. For example, according to the informant, German
troops were planning to awake the Scandinavian heads of state
in the middle of the night to inform them that Germany had
already taken control of their countries.

Earlier in March 1940 Hitler had issued his directive entitled "Case Weser Exercise" for the invasion of Denmark and
Norway. The German armed forces would mount a lightning
attack on the two countries simultaneously. The Navy would
seize Norwegian ports, while parachute teams would take control of the airfields—the first use of airborne troops in history.

On April 9 Denmark was overwhelmed, and German troops took control of key Norwegian ports and airfields. The British government, still in the midst of drawing up plans for the defense of Norway, was caught by surprise.

In May 1940 the same industrialist told Gaevernitz that a German attack on Belgium and Holland was imminent, and that Hitler hoped to force the British to make peace by the fall. Then Germany would turn against Russia, grabbing the Ukraine and territory extending toward the Ural Mountains. After that, perhaps, would come a move against South America. The Allies would have to destroy these gangsters, he repeated. He closed with a line that he must have learned in Latin class: the Roman Senate's declaration of a state of emergency—*"Videant consules ne quid res publica detrimenti capiat"* (Let the consuls see to it that the republic suffers no harm). Gaevernitz wrote his American diplomatic contacts that he shared the man's views.

While the United States was moving toward massive economic assistance to the British and the French, it is doubtful whether Gaevernitz's reports played a decisive role. Gaevernitz knew only one important contact in Washington—George Messersmith, the highest-ranking State Department official with detailed knowledge of Nazi Germany. Messersmith had been American consul general in Berlin from 1930 to 1934, American minister in Vienna from 1934 until 1936, and assistant secretary of state from 1937 to 1940. He had loathed the Nazis from the beginning. Unfortunately for Gaevernitz, Messersmith became ambassador to Cuba early in 1940, which excluded him from any policy making to do with Europe. Gaevernitz presented his reports to American diplomats in Switzerland, who passed them on to Messersmith and to Washington, but there is some evidence that the American minister in Switzerland, Leland Harrison, did not take Gaevernitz too seriously. German-Americans were not above suspicion during the war.

During the first months of the war, Schulte underwent a certain change. He was more intense, more resolved; he made fewer jokes than before. He listened regularly to foreign radio broadcasts, especially to the BBC, something that was strictly forbidden in the Third Reich, and eventually became a crime punishable by death.

Wolfgang Schulte served in the Polish campaign, where he was slightly injured during the last few days while retrieving telephone lines in the no-man's-land between the German front and the Russian one. When Wolfgang came home on leave, he mildly disapproved of his father's radio listening. But he knew that he would never change him, and since he was not himself a Nazi, only a loyal citizen, he did not persist in his criticism.

CHAPTER FOUR

News from Germany

Nazi Germany was a twentieth-century fortress under the command of a fanatical dictator. Power and knowledge were concentrated in relatively few hands, and the ubiquitous Gestapo and Abwehr (the German Military Intelligence Service) counterintelligence manned the ramparts to prevent information of value from leaking outside Germany's walls to its enemies. This was the imposing image presented to the outside world.

All of this was true, but only part of the reality. Eduard Schulte knew very well that for someone in his position gathering intelligence was a relatively simple matter. On economic matters he was well informed because he ran a large company that was an important cog in the war machine. But even on political and military matters the process of obtaining inside in-

formation was not all that difficult. He met generals and diplomats in the Berlin clubs; he constantly visited government
ministries in Berlin; he had well-placed acquaintances in the
capital and elsewhere. Schulte was thought to be above suspicion, and many of these men liked to talk, particularly to an
outgoing and intelligent man. For him there was plenty of information, almost too much information. One major problem
was to distinguish fact from rumor, but if Schulte heard the
same account from a number of different sources, that was
something approaching confirmation.

The difficulty was not in collecting information, but in
passing it on without undue risk. Schulte's frequent business
trips to Switzerland reduced that risk. No one in Germany
knew what he carried inside his head. The only danger of a
leak was in Switzerland itself, and he minimized that by
choosing his contacts very carefully. And in late November
of 1940 Schulte brought these contacts some very important
information.

On November 12, 1940, Vyacheslav Molotov, Soviet foreign minister and Stalin's most trusted aide, arrived in Berlin
for talks with Hitler and Joachim von Ribbentrop, the German
foreign minister. The last time the Nazi and Soviet representatives had met, more than a year earlier, the conference had re-
sulted in a treaty that had given Hitler the free hand he needed
to attack Poland and unleash the Second World War. Was the
new Berlin meeting a sign of another major attack?

As it turned out, Hitler had no intention of engaging in a
debate or even a dialogue. He harangued his visitor with a
speech about the new world order that would be established
after Germany's military victory. Molotov for the most part listened in stony silence. Occasionally he interjected very precise
questions that had nothing to do with Hitler's monologue. He
wanted to know whether Hitler would respect Soviet interests
in Bulgaria and Turkey, and why the Germans were keeping
troops in Finland, a country that really fell within the Soviet
sphere of influence. Molotov received no answers to these questions. Ribbentrop suggested that the Soviet Union join the
Tripartite Pact among Germany, Italy, and Japan. Molotov
was willing to discuss conditions for doing so, but Ribbentrop
could not authorize anything, and Hitler eventually told his
foreign minister to drop the idea.

None of the three men could carry on small talk, none had
a sense of humor. The only interruption of the icy atmosphere

came when a British air raid forced them to walk from the Soviet Embassy to the nearby shelter of the German Foreign
Ministry, an untimely reminder that the war was not quite
over. Molotov returned to Moscow with empty hands. It was
one of the most bizarre meetings in the history of diplomacy.

The reason for this lack of dialogue was simple. Four
months earlier Hitler had decided that the Soviet Union would
be the target of his next military campaign. The Führer had
given no written order, but he had discussed the issue with the
army leaders, and some blueprints were already worked out.
The conference with Molotov in November was a charade, although not a very good one, probably designed to mislead Stalin, and perhaps also to insure the continued delivery to
Germany of Soviet raw materials that were critical to the German war effort.

Schulte learned about the unproductive results of the
Hitler-Molotov-Ribbentrop meeting within a week and gave
the information to Chojnacki on his next trip to Switzerland.
This was unusually good and timely information. Only a few
people had been present at the meeting, and German diplomats for once were tight-lipped. Foreign diplomats and reporters in Berlin knew nothing. But a young anti-Nazi official in
the German Foreign Office named Hasso von Etzdorf, who
acted as liaison with the Army High Command, wrote up a
summary of the meeting that seems to have been one of
Schulte's sources.

The Polish link with British intelligence was strong, and
Schulte's information went quickly from Chojnacki's radio network to London. At the time the British War Cabinet had no
idea what Hitler's next step would be. In September 1940 he
had postponed Operation Sea Lion, the planned invasion of
Great Britain, but it was possible that he might renew the plan.
Other possibilities included German offensives in the Balkans
or North Africa, or perhaps even some joint German-Soviet operation. Britain had interests throughout the world, and its
forces were stretched very thin, indeed to the breaking point.
That the two dictatorships had not reached agreement, that
the meeting was such an inconclusive one, was of considerable
interest to London.

Then in April 1941 Schulte arrived in Zurich with much
more startling information: Germany was about to attack the
Soviet Union. He could even give the exact date. Schulte's
source this time was less mysterious. The German preparations

for the massive invasion involved many thousands of people.
Leading industrialists were more or less systematically can-
vassed: were they involved in trade with Russia? If so, they
were advised to slow down their deliveries. Could they supply
the military with enough raw materials for a major campaign?
And what did they know about Soviet installations, mines, and
factories? It was altogether obvious which way the wind was
blowing. There were even special mixed commissions—industry, government, and the Army—to prepare for the installation
of a German occupation government in Russia. To obtain the
date was a little more difficult, but not beyond Schulte's reach.
Originally Operation Barbarossa was to begin on May 15, but
on April 30 Hitler postponed the date until June 22 because of
the recent diversion of German troops to Yugoslavia and
Greece.

This information meant most to the Russians, but Schulte
did not have a link to Moscow. The Polish government-in-exile
regarded Russia as an enemy, and Switzerland had no diplomatic relations with Moscow. Neither Chojnacki nor the Swiss
could do anything to alert Stalin even if they had wanted to.
Not that this mattered very much: Stalin received warnings of
the German attack from dozens of sources, including his own
best agents in Japan and Western Europe. But he deluded
himself into thinking that the rumors were part of a Western
plot to embroil Germany and the Soviet Union. Hitler would
never betray him.

The British and the Americans also heard of the impending
German attack from a wide variety of sources. Schulte's report
through the Poles was by no means unique, but it was still significant, for despite all the reports and even the unrivaled British intercepts of German military radio transmissions, British
intelligence chiefs still doubted in April 1941 that a German
attack on Russia was a foregone conclusion. They could not
miss Germany's military preparations in the east, but there
were many in London who felt that Hitler was simply putting
some muscle behind German economic demands. As late as
June 12 the British War Cabinet discussed whether Hitler's
aim was to make war on the U.S.S.R. or to obtain greater
quantities of oil from the Caucasus, grain from the Ukraine,
and iron ore. On the next day, after the intercept of a cable
from the Japanese ambassador in Berlin, who had just talked to
Hitler, the British War Office finally concluded that the attack
would take place in the second half of June. Paradoxically,

Eduard Schulte's message might have had more impact in London had it come then, in June, rather than in April.

Between 3 and 3:30 A.M. on June 22, 1941, as Schulte and others had reported would happen, three million German soldiers stretched from the Baltic Sea to the Black Sea opened fire on Soviet positions and crossed the border. The Russians were unprepared, and their leadership inept. The Germans advanced more quickly, destroyed more divisions, inflicted more casualties, and took more prisoners than any army in history. But there were even more Soviet armies than they had anticipated, and these were better equipped than the Germans had thought. The German advance slowed down and eventually halted. There were great German victories, but the main aim of the campaign was not reached.

After his initial warning of the invasion of Russia, Schulte continued to pass on very valuable information about the eastern front. He was finding important new sources of intelligence. In the spring of 1941, on one of his periodic trips to Berlin, Eduard Schulte met with his cousin Hermann and heard unexpected news. The retired art gallery owner had decided to enter government service—and it was no ordinary civil service post either. Hermann explained that Colonel (later Major General) Hans Joachim Oster had contacted him. Oster was Admiral Canaris' deputy, the head of the Abwehr's Central Department (Z), and the soul of the anti-Nazi movement. Oster told Hermann that people like him, old soldiers with firsthand experience of foreign countries, were needed in the Abwehr. It was even more important, Oster said, to have level-headed people, not fanatics unable to differentiate between their own delusions about Germany's greatness and the realities of world affairs. Hermann offered some feeble resistance— he was now nearer sixty than fifty. But Oster brushed this aside; everyone had a special duty in wartime, and there were so few reliable people who could be trusted. Hermann understood and duly joined Oster's department. He was reactivated in April 1941 with the rank of captain (*Rittmeister*).

Eduard could not have imagined that his quiet and unpolitical cousin would find himself in a position in German military intelligence, and a central one at that. Hermann Schulte was seven years older than Eduard. Their physical resemblance was unmistakable. Hermann was a tall man, of elegant bearing; his pronounced forehead and his bushy eyebrows were clearly "Schulte." Like Eduard, he had been born in Düsseldorf. After studying law and art history in Berlin and Bonn, he had served in a leading cavalry regiment, and some of the friendships formed in those years lasted throughout his long life. As befitted a young art dealer, he went for a year to Paris and another to London to study modern art, but above all to familiarize himself with the profession. In 1910 he became a partner in the family firm. He served in the First World War as *Rittmeister* and, as far as can be established, had a good war record. Soon after the war he married Carola Andreae, a charming lady who came from a well-to-do family. She owned among other things the Trumpf building, an office building in the west end known to all Berliners. They had one son, Herbert, and also an adopted child, Werner.

Before the First World War the Schulte Gallery had been one of the leading art galleries in the German capital, if not the best known. But in the 1920s its importance declined, and in the early 1930s the Schultes decided to liquidate the company. There were several reasons for the firm's decline. Tastes were changing, artistic fashions came and went in rapid succession, and the Schultes had no desire to adjust themselves every few years to a new "ism," to neoromanticism and Dadaism, to Neue Sachlichkeit and eventually to the new official Nazi art. They still had some fine pictures in their storerooms. In 1934 their tax return showed that they sold a single picture, a major Böcklin, for which the Swiss were willing to pay a substantial sum.

Hermann and Carola entertained a wide circle of friends in their attractive Charlottenburg home. They found plenty to occupy themselves without being tied to a daily office routine. Hermann had friends and acquaintances in the world of politics, among his old military colleagues, but also among artists and business people. Eduard, to be sure, was closer to him than the others. This had not always been so. In their youth the discrepancy in age was too great to make for true friendship. They had become close friends only during the First World War when Eduard had served in the government in the German capital.

Unlike many of the people he knew, Hermann Schulte did not join the Nazi Party. He merely became a member of the SA-Reserve II, presumably on the assumption that at the age of fifty he would not be called to march through the streets of Berlin, in uniform or without, and that membership would be purely nominal. The assumption proved to be correct.

His attitude toward the new rulers was anything but enthusiastic, but he was not an active oppositionist. Throughout his life he had had little interest in political matters. The man for whom he now worked, Oster, a fellow horseman, was a different type altogether. Department Z of the Abwehr was Oster's brainchild. Its main official function was to keep the record of German military intelligence, to maintain a full list of employees and agents, at home and abroad. It was not supposed to engage in active ("positive") intelligence, but Oster disregarded this order from the first day. Department Z became an Abwehr within the Abwehr, with its own agents engaged in special missions. Many of these missions had in reality nothing to do with the aims of Hitler's strategy: on the contrary, they were intended to sabotage it from within. Department Z was divided into eight subdepartments dealing with finance, the legal aspects of intelligence work, the keeping of the chief archives, and so on. Hermann Schulte belonged to subdepartment ZO and headed subsection ZO 1, which apparently, consisted only of himself.

Hermann was not a big wheel in the Abwehr. Officially his assignment was *Offiziersangelegenheiten*—matters relating to the officers in the intelligence service, which could mean anything or nothing. His was a socially acceptable job in which he could be of help to friends. Hermann had some of the talents that were needed in this new career, and a guardian angel seems to have guided his steps. He did not show excessive zeal. Lacking ambition, he remained discreetly in the background, sharing an office and even a telephone with another official, Dr. Behnke, a relative of the man who had once been Canaris' chief—Admiral Behnke. His status, in other words, was not very high—and this would save him in later years, for as the war progressed, the Abwehr came under increasing attack from the SS and from Hitler himself. Eventually it was dissolved, and most of its functions were taken over by Himmler's Main Security Office, which included the Gestapo.

From 1942 on the Abwehr ceased to be effective. Some Allied observers of German intelligence later attributed this to the stupidity, lack of initiative, and corruption in the upper echelons. But the real reason for the decline of the Abwehr is to be found elsewhere: many of the senior officials of the Abwehr had reached the conclusion that Hitler would not win the war, and indeed that it was not desirable that he should. Some

began to engage in conspiratorial activities against the regime
they supposedly served. Some worked against it halfheartedly
or indirectly, others openly and with little regard for the risks
involved.

As the Gestapo began uncovering these things, some Abwehr
agents serving abroad defected to the Allies. The first in the
Central Department of the Abwehr to be arrested was Hans
von Dohnanyi, a part Jew by Nazi laws, with close ties to General Oster. A few months later Oster—who had been passing
German plans to the Allies from the beginning of the war—was
suspended, and finally in 1944, Admiral Canaris, the head of
the Abwehr, was removed. The extent of their "treason" (as the
Nazis saw it) became known only gradually. After the nearly
successful assassination attempt against Hitler on July 20,
1944, further evidence of treason in the Abwehr was obtained,
and a number of its leading officials were executed.

But Hermann Schulte had kept quietly in the background.
He made it his practice not to confide in anyone except two or
three friends whose loyalty he could trust. Not having been an
admirer of the Nazis from the beginning, he became even more
critical as the result of things he came to hear and witness in
the Abwehr during the war. His feelings were shared by his
wife; they lost both their sons in the war, one in particularly
gruesome circumstances.

Hermann saw and heard a great deal. It is a mistake to assume that only the chiefs of intelligence are the keepers of great
secrets. Such compartmentalization was perhaps possible in the
Middle Ages. But in twentieth-century bureaucracies complete
secrecy is impossible. Important information has to be typed by
secretaries, to be filed, to be communicated by way of the telephone or the telegraph, decoded and analyzed. It has to be
disseminated among a number of privileged recipients. Intelligence, after all, is not the collection of information for collection's sake or for the benefit of historians. It is meant to be a
guide to action. Dozens of people are bound to know even the
deepest secrets. Because he was in a strategic place at the right
time, there was little that escaped Hermann Schulte. Whatever
did not reach him through official channels was discussed in
the Abwehr canteen, or in the evening over a glass of wine. The
quiet captain, who does not figure in any of the postwar his-
tories of German intelligence, was bound to be among the best-
informed people in Germany simply by virtue of the location of
his office.

He met Eduard regularly, and since he trusted his cousin implicitly, there were few secrets that he kept from him. Did he know what use Eduard would make of the information he gave him? He must have guessed, but it is doubtful whether he was told in so many words. Hermann loathed the Nazis, but not with the same burning intensity as Eduard. He was not an activist.

Hermann was never suspected. Even after the Gestapo had an inkling that major leaks were occurring, he escaped detection. The Gestapo were looking for traitors much higher up, in Hitler's immediate surroundings. Given the nature of the information that leaked, the Gestapo was convinced that it could only have come from the "top people."

What kind of information had been passed to the Allies?

Late in 1941, following the German retreat from Moscow, Schulte reported to Chojnacki about impending changes in the German High Command. Soon afterward General von Bock replaced Rundstedt as head of Army Group South, Generals Guderian and von Brauchitsch were fired, and there were other important changes. In January 1942 Schulte brought information that was deemed of so much importance that after receiving the message from the Poles, the British immediately brought it to William Donovan's attention in Washington.* Schulte reported that huge operations in the east had depleted gasoline stocks to such an extent that the German Army was unable to undertake any large spring offensive on the whole eastern front. German strategists had therefore decided to carry out a "smashing operation" on the southern sector of the front only, via the Crimea and Rostov, so as to conquer the Caucasus in one drive and secure the oil fields there. This would be done as soon as weather permitted.

Schulte was in a unique position to know about German industry's dependence on raw materials. The country had enough coal and iron, but for most other raw materials it depended on imports. Bauxite for aluminum was imported from France, Italy, and the Balkans; nickel arrived from Finland, manganese from the Ukraine, wolfram from Spain and Portugal, and chrome from Turkey. But most important was gasoline, and the imports from the Rumanian oil fields were not sufficient. Germany was producing synthetic fuels—more than

* William Donovan was then Coordinator of Information; he became head of the new Office of Strategic Services in 1942.

seven million tons in 1942, almost 60 percent of which was used for military operations. But even this was inadequate, and Hitler's *Blitzkrieg* strategy was based on the erroneous assumptions that the war in the west would be over in a few weeks, and that the Russian oil fields would be seized soon after the invasion of the Soviet Union. Without fuel, German tanks would not move, and the air force would be grounded. Despite the enormous initial victories, by late August 1941 Hitler knew that the war would drag on well into 1942. The question of oil supply became crucial.

Hitler would have liked to occupy Moscow, partly of course because it was the symbolic heart of Russia. But the lack of oil dictated his strategy, and this meant a major offensive on the southern front only.* At the time, the Allies had no knowledge of Hitler's strategy on the eastern front. Information to this effect was of great importance.

Schulte's report of January 1942 to Chojnacki was a fairly accurate summary of Hitler's directives 41 (*Fridericus*) and Operation Blue, which were not to be implemented until May. The Allies received Schulte's report four months before the event, and it got the essential point right—that German offensive action would be virtually limited to the southern front in Russia. The same report also contained information to the effect that, in case the offensive failed, Germany was considering a plan to attack Turkey with the help of Bulgaria. This project was not, however, seriously contemplated, nor did Bulgaria join the war against the Soviet Union, as Schulte's source had predicted. Finally, the same long report dealt with the tensions between Hitler and his generals, which, while correct in broad outline, did not add much to what was known already, and contained some factual inaccuracies. Despite the errors, it was clear that the message could have come only from sources high in the German command.

Schulte continued to pass on important military information throughout 1942 and on into 1943. For example, he reported on the specifications of a new model of the JU 52, the

---

* The main bottleneck was not the *production* of synthetic oil (which continued to rise in Germany up to the Allied bombing raids in 1944) but the supply to the front line. German locomotives were not suitable for Russian railways. The roads were in bad condition, and as the German columns advanced, the supply trucks used up most of the fuel they carried for their own transport. In the end Army Group South was supplied partly by air, partly by camel. It was mainly because of the difficulties of supply that the passes in the Caucasus could not be taken by the German forward units.

main German transport plane. He updated the Allies on Hitler's relationship to his generals. To be sure, there were others providing similar information, including at least one other well-placed industrialist (to judge from his reports). But Schulte's information was generally quite good.

Schulte was an important source for Swiss intelligence as well. It is likely that he warned the Swiss as well as the Poles of *Fall Gelb*, the German plan to attack Western Europe in spring 1940. (Unfortunately, any documents that may exist on this matter have not been declassified.) The German treatment of Denmark and the Netherlands proved a most useful lesson to the Swiss authorities. These two countries had been scrupulously neutral, but Denmark was taken over in a few hours and Holland in a few days. Sweden, on the other hand, was not attacked. The reason was that it was better prepared; a German operation against Sweden would have involved twenty divisions, perhaps more, and they could not be spared.

More than once Hitler had made it known that he regarded the existence of small countries as an annoying anachronism. Switzerland was not the Netherlands or Denmark. It was neutral, but it would fight, and while the country was much smaller than Sweden, the terrain favored the Swiss. The Alps were not tank country, and even parachutists would find the going there difficult. Mobilization in Switzerland was more extensive than in any other country. At one time 850,000 men were under arms, one out of six of the total population. But if the Swiss kept all males in a state of military alert, the economy was bound to collapse within a short time. They had to know whether there was an immediate danger of invasion or whether they could afford to release half or more of those who had been mobilized. They knew that blueprints for an invasion had been prepared in Berlin, but blueprints existed for almost any eventuality. They had to know how real the danger was. Swiss military intelligence desperately cultivated reliable German contacts.

Under Lieutenant Colonel Roger Masson Swiss intelligence did a reasonably good job. Masson allowed decentralization of intelligence gathering. He gave those working for him a freer hand than was allowed by any other wartime intelligence chief. It was their own business if they did not want to tell him about their operations, networks, and agents; as far as he was concerned only results counted.

Switzerland had various friends in Germany who passed on

warnings fairly regularly. One source was the "Viking" line, which had been built up by Major Max Waibel, Masson's deputy, and which consisted of erstwhile colleagues from German military academies that Waibel had attended—military opponents of Nazism like Hans Oster, Georg Thomas, and Friedrich Olbricht, who had now risen to influential positions in the Abwehr or the German General Staff. But there were also others less conspicuous, businessmen such as Schulte who visited Switzerland regularly during the war.

In late 1941 Schulte told his Swiss associates what they desperately wanted to hear. For the present there was no danger at all of a German invasion. Switzerland's railways as well as its industries were far too important for Germany to risk damaging or destroying them. The fact that the bulk of the German Army was then tied up in the Soviet Union was by itself no guarantee of anything. Hitler would consider invading other countries if the German war economy needed their raw materials and could not get them otherwise. But as long as Switzerland continued to cooperate economically with Germany, it was safe. Such information, combined with similar reports from other sources, allowed the Swiss to function without all-out mobilization. If the danger of invasion arose again in the future, they could expect some advance warning from their German friends.*

Although Schulte continued to obtain much information from Tümpling and cousin Hermann, through Otto Fitzner Schulte had indirectly acquired a new and extremely valuable source: Karl Hanke, the Gauleiter and governor of Lower Silesia. More than once Adolf Hitler referred to Karl Hanke as the "very best of our Gauleiters." Hanke belonged to that young generation of Nazi leaders who had not been old enough to fight in the First World War, regretted this lost opportunity forever afterward, and sought to compensate for it by assertive military behavior. Hanke had risen to a very influential position from small beginnings. His father was a locomotive engineer, and the younger Hanke had not been able to finish high school (*Gymnasium*); instead he had some vocational training, first in a railway workshop and later in the mills. In the 1920s

---

* In March 1943 Schulte apparently warned the Swiss and the Poles that Switzerland would be in great peril if Italy collapsed under an Allied invasion: German forces would try to hold as much of Italy as possible and would therefore need Swiss routes of communication. In fact, the Germans did seriously consider an invasion of Switzerland at that time.

he had somehow attached himself to Goebbels in Berlin and become his advance man. He then came to Hitler's attention as one of the most promising young leaders and became a member of the Reichstag, the German parliament, at the age of twenty-nine.

In 1937 Hanke was made state secretary, the number-two job at the Ministry of Propaganda. Unlike Goebbels, he was not a speaker of genius, but a good organizer, a tremendous worker, always available when needed. Although his own career figured topmost in his order of priorities, he was capable of an occasional good deed. In the long conflict between Goebbels and his wife, Magda, who wanted a divorce because the little doctor's extramarital affairs had become a major public scandal, Hanke took the wife's side. His gallant activities on behalf of the helpless and neglected Mrs. Goebbels were perhaps not entirely altruistic. She not only appealed to his knightly instincts; he had also fallen in love with her and even proposed marriage. Magda Goebbels was lukewarm, and Hitler, in any case, invoked higher state interests: a divorce was out of the question.

By 1939 there was a reconciliation in the Goebbels household, and Hanke found himself out of a job. By instinct or through calculation he did the one thing that could save his career. He volunteered for the army, the only senior Nazi civilian leader to do so, and saw active service in an armored regiment as a mere lieutenant both in the Polish campaign and in France. Physically he was not a strong man, but his nervous energy saw him through the strains of army life; he returned with the Iron Cross, First Class, and a great deal of publicity. He was ready for a new career, and in January 1941 Hitler appointed him supreme party leader for Lower Silesia—and also head of the state administration in that province. Later on he also became supreme defense commissioner for the area.

There were chinks in Hanke's armor. Occasionally he showed weakness unbecoming to a top Nazi leader. He had been among the very coolest in the Night of the Long Knives in June 1934 when many of the most trusted storm-troop leaders were massacred. But later on, during the war, he warned his erstwhile protégé Dr. Albert Speer, the architect who now had become an influential minister, never to go near Auschwitz because (as he put it) some "horrible things" were taking place there.

This then was the man who over a glass of wine in the late

hours of the evening would discuss with Giesche's number-two man, Otto Fitzner, some of the problems troubling him and, generally speaking, the great issues facing the Reich during the war. There were some things an ordinary Gauleiter would not know, or would learn only indirectly and belatedly. But Hanke was no ordinary Gauleiter; he was always in line for further promotion, and in fact he succeeded Himmler as head of the SS in the last days of the war. State secrets that would not normally be made known to others would still reach him. In more than one respect the structure of the Third Reich resembled a medieval knightdom (or the Mafia). *Nul homme sans seigneur* (No man without a master) had been the hierarchical principle on which medieval society had been based. In the Third Reich, despite—or because of—the rigid application of the leadership principle, tens of thousands of people were but two steps removed from the top leadership.

Hanke was Fitzner's patron, and if Hanke could not keep his mouth shut, Fitzner was given to bragging. Whenever his colleagues, the senior Giesche staff, discussed politics, Fitzner would tell them that they really did not know what they were talking about. If they only knew what *he* knew . . .

Fitzner was a somewhat pompous, humorless man who did not even realize that Schulte was baiting him: "Do you really believe this, Herr Doktor?" Whereupon Otto Fitzner would prove that he did know, swearing his colleagues to absolute secrecy. Sometimes it took only a day or two and sometimes a month, but there were few secrets that did not find their way from the highly placed Gauleiter to the head of Giesche.

It is impossible to give a full list of those from whom Eduard Schulte obtained information. It is clear that Tümpling, Hermann Schulte, and Fitzner were his best and most frequent sources. Another useful contact was Jakob Werlin, a high executive of the Daimler-Benz automobile concern, which produced the Mercedes cars that Hitler liked so much. Werlin had joined the Nazi Party in December 1932, just before Hitler came to power. He subsequently met with Hitler a number of times, which turned out to be fortunate for other executives of the corporation, who had wives of Jewish descent. Werlin was able to keep his colleagues in key corporate positions over even Himmler's protests. In January 1942 Hitler appointed Werlin to a new government post, general inspector for automotive transport, and Werlin was an occasional visitor at Hitler's headquarters. Werlin and Schulte knew each other and would meet from time to time in Germany and Switzerland.

Of how much importance was Schulte's information for the Allied conduct of the war? This question cannot be answered with assurance at present, and it is not certain that there ever will be an authoritative assessment. The quantity of information received by the Allies was huge, but its quality was uneven, its provenance often unknown and sometimes dubious. Even a reliable source would sometimes convey a false or inaccurate report; Schulte, who was considered a reliable source, had to rely mainly on other informants who might have heard of a project in the planning stage but did not know that it was subsequently canceled. There were many rumors in wartime, and there was also disinformation—even on the highest level. Until 1943, Schulte gave his information to the Poles and the Swiss, and it is well known that the Americans and the British trusted their own secret services more than those of their allies or neutral sources. Worse still, though the information might be absolutely correct, timely, and of crucial importance, the recipients in London and Washington might still reject it because it did not fit their preconceived notions. Eduard Schulte was to discover this in a sadly tragic episode in the summer of 1942.

CHAPTER FIVE

The Mysterious Messenger

On Wednesday, July 29, 1942, the train carrying Eduard Schulte arrived at a station; he looked up from the newspapers he had been dozing over and saw that it was Stuttgart. The newspapers contained the usual official announcements from army headquarters. The High Command of the Wehrmacht had announced that the Russians were retreating beyond the river Don. In North Africa too, the situation had warmed up. There were frequent references to an obscure place called El Alamein. In peacetime, Schulte used to scan the business section of the papers, but there was nothing of great interest to be learned from these pages in wartime.

The train continued south. He had made this trip many times. From the window of his first-class compartment he could see a lovely and peaceful landscape. No one would have guessed that Germany was involved in the greatest and most fateful war in its history, that it was on the very eve of total victory, according to Hitler. The names of stations floated past: Böblingen, Ehningen, Herrenberg, and then the train entered a forest. It seemed like an eternity since he had last hunted in such a forest. Meadows, villages, and little towns with old castles, churches with onion-shaped towers, looking like mosques. Bondorf—Eutlingen—Horb—Neckarshausen—the train now ran beside a highway, but there was hardly any traffic. Then, for many miles, it ran alongside the river Neckar (the same river that was mentioned in an old elementary-school song about shepherds and their herds). There were no cows to be seen now and only a few sheep, but there were numerous little workshops and factories.

Big industry had bypassed this region, perhaps leaving it well placed for what was to come. Schulte had just been reading about Allied air attacks in places as far afield as Danzig and Königsberg. So far not much damage had been done, but one day, soon perhaps, these attacks would grow in intensity. Two months ago, one thousand British planes of Bomber Command attacked Cologne. A friend who had seen the devastation a short while afterward had given him a vivid account. Sulz passed by: he saw charming little covered wooden bridges over the Neckar, and then, for a fleeting second, there was a large gray building that he dimly remembered from a prewar visit. This was the Mauser works, where the famous revolvers and carbines were produced and now, in wartime, presumably also larger and more effective weapons.

How much attention did Schulte pay to the pretty Swabian landscape as the train made its way through the small villages and the quaint little towns? Again, as at the station in Breslau, his face betrayed nothing of his mood and feelings: and this same reticence was doubtless the reason he had never kept a diary.* He could not but feel great strain and apprehension.

---

* Except a hunting diary from which we learn that the summer of 1942 had been a good season for this passionate hunter. In late June he had managed to get away from his office, and for a week at his manor at Klein Voldikov he had gone out with Müller, the forester, each morning, and seldom did they return with empty hands. Except once: on the last day of his stay, exactly four weeks before his trip to Zurich, at a quarter to seven in the morning in a blue lupine aisle in the middle of the forest, Schulte spotted his biggest stag ever. He fired rapidly, but he was so excited that he missed by six or seven yards. "Long live abstinence . . ." he wrote in his diary. How peaceful had it been in deepest Pomerania—for hours he had been able to forget the accursed war.

Schulte was not a man beset by self-doubt—once he had made a decision, he did not look back. But he was also aware of the risks he was running—the fact that if, for whatever reason, he was caught, it would mean suffering and ruin not only for him but for his whole family. He was not an old man, nor poor, nor in bad health—if anybody in Germany had something to lose, it was Eduard Schulte. He had faced danger since the day the war broke out; every trip abroad, each contact with foreign intelligence, had involved great risks. But the mission he had imposed on himself when he heard of Hitler's order to exterminate Europe's Jews was different in kind from previous trips. On two or three prior occasions he had been the carrier of more important pieces of information as far as the course of the war was concerned. But these had to do with soldiers and diplomats, not with the systematic murder by gassing of a whole people, an event beyond human imagination. And there was no doubt that Hitler would get away with his design, just as he had surprised and defied the world every time in the past. This mission was a race against time and indifference, and there must have been many sad thoughts on Schulte's mind as the train approached the Swiss border.

In view of his heroic efforts, one might ask about Schulte's attitude toward the Jews. It was no different from his attitude toward other human beings. He had had business dealings with Jews in Germany, Britain, and Switzerland. There were some he had come to respect, and a few had become his friends over the years. There were others for whom he did not greatly care.

He had been concerned about the fate of the Jews of Breslau. Once there had been a flourishing Jewish community, among it wealthy merchants, physicians, and scientists of national and international renown. The majority, however, were neither rich nor famous, eking out a living for themselves and their families not without difficulty. Their contribution to the economic and cultural life of the city was quite disproportionate to their number.

Schulte used to discuss both hunting and politics with the owner of the neighboring estate, Ewald von Kleist-Schmenzin, who was one of the sternest opponents of Hitlerism. Shortly before the war he had traveled to London to warn Churchill and other British leaders of Hitler's intentions. Kleist was in direct contact with Canaris, and Kleist's brother-in-law was a leading figure in the Abwehr.

By 1942 the Gestapo had deprived Kleist of his hunting permit, as he was considered politically unreliable. There was much worse to come. Kleist did not escape in time.

Then Hitler came to power, and within six years their number fell from twenty thousand to ten thousand. Many emigrated, some committed suicide. Even during the first year of the war some succeeded in getting out, via Italy and the Soviet Union, both then still neutral. By late 1941 only 8,100 were left; only the Gestapo knew exactly how many.

Then they too began to disappear, quietly, without attracting any attention. First they were concentrated in certain streets and buildings, and then, after a few months, they were "evacuated" to some villages not far from Breslau. They were temporarily housed in buildings that had once belonged to Cistercian monks, but after a few weeks they were again removed, this time to an unknown destination. According to rumor, they were "resettled" in Poland, a version that Schulte found difficult to believe, for his firm was operating in Poland and had a wide network of informants there; surely he would have heard details if this resettlement had indeed taken place. Now he knew the real meaning of resettlement.

The conductor announced that they were in Singen, and warned that everyone had to leave the train for border control. In prewar days the passport and customs officers had boarded the train here for the convenience of the travelers. But now there were only a few travelers, and their convenience did not figure high on the list of priorities. Still, the control was not really that strict. The passengers were ushered into a room in the station building. Two men in police uniform and a civilian examined their passports. They consulted a long list, but everyone's papers seemed to be in good order, and the customs check that followed was perfunctory. There was not that much of value to be smuggled out of wartime Germany.

Within twenty minutes they were all back in the train. Schulte saw a Swiss flag on a little wooden house—an act of defiance or yet another border crossing? He had a fleeting view of the Rhine, which, now that the day had turned cloudy, did not look at its best. Then Schaffhausen. He must have passed the place a hundred times, yet he had never seen the Rheinfall, one of the wonders of Europe. Somehow there had never been time enough, never the chance to leave the train for a few hours. All he knew of Schaffhausen were the brown-roofed houses he had watched from the window of the train. He should at least once have visited the falls, the fountains, and the statues, but he had never really felt an interest in them. There had always been some urgent business meeting scheduled: a busy executive had no time to spare for such nonessential activities. There would be plenty of time for sight-seeing after the war (or perhaps there wouldn't, if the war ended in the way he feared it would).

Then, at last, Zurich's Hauptbahnhof, the main railway station. For the last few minutes the train moved very slowly and cautiously, and then it came to a halt. His office had wired the hotel in which he always stayed; there was a porter from the Baur-au-Lac waiting on the platform, and he carried Schulte's luggage to the big limousine that was waiting in front of the station. Zurich seemed strangely deserted in what used to be the height of the season; there were no tourists, and many men were in uniform.

They drove along the Bahnhofstrasse, Zurich's main thoroughfare, the headquarters of the big banks and of the most expensive shops. A policeman stopped the traffic at the Paradeplatz. On the right was Jelmoli, the largest department store. Near here Doris worked. The front of the store was decorated with Swiss flags, and a big sign announced that Swiss flags of every size could be bought inside the shop cheaply, and without textile coupons. Then after a few hundred meters the car slowed down and turned to the right. They had arrived.

Schulte had always been an honored guest at the Hotel Baur-au-Lac, as befitted an excellent customer. This time, no doubt because of the extreme slackness of business, the reception was warmer than usual—the concierge had a broad smile on his face, and the manager appeared within seconds to express his profound appreciation at the arrival of such an old and esteemed friend of the house. As always they would do their utmost to make his stay pleasant. At the Baur-au-Lac they remembered their guests' preferences, and so he was given his favorite suite overlooking the lake. There was rationing now, the manager said apologetically, but considering the circumstances he was sure that Dr. Schulte would find no reason for complaint. Certainly the quality of their wines had not deteriorated. Schulte told him his stay would probably be short, but he hoped to be back for a longer visit. The manager then withdrew, after renewed expressions of his esteem. Schulte saw flowers on a table, and a bottle of his favorite red wine (with the compliments of the management).

Schulte liked "Grand Hotels," and the Baur-au-Lac was one of his favorites. From the outside it was not particularly impressive, with its gray Biedermeier façade and the somewhat incongruous Ionic columns at the entrance facing the lake. A façade does not make a Grand Hotel, but as far as its location, the view, the little private park in front, and, above all, the discreet and efficient service were concerned, the Baur had few equals. Schulte felt at home in the public rooms with their big fireplaces, the Tudor paneling, and the Gobelin tapestries on the wall. The manager had told him that the hotel would be celebrating its hundredth anniversary in 1944. But 1944 seemed very far off.

It was now midafternoon; Doris would still be at work. He phoned her, and she was surprised and pleased. There had been no time to tell her about this visit. Schulte explained that there had been some sudden developments that made the trip necessary. He would be at her apartment in the evening, but it might be a little later than usual. He had things to do first.

It was pointless for him to call Chojnacki, or Schaefer, his close associate from the Swiss Union Bank. Both were men of discretion, well connected in the world of intelligence; but Schulte did not expect intelligence agencies to respond to the kind of news that he had obtained. The Poles and the Swiss were always eager to listen to him, but he knew that they had their own worries, and the fate of the Jews would not figure very highly among them. On other occasions in the past he had talked to Jacques Rosenstein, whom he had known in Berlin in the 1930s, a close business associate who often passed on information to Leland Harrison, the American minister (chief of mission), in Switzerland. But Rosenstein was now in New York.

Schulte had decided that his information about the impending tragedy must be passed on to the leading Jewish institutions in America. Only they had sufficient influence to sound the tocsin and to induce the American and the British governments to take some action. (Schulte, like many non-Jews, tended to overrate the influence of "World Jewry.") Who could be trusted to pass on this desperately important information, to be discreet and at the same time give it the necessary emphasis? Schulte went to the phone and asked to be connected with IKAP in Basel.

•   •   •

The person Eduard Schulte wanted so urgently to speak to at IKAP (*Internationale Kapital Anlage Gesellschaft*) was Isidor Koppelmann, Jacques Rosenstein's right hand man, his Sancho Panza, as their detractors said. Rosenstein had the brilliant, sweeping ideas, and Koppelmann was to follow them up and carry them out. Born in 1887, Koppelmann was a native of one of the eastern regions of the Austro-Hungarian monarchy. He had trained in a leading Vienna bank where Rosenstein had first met him in the late 1920s. Rosenstein had been impressed by his seriousness and competence but above all by his utter discretion, and he had hired him to take care of his Berlin office; it was there that Koppelmann had first seen Schulte. When Hitler came to power Rosenstein transferred Koppelmann to Basel to supervise his spreading business interests.

The function of IKAP was to advise investors, and it was attached to a well known Basel private bank, LaRoche. Its clients included such substantial firms as Giesche and also Schulte personally and thus Koppelmann was accepted, albeit a little reluctantly, by the Basel banking establishment, not usually very forthcoming in admitting outsiders to its ranks. With all his brilliance and entrepreneurial gifts, Rosenstein was too daring for the taste of some of the Basel bankers, and this too, affected Koppelmann's standing.

Koppelmann and his wife, a non-Jewish woman whom he had met and married in Vienna, were an outgoing, friendly couple. They had no children and entertained often in their house in Basel. Many years later Koppelmann's friend, neighbor, and physician, Dr. Friedmann, would still remember with some nostalgia the many interesting people from various countries he met in this hospitable home. Koppelmann was a man of wide interests, but politics was not among them. He was an extrovert and a great story teller.*

Koppelmann had already left his office in Basel when Schulte phoned, but a few minutes later he arrived at home, called back and when he heard that there was urgent business to discuss, he said he would take the first train in the morning to Zurich.

It was almost dark when Schulte left the hotel and turned toward the lakeshore. A little steamer called *Helvetia* was about

---

* But there was one subject on which he would never talk, his connection with Swiss intelligence and also the American and British secret services. Only many years later, after the war, in conversation with close friends, would he drop an occasional hint about meetings with Allen Dulles in a blacked-out Zurich street. Or he would mention in passing the fact that his friends from Swiss intelligence had strongly urged him never to travel to Zurich or back alone in an empty railway compartment—obviously there had been a warning from someone . . .

to leave the landing station and some drowsy seagulls were flapping their wings. On a wooden table there were announcements of coming local events: the annual Swiss fair on the other side of the lake, the music week in Lucerne, the tennis championship in St. Moritz and the Engadin golf competition. In the Bellevue Cinema a few steps away they were again showing René Clair's *Sous les toits de Paris.* It was one of the few films Schulte had seen and liked before the war. Elsewhere, "Kaiserwalzer," starring Martha Eggert, was being shown; so was a Mickey Rooney comedy, and another movie with James Cagney and Ann Sheridan. Switzerland was typically impartial in matters of culture: there was also a Le Corbusier exhibition. All the Swiss public knew of the war was from Cinebref newsreels showing the German version of the battles of Sevastopol and Mersa Matruh. How much longer would this idyll continue?

Soon afterward he rang the bell at an apartment in the Alfred Escher Strasse, a few hundred yards from the hotel. Doris smiled. "What a nice surprise." They embraced, not passionately, but like old, very close acquaintances.

They had known each other for several years, having first met not long before the war: Schulte was forty-seven at the time, Doris in her early thirties. She was an attractive, vivacious woman; some of her acquaintances said that she looked like a sister (a little fuller perhaps) of Gene Tierney, the movie star, who, coincidentally, had gone to school in Switzerland. Doris had been born in Zurich of East European Jewish parents. She was unattached, and flattered by the attentions of this important industrialist. She came to love him. Schulte had never been a womanizer and he was no longer of the age at which romantic attachments are easily formed. Yet he fell in love with this young woman, of a background so different from his own. Perhaps he was attracted by her lack of inhibitions, so different from his own character; perhaps it was her warmth, perhaps the fact that unlike his wife she was not an intellectual and had no pretensions in that direction. It is difficult to fathom the human heart; all we know is that this was Schulte's only serious affair and that it was to become a lasting relationship. It is even more difficult to know to what extent his love for Doris had impelled him to engage in this rescue mission in the middle of the war. Surely it had been an important factor in his decision, but from all we know of Schulte, it cannot have been the decisive impulse.

Doris said that he looked worried. Schulte answered that

there were problems, but for once not connected with his business. Doris was discreet; she did not persist. They sat down for a late dinner.

When Schulte and Koppelmann met in Zurich the next morning, the industrialist went straight to the point. He had come into the possession of some information that sounded incredible but was absolutely authentic. It concerned the fate of the Jews of Europe, not just some, but all of them. This information had to be transmitted immediately to the leading Jewish organizations in America. Above all, unless action was taken to thwart the diabolical Nazi scheme, few if any Jews would be left in Europe by the end of the year. Schulte gave Koppelmann the substance of the information and repeated that it was absolutely genuine. There could not be the slightest doubt of its truth, and this ought to be made very clear to Koppelmann's contacts.

Koppelmann sat in silence. He knew Schulte as a sober businessman, anything but a panic-monger. He had been proved right on many occasions. Nor was it any secret that many Jews had already been killed in Eastern Europe, some quickly, in pogroms, some slowly starved to death. Only a few weeks earlier Koppelmann had received terrible news from a lawyer in Bucharest, Rumania. His beloved only sister had been deported to Transnistria, which meant almost certain death for her. Her last desperate cry for help was "Get me a visa to some foreign country." There was a faint chance that a passport or even a visa from some Latin-American republic would get her and her family out of the hell of Transnistria. Koppelmann had heard that such documents were useless once people had been deported, but Jews were clutching at any straw, and who could blame them. Koppelmann had phoned the Palestine Office in Geneva, but his friend Scheps had told him that they had no "certificates," as the immigration permits to Palestine were then called, and even if they had them, they would not be given to Rumania, which was enemy territory.

Koppelmann agreed that Schulte's information was of the greatest importance. Unfortunately, he did not know the Swiss Jewish leaders and the diplomatic emissaries that well—he did not really move in those circles. Schulte asked him to think again. Koppelmann thought of Sagalowitz.

Schulte remembered the man; he had met him a few times in the Rosensteins' house. A pleasant man, he said—a journalist. But did he really have the right connections? And above all,

could he be trusted? Koppelmann said that Sagalowitz knew
everyone of consequence, that he was one of the leading experts
on Nazi Germany in Switzerland, and that he was taken very
seriously by people in authority. Before Rosenstein had left for
America he had impressed on Koppelmann that if ever he
needed political advice on Jewish affairs, his former classmate
Sagalowitz was the man to consult, not the babblers heading
the Jewish community. There was not much love lost between
Rosenstein and the local Jewish establishment.

Koppelmann decided to telephone Sagalowitz on the spot.
A female voice answered: it was Sagalowitz's companion Annette [not her real name]. No, he was out of town. He was in
Lausanne participating in the annual Swiss chess championship. He would be back in five or six days. Koppelmann called
the Beau Rivage in Lausanne. Sagalowitz was not registered
there. He tried the Hotel du Château. Yes, the operator told
him, the doctor was among their guests. But the competition
continued, and he had strict instructions not to page any of the
players—they must not be disturbed. Koppelmann left an urgent message.

Within an hour Sagalowitz called back. Koppelmann explained that a matter of the gravest importance had arisen.
Only Sagalowitz would be able to deal with it—could he possibly come to Zurich for a day? Sagalowitz replied that it was out
of the question. This was the first major chess tournament since
the outbreak of the war. Chess was his great passion; he was
vice-chairman of his chess club in Zurich, and at one time he
had corresponded with the great Emanuel Lasker. If he left the
tournament even for a day, he would be in serious trouble; his
chance for a good finish, slim though it was, would be gone.
Surely a delay of a few days would not make much difference.
Koppelmann said he would not have made the suggestion if it
were not a matter of life and death.

Sagalowitz wanted to know further details before making
up his mind. Koppelmann dropped hints about a visitor from
abroad who had arrived with information of the utmost importance. But he did not mention any name or the contents of the
message. The perplexed Sagalowitz complained that every
misfortune seemed to happen to him! He had looked forward
to the tournament for a long time. In early July, he had had to
undergo a hernia operation, and for a while it seemed doubtful
whether he would be able to compete in Lausanne. But he had
recovered in time and gone to Lausanne, where he had met

many old friends and rivals from all over Switzerland. His chance to finish at the top of his section was not good. Still, it was an imposition to ask him to leave the tournament in the middle—there was so much of interest going on, and so much to be learned.

Why the hurry? It sounded very mysterious and not altogether convincing. But Sagalowitz had never refused an appeal for help. And so after some reflection he agreed to take a train to Zurich the next day. Before leaving he talked to the chief judge of the tournament, who told Sagalowitz that he would reschedule his match.

Koppelmann then asked Schulte whether he wanted to meet Sagalowitz in person. Schulte preferred not to see him, at least not now. Later on there would no doubt be more information and another opportunity to meet him. But he had an important conference in Berlin in two days which he couldn't miss. Sagalowitz already knew of Schulte; that was enough. To others, Schulte's name would mean nothing.

Koppelmann left the hotel. A little later Schulte checked out and returned to Germany.

Sagalowitz slept fitfully, rose early, and took the first train to Zurich. He walked from the station to his apartment in the Nüschelerstrasse, a fairly undistinguished street a few yards from the central synagogue, a red-and-white sandstone building. It had been designed, like so many non-Orthodox synagogues around the turn of the century, in what was thought to be Moorish style. Sagalowitz's proximity to the synagogue, however, was not of great symbolic importance, for though known as a "good Jew," Sagalowitz was a freethinker and was not often seen in the house of God.

Benjamin Sagalowitz, the man who was to play a major role in the story now unfolding, was forty-one years old at the time. He was a pleasant and friendly person, a truly good man with probably not an enemy in the world. He was of above-average height, his face was slightly elongated, his ears prominent. He smiled frequently and could usually come up with a joke, an anecdote, or an encouraging word, however dismal the situation. He had the gift of inspiring confidence and making friends without even trying very hard. He was a man of great natural tact, truly altruistic and highly educated. He was perhaps a little too soft and vulnerable for the rough-and-tumble of this world, and thus his career had not been commensurate with his many talents.

Sagalowitz was a native of Russia. His father, Hersch, had been a wealthy merchant in Vitebsk, Chagall's birthplace. But Benno (as all his friends called him) hardly remembered Russia; he had been four when the family left Russia, following the pogroms of 1905. His father, his mother Jetta, and the five sons, of whom Benno was the fourth, settled first in Berlin and later in Wiesbaden. They were fairly well off; monthly remittances from Russia continued to arrive. Despite all their sad experiences in Russia, they still felt a strong link to their country of origin, and when the First World War broke out they had moved on to neutral Switzerland. They lived at first in the Waldhaus, on the Dolder, overlooking Zurich, a big wooden hotel at the edge of a forest. The hotel could be reached by way of a funicular railway. Benno was an individualist even in his younger years: to reach school in Raemistrasse he preferred the excitement of a sled, even if it meant hauling it uphill on the way back.

It was in the *Literargymnasium* that Sagalowitz met some of the youngsters who were to become his friends later on. One of them was Jacques Rosenstein. Jetta was not too enthusiastic; the Rosenstein family had an establishment in Zurich's entertainment quarter, an altogether harmless affair, but still not quite respectable by the strict standards of the time. Benno in any case was not deterred by considerations of this kind. There were heated discussions at school about the war. Switzerland was neutral, but this did not prevent people from choosing sides. In Zurich most hoped for a German-Austrian victory. There was, after all, a close Swiss cultural affinity with Germany; the Entente included not only Republican France but also despotic Russia. Benno belonged to the minority that did not hope for a German victory. Was there in him a vestige of Russian patriotism, a feeling for a Russia he had hardly known? Or was it because Benno the socialist expected the future Russia to be free and democratic?

The Sagalowitzes were different from the typical Russian-Jewish families that had arrived in Western Europe during the prewar decade. Benno's family had money, they were cultured, and they had no wish to emigrate to America. Their house was a center for young Jewish intellectuals from Eastern Europe— poor students, but also men and women who had already made their way in the world, leading Zionists but revolutionary socialists too. From the passionate debates at home Benno drew as much inspiration as from the lectures at school.

He somehow managed to complete law school in Zurich. He was a favorite of Professor Hafter, one of the leading legal experts of the time. His dissertation (*summa cum laude*) was on certain aspects of the law of journalism. But unlike Rosenstein, who had also studied law with him, Sagalowitz did not immediately find a job in the Zurich public prosecutor's office, for he was not a Swiss citizen. He had not been naturalized because the authorities had reached the conclusion that this young foreigner, with all his gifts and despite the fact that he had become very much a part of the Zurich scene, somehow led the life of a profligate.

Sagalowitz, to be sure, was a man of the highest ethical standards—too much so, his friends said. But he had one major weakness—he was very attractive to women, and he found it difficult to resist them. Furthermore, the ladies concerned were not of the demimonde but, on the contrary, came from good families; some were even married women. And this, in the eyes of the authorities, made things even worse.*

Since his lack of citizenship made a career in law out of the question, Sagalowitz had gone into free-lance journalism. But life for a free lance in a small country was not easy. Always eager to help others, Sagalowitz frequently found himself without money for his own basic needs. When the Second World War broke out he volunteered for the Swiss Army, but he, like all "foreigners," was rejected.

He had obtained his first regular job not long before the outbreak of the war: the Association of Swiss Jewish Communities made him head of their information bureau (JUNA, or Jüdische Nachrichtenstelle). There had been no institution of this kind before, for most Swiss Jews believed in keeping a low profile. The country had been good to them, and if there were no Jews in high places in government or the army, it was also true that few had wanted such careers. Even in 1938, when Sagalowitz was appointed, many doubted the need for a research and press office, however small. (It consisted of Sagalowitz and a secretary.) But a few other members of the community had opposed the ostrichlike, parochial attitude of their coreligionists, who hoped against hope that the great wave of anti-Semitism would somehow abate or at least pass them by and that it could be safely ignored. A Swiss fascist movement, the Fronten,

---

* Sagalowitz became a Swiss citizen in the 1950s, forty years after he had arrived in the country. He was still living with a woman to whom he was not married. But the authorities at last relented.

had lost some of its influence, but Nazi propaganda continued
in various ways. There were political scandals, such as the
Elders of Zion trial,* which attracted worldwide attention.
And there was no one better qualified than Sagalowitz to
collect the material, to analyze and comment on the sinister
developments. This then was Benno Sagalowitz in 1942, a profoundly decent man in his best years, slow-moving, mild, and
quite vulnerable.

During the early summer, word had reached him that
Valia, one of his brothers, a painter, was in danger as a stateless
person in Vichy France. Valia had felt he could not leave his
elderly parents, who had moved on to France after Hitler had
come to power in Germany. Now they were all trapped. In
June 1942 there seemed no way to get a stateless person into
Switzerland—Minister Eduard von Steiger and Heinrich
Rothmund, the chief of police in charge of foreign nationals,
had announced that the "boat was full." Those who managed
to enter Switzerland illegally were sent back.

There was one Swiss citizen who was determined to save
Valia. It was a story appropriate to a Hollywood movie. When
the Sagalowitz family had lived in Zurich, they had been
friendly with a non-Jewish Swiss family with a pretty little
daughter aged eight or nine. The five Sagalowitz boys had all
been handsome, reasonably well behaved, and promising, the
pride of their mother. One day Jetta had jokingly asked Lucie,
her friends' daughter: "And which of my boys do you want?"
Lucie had quickly pointed to Valia.

Valia had gone first to Berlin, later to Paris. He and Lucie
had exchanged occasional letters but had then lost contact.
One day in 1942 Lucie met Benno in the street and heard that
Valia was in grave danger. From that moment on she dedicated herself to getting him out. She found in the Bern police
department a senior official whom she had known since childhood. In the 1930s he had unwisely sympathized with the fas-
cists, and Lucie pressed him to atone for his sin by helping to
save her fiancé. And the man did help. Valia entered Switzerland illegally, but unlike many stateless persons at that time, he
was not returned to where he came from. Instead he was kept
in a Swiss prison. For a Jew in 1942 that was the difference be-

---

* The *Protocols of the Elders of Zion*, the most famous anti-Semitic forgery of modern times, was widely publicized by the Nazis and other anti-Jewish movements. Jewish organizations went to court in Bern in 1934 to prove that the
book was a forgery.

tween life and death. Soon afterward Lucie became Frau Sagal—Valia had shortened his name for professional reasons—in a simple ceremony.

On a late July afternoon Benno Sagalowitz now had to face his own crisis—not a personal crisis but one confronting an entire people. Koppelmann arrived a few minutes early. He said that the German industrialist of whom Sagalowitz had heard from Rosenstein had been in town and wanted to convey an urgent message to Sagalowitz. He took a piece of paper from his pocket on which he had made notes and began to read: "I have received information from absolutely trustworthy sources that Hitler's headquarters is considering a plan to kill all remaining European Jews." It was no longer a question of a few thousand Jews here and there; the Nazis were talking of three to four million who were to be transported to the east and gassed with prussic acid. An enormous crematorium had been built. About the date of the operation the industrialist had been a little vague: it was not clear whether the plan was in the last stages of preparation or whether the mass murder had already started.

The whole affair was kept in great secrecy by the Nazis. But even if the mass executions had not yet started, it was only a matter of days or weeks. Unless the Allies took action at once, it would be too late. The industrialist had also made it clear that by "action" he did not refer merely to protest or warnings. End of message. Koppelmann also said that the man thought that he, Sagalowitz, was the best person to convey this message to the world Jewish institutions and the Allies. Sagalowitz thought for a few moments. "Did he give his source?"

"He would not tell me."

"May I quote him when I pass it on?"

"Under no circumstances; in fact, he wanted your word of honor that his name will be kept out." Koppelmann went on to say that the man was personally unafraid, but there were others involved and he owed it to his family. The industrialist had also said that he would be in Zurich again in a few weeks, very likely with more information. But they should not wait for his next visit. Sagalowitz said that while he thought that almost anything was possible as far as the Nazi leaders were concerned, others would want more tangible evidence. He tended to trust the source, but others would reject what had been said as mere rumor: there were all too many rumors in war.

Koppelmann wanted to take a late train back to Basel, and

he left. Sagalowitz went out for a walk. He needed some fresh air. It had been unseasonably cold in Switzerland that July, but during the last days of the month summer had come with a vengeance. Sagalowitz walked toward the Limmat, crossed a bridge over the river, and found an empty seat in the corner of his favorite coffeehouse, the Odeon. He was greeted by a group of chess players who were greatly surprised to see him in Zurich. They knew, of course, about his participation in the Lausanne tournament. Sagalowitz joined them for a few minutes and told them that, to his great regret, he had had to return to Zurich suddenly. It was a fine competition, and they had been given a wonderful reception in Lausanne. And then he apologized—he had an urgent letter to write. They understood and left him alone.

A great many letters had been written in the Odeon, and also poems, plays, novels, political manifestos, and even scientific lectures. The Odeon was an institution; it was the kind of literary café that had flourished in Vienna and Paris, and had all but disappeared in Berlin. Ever since it opened in 1911, anyone who was someone came there. Of course, that helped to attract a broader crowd—young people as yet unknown, older people who never made it, eccentrics and eminently sane bourgeois, pro-Nazis and Communist sympathizers, and artists who could not care less about politics. It seated more than two hundred people, not counting the first-floor cabaret, and in more peaceful days it had been difficult to get a seat at any time of the day.

But this was a time of war. Almost everything in Switzerland was rationed; there were three meatless days each week, and guests in restaurants needed a coupon. There was a total blackout, and very few private car owners were allocated gasoline. Hotel owners complained that only one tenth of their rooms were taken even during the prime season—how could they survive? Many of the smaller shops had closed. And it was no longer difficult to get a seat in the Odeon, even during the busiest hours.

Sagalowitz had not been back to Germany for many years, but he had followed events there very closely indeed. And what necessary information he did not have in his head, he would find within a very few minutes in the press archive in his office. He was a fanatical newspaper reader. Whenever he noticed an interesting item, which might happen a dozen times a day, he would cut it out, scribble a letter or a number on it, and leave it for his secretary to be filed in his large, sprawling, and, to the uninitiated, utterly confusing collection.

A week ago he had cut out a report of more than ordinary interest from the *Neue Zürcher Zeitung*, the leading Swiss newspaper. It was a message by Winston Churchill to a mass meeting of American Jews in Madison Square Garden: the Jews had been among the first victims of Nazism; more than one million had been killed. Churchill said, "Hitler apparently will not be satisfied until the cities of Europe in which Jews live are turned into giant cemeteries. But the Jewish people will not bow to the decision of its extermination."

Sagalowitz had studied this revealing item, which had appeared on page two, very carefully. Usually, news about mass pogroms and the killing of thousands of Jews in Eastern Europe was suppressed by the Swiss censorship. The editors and some journalists had seen despatches from foreign wire services, and there had also of course been some information from Swiss sources. This, the censors said in their internal guidelines to the editors, was "atrocity propaganda" of which there had been so much in the First World War. There was no hard evidence to back up the stories. The reports also annoyed the Germans no end. Every few weeks Otto Köcher, the German minister in Bern, would lodge a protest about the hostile attitude of the Swiss press. And sometimes there would be more than just protests: Goebbels himself had recently hinted that he would despatch recalcitrant Swiss journalists to Siberia when the hour came.

If the newspapers now published Churchill's message, it meant that an official statement by a prominent Allied leader was privileged: such statements would not have trouble passing the censors. The substance of Churchill's message—did it not confirm the information he had just received from Schulte? For Churchill had spoken not only of a million Jews who had already been killed. He had mentioned a decision to exterminate all of them. Was it just a manner of speaking, a dramatic turn of phrase?

Of course, Sagalowitz had to act, but what were the options open to him? It was not the first time that he had been asked to convey information that demanded political action. Every journalist found himself in such a position at one time or another. But this was no ordinary message. What if Churchill's phrase were literally true? If Sagalowitz had learned anything during the previous three years, it was that almost everyone had underestimated Hitler. The utter consistency of his policy, the total lack of scruples and humanitarian considerations, his radical measures, his sudden, massive attacks, had taken the world by surprise time and time again. Even Sagalowitz had misjudged him. Hitler was now at the height of his power. His sway extended from the English Channel to the Caucasus, from northern Norway to North Africa. If he had reached the conclusion that the time was ripe for a "final solution" of the Jewish question, who was there to restrain him?

Should Sagalowitz alert his superiors, the heads of the Swiss Jewish community? Of course, they would have to be told one way or another. But these little, fearful, parochial people who had been successful in business and thus risen to positions of influence in the community would hardly know how to reach the Allied leaders and mobilize public opinion abroad. As far as they were concerned, Sagalowitz was far too much of a *Weltmensch.* Why did he always have to concentrate on affairs that were not directly concerned with the fate of Swiss Jewry? Sagalowitz had little sympathy for the ultra-Orthodox Jews of whom there were not a few in the country. Some of them were very active in rescue missions, but their concern and compassion were limited mainly to their own kind of Jews.

Swiss Jewish leaders had few links with the Jewish organizations in London and New York. A Swiss Jewish statement would not carry much weight. Probably, Swiss Jews would be too afraid to make a forceful statement in the first place. For Switzerland was a neutral country, and the Jews would not want to be accused of endangering its neutrality. How often had he listened to arguments of this kind? And there was, of course, some grain of truth in them as there always is in such arguments. It was easier to defy and attack Germans from a safe distance. Switzerland was surrounded by the Axis powers, and no one could say with any assurance that the Nazi leaders would leave this island of relative freedom alone forever. In 1940 a German invasion had seemed very likely. That alarm had passed, but the danger of a German invasion was by no means over. Was it not natural that the Swiss government opted for a low profile, that it tried not to provoke its mighty neighbor?

No, this was not an assignment for Swiss Jewry. The message should reach Roosevelt as quickly as possible. Who had the ear of the U.S. President? The American diplomats in Switzerland had what they considered to be more important concerns. And for the foreign journalists this would be just another story. Sagalowitz thought of Richard Lichtheim, the Geneva representative of the Jewish Agency for Palestine, whom he had known for years. They were not exactly political allies, but they respected and trusted each other. But Lichtheim had no direct contact with London and Washington. There were some other representatives of Jewish organizations in Switzerland, but none of experience and stature. Some had been appointed simply because they happened to be on the spot when the war broke out, because of family links, or professional interests. Contrary to widespread belief, all the Jewish institutions were quite poor; their representatives did not lead the life of diplomats. Sometimes even an extra trip from Geneva to Zurich or a long-distance phone call constituted a problem, because there was no provision in their budgets for such extravagances.

Sagalowitz thought of Gerhart Riegner in Geneva, a young man to be sure, but earnest, eager, and reliable, who reported directly to the leaders of the World Jewish Congress in New York. The very name "World Jewish Congress" sounded impressive, something like a modern version of the Elders of Zion, a wealthy and powerful organization with a network of representatives all over the world, excellent connections, and enormous lobbying power. Its constitution said it was a "voluntary association of representatives of Jewish bodies throughout the world to assure the survival and to foster the unity of the Jewish people."

Sagalowitz knew better than most what the World Jewish Congress really was. He had been present at its creation in Geneva in 1936. It had no power, no apparatus, no substantial budget of its own; it had small offices in New York and London, a few correspondents in various other centers. Its real center was whichever hotel room Nahum Goldmann, its peripatetic general secretary, happened to be in at the time. Goldmann was also involved in a dozen other activities. The aim of the World Jewish Congress was to fight the Nazis and to protect the rights of the Jewish communities in Eastern Europe. Its weakness represented fairly accurately the weakness of world Jewry, a lack of cohesion and cooperation. Numerous Jewish organizations refused to have anything to do with the Congress. But with all its shortcomings, the Congress had a direct channel from Switzerland to America. Through its president, Rabbi Stephen Wise, a man of great renown in the

Jewish world and an unofficial Jewish spokesman to non-Jews,
it was in a position to make its voice heard in New York and
Washington. And so Sagalowitz concluded that Riegner was
his best chance.

It was near closing time as Sagalowitz left the Odeon, not
without apologizing once again to his fellow enthusiasts at the
chess table. The heat had hardly abated, the street was virtually deserted; a few men in uniform hurried toward the railway station to catch a late train. Café Select, the Odeon's rival,
had already closed.

"You have been long, I was worried," Annette said when
Benno entered the apartment. He said he was sorry, kissed her,
and went to bed. From there he called Riegner in Geneva,
apologized for the late hour, and said that a very urgent matter
had suddenly arisen. Could they meet the following day in
Lausanne? Riegner agreed without hesitation.

On Saturday, August 1, Sagalowitz arrived at the station in
Lausanne on the first train from Zurich. When he had come to
Lausanne earlier that week, he had regarded his stay there as
something like a holiday after his recent operation. He had
been in a good mood; at the party given by the local municipal-
ity in honor of the chess masters he was, as so often, the life of
the party, joking and consuming liberal amounts of the excellent local wine, the Dezaley. Only a few days had gone by, but
now a great sadness had come over him.

Instead of taking the funicular down the steep decline to
the lake, he went for a short detour through the park. There
was an hour or more before Riegner would arrive, and he went
into the great hall of the Beau Rivage. Sagalowitz was drawn
to the central chess tables, where now, in the late stages of the
tournament, the decision was about to fall. He had not
watched the game for long when a bellhop told him there was a
man waiting for him at the reception desk. Sagalowitz left the
hall, greeted Riegner, and the two went to the nearby Hotel du
Château, where they sat down on the terrace.

Gerhart Riegner, a rather small man, was then aged thirty.
But for Adolf Hitler he would have been well on the way to an
academic career. His father was a lawyer, and Gerhart's interest too was in jurisprudence, with emphasis on the philosophy
of law. The family was deeply rooted in German culture. Hermann Cohen, the great Kantian philosopher, was Gerhart's
uncle. Some Riegners had also been involved in public affairs.
Gerhart's mother had been a member of the executive of the

German Democratic Party. Yet Jewish tradition was also alive in the family: Lewandowski, the foremost nineteenth-century composer of synagogue music, had been a close relative.

The Riegners had lived in comfortable circumstances in Berlin-Charlottenburg. Then came April 1, 1933, the day of the Nazi boycott of Jewish businesses, followed by a host of official restrictions on the number of Jews in the civil service and professions. Riegner's father could no longer practice law. His older sister lost her job as a teacher, his younger sister had to leave school, and Riegner, a trainee law official, a *Referendar,* at the Wedding law court in the midst of working-class Berlin, also found himself unemployed.

As was the custom in those years, Riegner had studied at various universities—Berlin, Heidelberg, Freiburg—and he had been a member of the Republican Front, a left-of-center student group. The group had faced an uphill struggle, for the Nazis had conquered the German universities well before they emerged as the strongest political party in parliament. There were few student debates but a great deal of student violence. On one occasion he and his friends had to jump from the windows of an auditorium to escape an attack by Nazi storm troopers. It sounded funny when he related such incidents many years later, but at the time no one thought it very amusing, and a number of people were in fact killed, and more injured, in the street battles of the late Weimar years. The fanaticism he had encountered among not a few of his contemporaries had frightened him. It had also helped him to perceive the gravity of this new political phenomenon, which for many others remained strange and puzzling.

Riegner considered moving to Palestine. He had come into the orbit of the Zionist student organization during his last university year. But he still wanted to pursue his studies, and so, after Hitler took power, he enrolled at the Sorbonne, rather than join a kibbutz and work in agriculture. Then came another setback. After Riegner passed his second bar examination in Paris, the French authorities promulgated a law according to which foreigners could not practice law until ten years after their naturalization. Yet another door was closed. Riegner's discouragement ended after the internationally known legal and political philosopher Hans Kelsen gave a number of guest lectures in Paris. Riegner admired Kelsen more than any other contemporary thinker in the field. He approached the scholar and asked for advice. Kelsen suggested a move to Geneva where Riegner might be awarded a grant in the not-too-distant future.

The Graduate Institute at Geneva was at the time a center for the study of international relations. In the field of law it had William Rappard (formerly at Harvard), Paul Guggenheim, and Kelsen as its luminaries. International law had not been the area Riegner had contemplated taking up, but this was hardly a time to pick and choose, and so he found himself in Geneva in 1936. His grant actually materialized.

Geneva was also, of course, the seat of the League of Nations. It was no accident that the founding meeting of the World Jewish Congress took place there. One of the assignments of the League was monitoring the rights of minorities guaranteed by the post–First World War treaties, especially in Eastern Europe. While the real power of the League was strictly limited, it was one of the few channels through which Jewish organizations could air their complaints against blatant anti-Semitic measures in countries such as Rumania and Poland.

Nahum Goldmann, chairman of the World Jewish Congress's Administrative Committee, was looking for a young lawyer to represent the Congress at the League. Goldmann asked the three leading Geneva law professors to recommend someone with experience in international law to take over the day-to-day work at Geneva. They recommended Riegner, who was very surprised to be offered the post. There were not many interesting jobs for young émigré lawyers at the time (nor for their more distinguished senior colleagues), and, above all, Riegner felt that he could not refuse to cooperate in the fight against Hitler.

For the next five years he had managed Congress affairs from his little office, first in the Rue de Lausanne, later the Rue de Paquis, and finally the Quai de Wilson, in the building of the former Hotel Bellevue. Richard Lichtheim of the Jewish Agency for Palestine had his office on the same floor. They had one of the best panoramas in the city, with the lake to their feet, little boats, fountains, the Parc Mon Repos to their left; on the other side, the Parc de la Grange, with the finest roses in the country; and beyond it, in good weather, the mountains Mole, Salève, and a snow-covered Mont Blanc. Many years later Riegner would say: "I had one of the most beautiful landscapes before my eyes, and I knew that all over Europe the most terrible things were happening."

As the war clouds gathered, Riegner's work in Geneva was no longer restricted to submitting memoranda to the League of Nations, which for all practical purposes had ceased to exist. Geneva suddenly became one of the most important listening posts in Nazi-occupied Europe, as the seat of the International Red Cross, the one organization that maintained some form of liaison among the combatants. Riegner found himself dealing with problems for which in many ways he was not prepared; but then neither was anyone else.

Over lunch Sagalowitz told Riegner about his meeting with Koppelmann. Riegner wanted to know more about Koppelmann, whom he had heard of but never met. In particular, he wanted to learn more about Koppelmann's source. How reliable was the industrialist; why couldn't his name be mentioned, even in the strictest confidence? Sagalowitz said that he was not at liberty to divulge it. He had known the man, though not intimately, for a number of years, through a common friend. He knew him as a totally reliable person; there was not much more he could add.

They talked for more than five hours, going over the same ground again and again. They finished lunch and went for a walk along the Quai de Belgique and the Quai de Ouchy; they watched the little steamers arriving and leaving; they stood for a while at the landing stage, glancing at the tropical flowers adorning the beach. After sitting on a bench the men walked again, and when they were tired they rested in a nearby coffee-house.

Lausanne is a beautiful and charming city. Rilke once wrote that its atmosphere reminded him of Montmartre. There is no denying that the shores of Lake Geneva stand comparison with the finest part of the Riviera. There is something Mediterranean in the air, and it is no accident that the place has attracted so many famous writers from the countries of the north, Gibbon, Shelley, and Byron among them, and, in a more recent age, T. S. Eliot. At any other time Riegner and Sagalowitz would have enjoyed the colors, the smells, and the scenery. On this occasion the beauty of nature was lost on them, and instead they asked themselves, over and over, the same questions: Could it be true? Or was it a case of disinformation, or even a provocation? Did the information that had just reached them fit into the general picture?

They could see that throughout the war the situation of the Jews in the Nazi-occupied countries had deteriorated rapidly.

Hundreds, perhaps thousands, of Jews had been killed during the German invasion of Poland and in the months after. They had been persecuted in every possible way; they were herded into ghettos and sent into slave labor. They had lost all civic and legal rights, and thousands had died of starvation, disease, and even suicide. But prior to June 1941 there had been no systematic mass killings, and Hitler's prediction in a speech on January 30, 1939—repeated three years later—that in a new world war the Jewish race in Europe would be destroyed, had not yet come true. The Jews had suffered grievously, but the great majority of them were still alive.

Then, following the German invasion of the Soviet Union, special Nazi murder squads had gone into action. By the end of 1941 some 500,000 Jews in the German-occupied Soviet territories had been murdered. But shooting proved too slow and cumbersome, and in January 1942, Reinhard Heydrich convened a conference in Wannsee, a Berlin suburb, to plan and coordinate the so-called "Final Solution" of the Jewish question. During the first half of 1942 most of the death camps were built in Poland. But Eastern Europe was largely sealed off from the rest of the Continent, and while some reverberations of these events reached the outside world, and a few people suspected that something dreadful was going on, there were not many details or much evidence before April 1942, when round-ups and deportations started in various European countries. There were some reports about mobile gas vans, but nothing yet about gas chambers. The Wannsee Conference was still a well-kept secret. There were no certainties, but there was reason to fear the worst. In October 1941 Riegner had written to Goldmann in New York that it was not at all clear how many—if any—Jews would survive should Nazi persecutions continue on the same scale.

Riegner was not the only Cassandra in Switzerland. Richard Lichtheim was one of the most gifted and experienced Zionist diplomats of his generation. Yet because of his nonconformism, he was not a member of the Jewish Agency for Palestine executive in Jerusalem, London, or New York when the war broke out. He was in Geneva, considered an unimportant outpost. His appointment came more or less by accident. He had attended the World Jewish Congress in Geneva in August 1939 and was asked to stay on to head the new office of the World Zionist Organization there—to keep contact with Zionist organizations in both camps. Then, because of the war, the

Geneva backwater became crucial. In the First World War the Zionists had operated out of Copenhagen and Amsterdam, but these cities were now in Nazi hands. Only neutral Switzerland remained as a base of Zionist European operations.

Lichtheim, like Riegner, spent much of his time in Geneva in the early years of the war gathering the best information available about Nazi persecution of the Jews and trying to suggest means of saving lives. In November 1941 he reported to the Jewish Agency executive in Jerusalem: "With regard to Germany, Austria and the Protectorate [Czechoslovakia], it must be said that the fate of the Jews is now sealed. Generally speaking this whole chapter bears the title 'Too late.' " And in another letter, sent to the head of the Emergency Committee in New York in early 1942, Lichtheim wrote: "The number of our dead after the war will have to be counted not in thousands or hundreds of thousands but in several millions. . . ."

A short time before the meeting in Lausanne, Riegner and Lichtheim had handed a memorandum to the papal nuncio in Bern, Filippo Bernardini, in which they requested the intervention of the Holy See to save the Jews in Catholic countries such as Croatia and Slovakia. They were already convinced— and said so—that the Nazi measures pointed to the physical extermination of the Jews. But again there was no tangible evidence that an explicit order had been given. Then, in June 1942, information was received that more and more regions were to be made *judenrein*, emptied of Jews. Mass deportations from France, Belgium, Holland, Germany, Austria, and other countries began. But since Poland was also to be made *judenrein*, where were these Jews to be settled? Perhaps in the occupied regions of the Soviet Union? Hardly so; there were no Jews left in the Ukraine, White Russia, or the former Baltic republics. They had either fled to the east or had been murdered. Those deported were told that they were to be "resettled" in Poland. There was an obvious contradiction, and the only plausible explanation was that those in charge of the "evacuation" did not expect the Jews to live long at their place of deportation. The deportations, in other words, were based on the assumption that the Jews would disappear, and only the question of how their deaths would be accomplished seemed left open. But well-functioning bureaucracies do not leave essential questions open. Thus it should have been clear that there was only one logical conclusion as to the fate of the deported Jews.

Human beings frequently shy away from logical conclusions in search of more reassuring ones. This was, after all, Europe in the middle of the twentieth century. Hunger and deprivation and inhuman conditions, these one could imagine, but the murder of millions of innocent civilians by poison gas in death factories seemed altogether impossible. Most Jews, too, refused to accept the horrible truth—and Jews from Eastern Europe probably more so than those from Germany. Some Jews had regarded the Germans as liberators in the First World War, as *Kulturträger* who may have looked down on the Jews, but who were, if anything, less anti-Semitic than the average Pole or Russian. With Germans one could reach an arrangement, many Jews thought. Many also remembered the false atrocity propaganda of the First World War, the stories about Belgian babies being eaten alive by German soldiers.

Sagalowitz had followed events in Germany closely—and Riegner had lived through them. They both knew that there was a world of difference between the Germany of the Kaiser and the Third Reich. But the old images die hard. Riegner remembered private meetings in Geneva in which he had been bitterly denounced as a panic-monger by some of those who had witnessed the German soldiers in Kiev and Warsaw in the last war. "You are a young man," he had been told by more than one of them, "our experience with Germans goes back farther than yours: there is nothing new under the sun. . . ." The Jewish leaders in New York, Jerusalem, and London had also tended to dismiss the reports they had received from Riegner and Lichtheim as too alarmist. There had been major pogroms, but no information so far that all Jews were to be killed in the near future.

Riegner and Sagalowitz, at their meeting that afternoon, also had such doubts. Some aspects of the industrialist's report seemed unlikely. But they knew that it was not up to them to pass judgment, for they were in no position to check the story. The question facing them was whether it was at all *possible* that the Nazis were preparing for the mass murder of European Jewry.

They could wait until further information became available from other sources: this would surely be the safest course. Murder on such a gigantic scale could not possibly be hidden for long. Perhaps they should wait; by acting immediately, they would invite criticism. They might be accused of spreading all kinds of wild rumors.

But as the two walked along the quay, they concluded that

they would have to run this risk: for what if the report were true? In this case every day mattered, for even the Nazis might hesitate to carry out their design once it became known to one and all. In short, Riegner realized that a tremendous responsibility rested on him, and together with Sagalowitz he decided on a course of action. They would interrogate Koppelmann (whom Riegner had never met), and then Riegner would consult Professor Guggenheim. It was close to dinnertime when they parted, having agreed that unless anything unforeseen happened they would meet again on Monday in Zurich. Riegner spent an anxious weekend in a sunny and half-deserted Geneva.

CHAPTER SIX

The Riegner Telegram

Back in Breslau, Schulte was dealing with production schedules, the supplies of raw materials, and plans for his next visit to the ministries in Berlin. There were difficulties with the War Ministry: the armament experts were insisting on the delivery of pure, unalloyed zinc for the production of ammunition. But to achieve absolute purity was a tricky technological problem.

In between appointments and conferences Schulte tried to obtain further information about the plan to exterminate European Jewry. This was not easy. Such a topic could not be brought up incidentally in conversation; it would involve persistent probing, and this was bound to attract suspicion. Schulte hoped that his contacts in Switzerland had been able to find out more now that he had given them the lead.

. . .

After his unquiet weekend in Geneva, Riegner was in
Zurich with Sagalowitz to see Koppelmann. On Monday, August 3, the men met in the office of Rosenstein's firm. A few
minutes' conversation was all Riegner needed to size up Koppelmann as an extrovert; he was broad shouldered, heavyset,
obviously no intellectual, but a practical man, probably a
shrewd judge of character. Sagalowitz made it clear at the out-
set that he and Riegner did not disbelieve the shattering report.
Their intention was simply to find out whether there was anything else the industrialist had told Koppelmann, however insignificant, that could shed some light on the report.

Koppelmann thought hard and said that there was nothing
he had forgotten to convey. But he had meanwhile received
similar information from other sources. Highly placed Germans visited Basel frequently, and while the reports that had
come from them were a little vague, they had all amounted
substantially to the same thing. Some major, unprecedented
action against the Jews was under way, and it involved more
than just their deportation to the east.

As an afterthought he added: "The man I saw a few days
ago thought that instant countermeasures are imperative. Unless the Nazis are faced with some tangible, major threat, such
as the arrest of hundreds of thousands of Germans living in
America, they will not be impressed. My German guest also
thought," he added somewhat incongruously, "that the Arch-
bishop of Canterbury rather than some politician should be the
first to make the whole affair public."

Riegner said that it would be hard to convince his own
people if he were unable to mention the source. If he could not
have the name, he needed at least some information to show
that the industrialist was a man with the right contacts.

Koppelmann thought for a moment: Riegner could safely
say that the source was one of Germany's biggest industrialists,
employing more than thirty thousand people. He had excellent
connections in highly placed political and military circles in
Berlin; he even had access to Hitler's headquarters. But this information was not to be made public; it was to be used only
in private communication.

Riegner wanted to know more about the industrialist's politics and his reliability on past occasions. Koppelmann said he
had not the slightest doubt about him on these two counts. The

man was a firm anti-Nazi; he was convinced that the criminal adventure in which Hitler and his followers had engaged would lead to total disaster. Yes, his information had been correct on past occasions. After Soviet Foreign Minister Molotov's visit to Berlin in November 1940 the industrialist had immediately reported that no agreement had been reached between the Russian and his German hosts, very much in contrast to the official communiqués. Later on, in April 1941—but this too they had to keep absolutely secret—he had known the date set for the German invasion of Russia. There had been other such instances. What possible interest could the man have in passing on false information on the fate of the Jews? If it were a matter of military information, there might be reason to doubt him. But what conceivable benefit could the Nazis derive from making their own crimes known?

Riegner took the night train back to Geneva. Early the next morning he wrote Professor Guggenheim, who, like many Genevans in August, was on vacation somewhere in the mountains. Guggenheim had been one of Riegner's patrons at the university. He was also legal adviser to the World Jewish Congress and thus a natural person for Riegner to turn to. Moreover, Guggenheim was well connected. Carl Burckhardt, the "foreign minister" of the International Red Cross and a well-known historian, was a former colleague, and Guggenheim also knew quite well the American consul in Geneva, Paul Squire. The American Consulate was located in the Rue Mont Blanc, in a building owned by an insurance company for which Guggenheim acted as counsel.

Paul Guggenheim belonged to one of Switzerland's leading Jewish families, hailing from one of the two villages to which Swiss Jews had been more or less confined prior to the nineteenth century. His father had been a founder of the Association of Swiss Jewish Communities; in later years the son was to become its president. Paul Guggenheim also knew Germany well, having taught international law at Kiel University at a time when the Nazis emerged as the strongest party in that northernmost German province.

"Dear Professor," Riegner began his letter, "I was yesterday with Sagal in Zurich and wanted to report at once since this concerns a very serious matter, and I do not want to act without your knowledge."

He summarized what he had learned from Sagalowitz and Koppelmann and added his own interpretation: "At first sight the affair sounds totally fantastic. But one cannot exclude the consideration that these measures are rooted in the inner logic of the regime and that these people have no scruples whatsoever." Riegner quoted Hitler's speech of January 30, 1939, prophesying that European Jewry would perish in the war and reviewed the news about deportations that had been received within the past month. The source of the Final Solution report was absolutely reliable. What could, what should be done? He intended to approach the American and the British consuls and to ask them, first, to inform their governments and, second, to despatch a coded message to Rabbi Stephen Wise in New York and to Sidney Silverman, a Labour member of the British Parliament who also headed the British section of the World Jewish Congress in London. It would be up to them to make the Nazi design known in their countries.

Riegner stressed that time was of the essence in view of the fact that the mass murder was to take place in the autumn. Wise and Silverman would also have to consult with their governments about possible countermeasures. Riegner did not think it advisable to contact the other Allied (exile) governments from Geneva; this could best be done in New York or London. Nor had he informed anyone else, not even Lichtheim. For this was obviously an affair for the World Jewish Congress to deal with.

Guggenheim telephoned Riegner the next day, discussed the information that Riegner had received, and then sent him a short note in French that Riegner could use as a letter of introduction to Paul Squire, the American consul, a man worthy of the highest confidence. He also advised Riegner to tone down the message somewhat. It would be better to omit the reference to a giant crematorium, and a sentence should be inserted to the effect that the information about the Nazi plan was transmitted with reservation, as its accuracy could not be checked from Geneva. Such language was more befitting a legal document than a political report, for it was obvious that those in Geneva were in no position to confirm decisions taken in Hitler's headquarters or during secret preparations in Poland.

Why did Guggenheim counsel caution? Prudence was second nature to a distinguished jurist who knew better than other mortals the vital importance of full evidence. But this, alas, was not a legal case, and the evidence was bound to be incomplete and imperfect. Guggenheim did not rule out the possibility that the Nazis had some sinister scheme aimed at the Jews, and he promised to investigate further. Above all, he would ask Burckhardt, the Red Cross official. Although the Red Cross's sources were limited, it was bound to have heard of something if there was any truth in Schulte's report.

Riegner made appointments to see officials at the British and American consulates in Geneva. After receiving Guggenheim's letter, he set out on the morning of August 8 to present his case. If he had known the industrialist's name, he might have felt more secure, but there was no point in belaboring that now. Sagalowitz had given his word to Koppelmann; Riegner had to do the best he could without knowing the source. The British consul, Livingston, was on vacation, and Riegner was received by a vice-consul named Armstrong. Riegner conveyed the industrialist's information "with all due reservations." He asked Armstrong to inform the Foreign Office in London and to convey the message to Silverman. Within an hour he was informed that the cable had gone off to London. So far, so good. In a letter he wrote that afternoon, Riegner told Guggenheim that things had gone well with the British. Then Riegner went over to the American Consulate in Geneva. He had a letter of introduction; the prospects seemed good.

Paul Chapin Squire, fifty-two years old, had been a career Foreign Service officer since 1919 and spoke good French and German. Since the outbreak of war in Europe, he had established a reputation with his superiors in Bern as a knowledgeable analyst of political and economic intelligence. But on August 8, Squire was on vacation in the southern Swiss Alps, in the pretty town of Crans-sur-Sierre overlooking the Rhone River. As Riegner walked into the American Consulate, he was met by a tall, pleasant young man named Howard Elting, Jr., who, he learned, was Squire's subordinate.

Riegner had been under considerable strain these last few days: the more he thought about it, the more likely the industrialist's report appeared to him. Riegner was normally a quiet, reserved, even impassive man. Yet in his account of the meeting Elting found him "in great agitation." Nor did Elting remember anything about "all due reservations." When Elting told Riegner that the plan to carry out mass murder by means of prussic acid seemed fantastic, Riegner answered that he had reacted the same way at first. But now the information about deportations all across Europe strengthened the case.

Riegner's earnestness and insistence overcame Elting's doubts, and convinced him of the need to act. Elting said he would report the story to the American Legation in Bern. He warned Riegner that he could not guarantee results: the higher-ups in Bern might discount the report as being from an unknown source and reject the request to convey it to Rabbi Wise. Riegner pressed, but Elting knew what he was talking about: the State Department did not look kindly upon private individuals using diplomatic channels of communication. Elting was also well aware that he was a very junior vice-consul, the lowest rank in the Foreign Service hierarchy. If the legation did not credit Riegner's information, Elting's own view would matter little. Riegner consoled himself with the thought that at least the British would notify Silverman.

Seven days had now passed since Riegner and Sagalowitz had met in Lausanne, ten days since Schulte had arrived in Zurich. The "secret messenger" was now back in Germany, but his thoughts must have been in Switzerland, Washington, and London, and of what was being done, if anything, about the terrible information of which History had made him the bearer. Whatever they may have wondered, none of them knew that the death factories at Belzec, Sobibor, and Treblinka were already in operation, that Auschwitz had begun the use of prussic acid, and that the liquidation of the huge Warsaw ghetto was under way.

Losing no time, Elting sent his own memorandum and Riegner's proposed telegram to Stephen Wise to the American Legation in Bern. He went as far as he could to assist Riegner:

> My personal opinion is that Riegner is a serious and balanced individual and that he would never have come to the Consulate if he had not had confidence in his informant's reliability and if he did not seriously consider that the report may well contain an element of truth. Again it is my opinion that the report should be passed on to the Department for what it is worth.

Counselor of Legation Jerome Klahr Huddle immediately advised Elting to draw up a formal report to be telegraphed to Washington. In his cover letter addressed to the secretary of state on August 10, Elting conscientiously repeated his "belief in the utter seriousness of my informant [Riegner]."

But Huddle and American Minister Leland Harrison thought the situation required more than the usual diplomatic caution. In a despatch accompanying Elting's report Harrison called Riegner's story "war rumor inspired by fear and what is commonly understood to be the actually miserable condition of these refugees who face decimation as a result of physical maltreatment, persecution, and scarcely endurable privations, malnutrition, and disease." Harrison and Huddle apparently believed that a lot of Jews were dying, but not that the Nazis had decided to kill all of them.

In a summary sent to the Office of Strategic Services, State Department officials in Washington termed the legation's message a "wild rumor inspired by Jewish fears." Even Harrison's admission that many Jews were dying was dropped. The State Department now had to decide whether to pass Riegner's information on to Rabbi Stephen Wise in New York.

•   •   •

An American Jewish population divided by different interpretations of faith, by national origin, language, and to a certain extent politics, had no single leader, but most American Jews at the time had heard of Stephen Wise. He had been brought by his German-speaking parents from Hungary to New York at age one in 1875 and had gone on to graduate from Columbia University. Wise was ordained in Vienna as a Reform rabbi and eventually became the founder of the Free Synagogue of New York, an unusual congregation that depended upon voluntary contributions from its members and gave its rabbi complete discretion to preach as he wished.

His energy and oratory spread his message widely inside and outside the Jewish community. He was an impressive figure by any standards. In the words of a contemporary, Wise's big, full forehead, aquiline nose, jutting chin, and steely jaws gave the impression of enormous driving power, of indomitable will. Flowing dark hair graced his forehead; his tall, aristocratic bearing added to his presence. As he gained visibility and support among the liberal New York establishment, Wise became more and more confident about exerting political influence.

As a young man in Europe he had met the founder of Zionism, Theodor Herzl, and became one of the earliest American Zionists. By 1942 he was the principal figure in two pro-Zionist organizations, the American Jewish Congress and the World Jewish Congress. Wise combined his Judaism with a commitment to social causes that brought him to the left wing of the Democratic Party and occasionally beyond. Despite his speaking ability, however, Wise's temperament was not altogether ideal for politics. He tended to divide the world into those who were in favor of the right things and those who were opposed; he often neglected the uncommitted and indifferent. His ability to judge people was at best erratic.

After refusing to support Franklin Roosevelt in 1932, Wise was won over by the New Deal and the President's charm. A celebrated orator himself, Wise also appreciated FDR's mastery of the art. He solidified his links to the Roosevelt Administration with personal ties to prominent Roosevelt advisers and officials such as Felix Frankfurter, Henry Morgenthau, Jr., David Niles, Frances Perkins, and Harold Ickes. The State Department was less favorable terrain—there were few New Dealers there. As a member of the President's Advisory Committee on Political Refugees, Wise had pleaded frequently at the State Department for emergency visitors' visas for European rabbis and others threatened by the Nazis. Well before 1942 he had made himself *persona non grata* with several State Department officials. To put it crudely, Wise was a major nuisance as far as some State Department bureaucrats were concerned. Still, he wielded too much influence and knew too many important people to be dismissed unceremoniously.

It was perfectly true that those about to be sent to the gas chambers were not, as a rule, holders of American passports, and in this sense no definite "American interests" were involved. But if Eduard Schulte in Breslau had subscribed to a similar interpretation of "interest," he would not have risked his neck to get the information to Switzerland. And the State Department had not yet been asked to do anything beyond transmit a telegram to an American Jewish leader.

Paul Culbertson of the Division of European Affairs at the State Department noted that Rabbi Wise might "kick up a fuss" if he found out that the State Department had withheld Riegner's message. But in an internal memorandum his colleague Elbridge Durbrow bluntly stated the case for shelving the message:

> It does not appear advisable in view of the Legation's comments, the fantastic nature of the allegation, and the impossibility of our being of any assistance if such action were taken, to transmit the information to Dr. Stephen Wise as suggested.

A draft instruction to Harrison continued:

The Department feels that it would be unfair to
the American public if stories of this kind are
given publicity unless careful efforts by our officers abroad have been made to obtain confirmation at least tending to support them. It is
suggested, therefore, that in the future the Legation refrain from accepting information of
this kind for possible transmission to third parties unless, after thorough investigation, there is
reason to believe that such a fantastic report has
in the opinion of the Legation some foundation
or unless the report involves definite American
interests.

Slightly more cautious sentiments ultimately prevailed in
the long marble corridors in Washington. On its route around
the State Department the slap at Harrison was deleted. The
final State Department cable to Harrison noted that State had
not seen fit to forward an unsubstantiated rumor to a private
individual. Huddle accordingly wrote to Elting on August 21
suggesting that if Riegner could find corroborating information, the department would reconsider. Riegner accepted the
decision with as much grace as possible under the circumstances.

On the very same day that Huddle told Elting of the State
Department's decision, Franklin D. Roosevelt held a press conference. The President summarized for the White House press
corps a document that he had recently received from the governments-in-exile of the Netherlands, Yugoslavia, and Luxembourg about barbaric Nazi occupation policies in Europe that
"may even lead to the extermination of certain populations."
He then defined his own official stance:

Our Government has constantly received additional information from dependable sources,
and it welcomes reports from any trustworthy
source which would assist in keeping our Government—our growing fund of information and
evidence up to date and reliable. In other
words, we want news—from any source that is
reliable—of the continuation of atrocities.

Ironically, the news of the Final Solution had already come
from a trustworthy source, but it had been rejected, and the
President had not even been told.

Riegner had better luck with the British, but not because London was more perceptive or more sympathetic. Riegner had calculated the odds correctly. Rabbi Wise was a private citizen; the State Department might not want to do him any favors. But the British representative of the World Jewish Congress, Sidney Silverman, was a member of Parliament and a well-known barrister. For a Foreign Office bureaucrat to withhold an important message to a member of Parliament would have been contrary to established political rules—even in wartime.

But in London, as in Washington, the foreign-policy experts were skeptical and disinclined to act. The under-secretary of state for foreign affairs, Richard Law, asked for background on Riegner, but the Refugee Department knew nothing. On August 15 a junior diplomat named Frank Roberts, who became one of Britain's leading ambassadors after the war, wrote: "I do not see how we can hold up this message much longer, although I fear it may provoke embarrassing repercussions. Naturally we have no information bearing on the story." Two days later Silverman received the telegram from Riegner. Silverman sent the cable on to Wise via the Western Union office, as Riegner had asked him to do. In wartime, private telegrams had low priority and also had to go through the censorship office. Not until August 28 did Wise finally learn what Riegner had tried to communicate to him three weeks earlier.

• • •

August 28, the day the Riegner-Silverman telegram arrived in New York, was a Friday. Rabbi Wise was preparing for Sabbath services. Over the weekend and early the next week Wise conferred with other officials of the American Jewish Congress and the World Jewish Congress. By Wise's account, they were all "reduced to consternation." Riegner they knew to be a reliable man, conservative in his judgments, a scholar who would not be swayed easily by rumors. But it was not enough for them to believe Riegner. The government had to be convinced and had to take action.

Undersecretary of State Sumner Welles, whom Wise contacted on September 2, was the best bet for getting to FDR. The wealthy and dapper undersecretary, the image of the old-line diplomat, was a personal friend of the President's. Moreover, he was more adept and energetic than his superior, Secretary of State Cordell Hull, a former senator from Tennessee.

For years it had been Welles versus Hull at the State Department—and Welles had been winning the battle for FDR's ear.

It was just as well for Wise. Despite the fact that Hull's wife was Jewish, the secretary had always refused to bow to "special interests" and concerned himself with general issues of foreign policy, particularly economic relations. Perhaps he knew too well what many southern congressmen thought about the admission of Jews to the United States. Welles, however, had a humanitarian streak and was friendly with Eleanor Roosevelt, who had long demonstrated her concern about Nazi persecution of the Jews. Welles might not do all Wise wanted, but he would certainly not ignore the rabbi.

But Welles too had to rely upon State Department experts for information. European Division chief Ray Atherton pointed out to Welles that there was no confirmation of how many Jews were deported to the east, let alone whether they were being "exterminated." The State Department's understanding was that the deported Jews would be put to work, like Poles and Russian prisoners of war, on behalf of the German war machine. Welles telephoned this information to Wise on September 3 and asked Wise not to publicize the Riegner telegram until it could be confirmed. Wise agreed. He probably had no idea how slowly the wheels of bureaucracy would move.

In the meantime more information was coming from Switzerland. Koppelmann had called Sagalowitz and Riegner and told them that he had just received a further report, according to which the order to exterminate European Jews had been proposed by Herbert Backe, the Nazi commissar for food, who had a vested interest in conserving scarce food supplies; however, Hans Frank, the Nazi governor of Poland, had said he needed Jews as laborers for the war effort. Whoever was the source of this report, it certainly was not Schulte or anyone else familiar with the top Nazi leadership. Backe did not belong to the Nazi old guard and to Hitler's inner circle; he simply would not have been consulted on matters of high policy. He was solely an agricultural expert.*

Koppelmann had many informants: business associates of Rosenstein, resident Basel lawyers and bankers with ties to Ger-

---

* Backe was also one of the few Nazi leaders to express shame and guilt after the war. Although disclaiming knowledge of Auschwitz, he admitted indirect responsibility: "The torments of my soul are immeasurable." A few days after saying this he committed suicide.

many, a few émigrés who still had channels to Berlin. (One of the émigrés based in Basel had served with Göring in the German air force during the First World War.) However, Koppelmann was not a trained intelligence analyst, with the result that sometimes, when collating various pieces of information he had received from his different sources, he would unwittingly run together facts, partially accurate material, and material that was unsubstantiated or even false.

But if there were inevitable mistakes on details, the general picture coming from Switzerland was, as we now know, in all essentials correct: the Jews were being exterminated. In fact this was happening faster than the reports indicated. If additional information were still needed, it came from the man whose qualifications could hardly be doubted. In a speech in the Berlin Sportpalast on September 30, 1942, Adolf Hitler reminded his listeners that in a previous speech before the war he had warned that if world Jewry should bring about another war (his phraseology, of course), it would not be the Aryan peoples who would be exterminated, but Jewry. Now Hitler proclaimed: "I shall be right also regarding this prophecy. . . ."

America had been in the war for nearly a year; yet how far was the reality of the war from Americans and how far were they from understanding it. The headlines in the New York papers featured the arrest of seventy-five gamblers in a raid in New Jersey, a strike of newspaper vendors in New York, and charges of neglect against Mayor Fiorello La Guardia. The media debated whether drivers should have an annual mileage ceiling of 7,700 or 5,000 miles.

The President dealt with such issues as the Price Control Act, the establishment of a commission to decide claims of American nationals against Mexico, and the launching of a great fund-raising campaign for the Red Cross.

On September 10 Stephen Wise went to Washington where he saw State Department officials, Vice-President Henry Wallace, and others, and showed them the "awful cables."* He heard from the ambassador of the Polish government-in-exile that Hitler might conceivably destroy Europe's Jews, but that for the moment they were being sent to the Russo-Polish frontier to build fortifications. There were some constructive suggestions in Washington. Assistant Solicitor General Oscar Cox

---

* Riegner's telegram and another report of mass killings in Poland from Orthodox Jewish sources in Switzerland.

thought the two cables might be "the [last] straw" to bring about the creation of a United Nations War Crimes Commission.

FDR and Welles had already instructed the President's personal representative, Myron Taylor, to consult with the Vatican about Nazi mass killings. Taylor, a former U.S. Steel executive, spoke with Secretary of State Cardinal Luigi Maglione on September 25, requesting the pope to speak out publicly against the inhumane treatment of refugees and hostages—especially Jews—in the German-occupied territories. Maglione recited what the Vatican and Church officials had already done. The pope had threatened that God would bless or condemn rulers according to the way they treated their subjects. The cardinal told Taylor that this was as far as the pope could go without "descending to particulars," in his view a risky political step that would require documentary proof.

The next day, through a circuitous route, Taylor received more information about Nazi crimes from Richard Lichtheim, who had contact with two men recently arrived from Poland. (Lichtheim's despatch went through State Department channels to Stephen Wise, who gave it to Undersecretary of State Welles. Welles cabled it triple priority to Bern, from where it was sent by pouch to Taylor in Rome.) This despatch revealed that the Jews of Warsaw were being removed from the ghetto and killed in special camps, one of which was identified as Belzec. Jews deported from Germany, Belgium, Holland, France, and Slovakia were to meet the same fate. Lichtheim's sources did not know about the gas chambers, but they understood that non-Jews sent to the east were being used as laborers, whereas most Jews met a different fate.

Sumner Welles wanted Taylor to obtain confirmation and suggestions for action from the pope. But Taylor's renewed inquiry in Rome drew only an admission that the Vatican too had received unverified reports of "severe measures against non-Aryans." The Holy See had no practical suggestions to make; only physical force from the outside could end Nazi barbarities. Several months later Pope Pius XII himself told another American diplomat that he could not publicly condemn Nazi atrocities without explicitly condemning the "Bolsheviks" as well.

. . .

To receive a triple priority message from the State Department on Nazi killings of Jews must have startled Leland Harrison, the U.S. chief of mission in Switzerland, for the European Division had not shown great interest in the issue previously. In early October Welles added a personal message to Harrison requesting him to meet with Riegner or Lichtheim and see what additional evidence they had. Wise had just pointed out to Welles that the two Jewish officials were probably afraid to send such information through the open mails.

Leland Harrison was neither lazy nor incompetent. He enjoyed the pleasant side of diplomatic life in Bern—the formal dinners, fine wines and brandies, the friendly golf matches. Before the war he had refused a presidential request that he move up to become ambassador to Canada, because he and his wife were so settled in Europe. To sift through the evidence about the killing of millions of human beings—that was not one of his more pleasant tasks.

But Welles's persistent interest broke the logjam in Bern and Washington. Harrison alerted Welles the very next day that numerous reports from Jewish and non-Jewish sources, supplemented by information from Paul Squire in Geneva, indicated that the Nazis were indeed sending Jews from Western Europe to an unknown fate in the east. Polish diplomats confirmed that the Warsaw ghetto was being emptied. Harrison was now willing to assist Riegner and Lichtheim, and he passed word to Squire that the two would be welcome at the legation. Counselor of Legation Huddle even added to Squire that the matter was urgent. Meanwhile, Welles showed Harrison's ominous cable to Wise.

On October 7 the White House issued a press release indicating that Nazi war crimes were continuing. FDR declared that war criminals would be punished at the end of the war, and toward this purpose the U.S., Britain, and other governments were establishing a United Nations Commission for the Investigation of War Crimes. That was little enough, but still a small step forward. It was also a sign that the White House had seen some of the information from Switzerland about the Final Solution.

Riegner and Lichtheim came to the legation in Bern on October 22 and presented Harrison with a set of documents they had prepared about the Nazi policy of extermination. They watched as Harrison opened the cover sheet and read on the first page:

> Four million Jews are on the verge of complete
> annihilation by a deliberate policy consisting of
> starvation, the Ghetto-system of slave labour,
> deportation under inhuman conditions, and or-
> ganized mass-murder by shooting, poisoning
> and other methods. This policy of total destruc-
> tion has repeatedly been proclaimed by Hitler
> and is now being carried out.

The Riegner-Lichtheim report called for the collection of specific evidence on those responsible for the killing and the punishment of the guilty. More importantly, it urged the strongest
possible pressure on the partly independent governments of
Italy, Hungary, Rumania, Bulgaria, and Vichy France not to
cooperate in the deportations. The Vatican might be of service.

Harrison read further and found a country-by-country
breakdown of estimated Jewish mortality. He had some doubts
about the figures compiled there and later put question marks
in the margin.

Then came the crucial part—the section about a reliable
German source who claimed that Hitler's headquarters had
considered and accepted a plan for the extermination of three
and a half to four million Jews. Riegner and Lichtheim had not
spared the State Department. Their report summarized how
they had delivered this information to the American Consulate
at Geneva on August 8 and how they were later informed that
the State Department had refused to deliver it to Stephen Wise
because it was unsubstantiated.

Harrison finished reading the last part of the nearly thirty-
page report—some letters from Poland received via the Stern-
buchs (a Jewish Swiss family very active in rescue operations),
as well as an eyewitness account of mass killings of Jews in Lat-
via. Although he had already been reading for twenty minutes
in the presence of his guests, Harrison began to reread some of
the key sections. Then, with an almost expressionless face
(Lichtheim called it a "poker-face"), he began to ask questions.

Harrison wanted to know the sources for each of the documents that Riegner and Lichtheim had appended to their report. He particularly wanted to know the name of the German
who supplied the information about the discussions at Hitler's
headquarters of the Final Solution. Although they had not met
the industrialist, Riegner and Lichtheim by then knew the
man's name—Sagalowitz had reluctantly given it to them in a

sealed envelope. Lichtheim had opened the envelope, and now they faced a moral dilemma. To reveal Schulte's name might cost him his life, for the Germans were quite capable of intercepting and decoding American diplomatic transmissions. Not to reveal the name meant that Harrison and the State Department would be less likely to credit their information, and more time would be lost.

In the end they gave in. The slip of paper in the envelope read: "Managing director Dr. Schulte, mining industry. In close or closest contact with dominant figures in the war economy." But Harrison was not to send this name to Washington. Riegner also told Harrison about new, independent confirmation of the order for implementing the Final Solution that he had recently received from Paul Guggenheim, who had obtained it from a high official of the International Red Cross. Harrison wanted more details as soon as possible. The two Jewish officials promised to get proof and more specifics. Harrison expressed his thanks.

Harrison then called Paul Squire in Geneva and asked him to come to the legation the next day. He needed Squire's opinion on the evidence, and they could not discuss this problem adequately by phone. Squire apparently told his superior that he was already convinced—he had in fact seen much of the Riegner-Lichtheim information before. Harrison gave Squire the task of obtaining sworn statements from those individuals in Switzerland who had supplied the information to Riegner and Lichtheim.

On October 24 Harrison wrote a personal letter to Undersecretary Welles, describing his meeting with Riegner and Lichtheim. Harrison informed Welles that he had the name of the German industrialist. He also stated that the International Red Cross official mentioned by Riegner and Lichtheim was probably Carl Burckhardt. At a luncheon Harrison had overheard Burckhardt discuss an order for the Final Solution with Professor Guggenheim. Harrison promised to send sworn statements as soon as they were obtained.

Five days later Squire persuaded Professor Guggenheim to write and sign a detailed statement, provided that Burckhardt's name was not used. Guggenheim had learned from "a citizen of Switzerland" that Hitler had allegedly issued an order for the extermination (*Ausrottung*) of all Jews in Nazi-controlled territories. Hans Frank and even Heinrich Himmler were said to have opposed the plan on practical grounds, but

Hitler had repeated his order in September 1942. The information about the order was believed to have come from two independent sources: an official of the German Foreign Ministry in Berlin and an official in the Ministry of War. Moreover, other sources had provided information that was consistent with the Final Solution plan. By this time Squire had also obtained a sworn affidavit about the execution of the Jews of Riga from a Latvian Jew who had escaped to Switzerland. Harrison sent both affidavits to Welles, warning him to keep the names confidential and promising to send a statement from Burckhardt himself if it could be obtained.

The State Department must have known that Burckhardt was no ordinary citizen of Switzerland, but one of Europe's leading intellectuals and an international civil servant of great renown. After studying at various Swiss and German universities, the patrician Burckhardt had gone into the Swiss diplomatic service, then switched to the academic world. While professor of history at Geneva he wrote numerous highly praised works on European history. But he was also a diplomat and a man of action. From 1937 until 1939 he served as League of Nations High Commissioner for the Free City of Danzig, which was coveted by both Germany and Poland. Later he would write a book on his experience.

Burckhardt met personally with Adolf Hitler in August 1939 in an unsuccessful attempt to settle disputes over the Polish Corridor and Danzig. He got a rude awakening; the Führer did not particularly want a peaceful settlement and threatened to wipe Poland off the map. Hitler told Burckhardt bluntly that Germany wanted to go to war in the east to obtain vast stretches of land. But if the Western nations insisted on declaring war to defend Poland, Germany would beat them first and attack Russia later. Beyond his firsthand knowledge of Hitler, Burckhardt enjoyed close contacts with many other high German officials, some of whom he had known since his university days. His Red Cross organization also had sources in Germany. It would be difficult to dismiss whatever Burckhardt put on the record about Nazi killings of Jews.

Squire spoke directly to Burckhardt on November 7. Burckhardt confirmed privately and not for publication what he had earlier told Guggenheim, although he admitted that he had not actually seen the order itself. Squire asked whether the order explicitly used the word "extermination." Burckhardt replied that the order had required the territories to be "free of

Jews." But since there was no place to put the Jews, it was quite clear what the result would be.

Burckhardt told Squire that he had tried to get the International Red Cross to make a public appeal to the world on the question of Jews and hostages in Nazi Germany. The executive committee of the IRC, however, had rejected the idea on October 14, 1942, on the grounds that it would serve no purpose, might make the situation more difficult, and could jeopardize Red Cross work on behalf of prisoners of war and civil internees—"the real task of the Red Cross." The Nazis considered the Jews political enemies, but no other government considered them worthy of special protection. They were not POWs, not civilians, not Americans, not Britons. Only the governments-in-exile of countries conquered by Germany intervened for their Jewish citizens, and these governments had little leverage. Burckhardt's information, sent to Harrison on November 9, confirmed Schulte's original report.

After the new information went to Washington on November 23, Welles could no longer withhold judgment. He summoned Stephen Wise to Washington the next day and told the rabbi that he regretted to confirm Wise's deepest fears. But Welles must have thought it undesirable to notify his faction-ridden department of what he had told Wise. He wrote no official memorandum of the conversation at his meeting with Wise. And despite all the time and effort devoted to confirming Schulte's original report, a number of State Department officials continued to deny the existence of a Final Solution.

Wise, however, had not been idle while waiting for Welles. On September 28, one month after receiving the Riegner telegram via London, Wise spoke at a rally against Nazi atrocities held at Madison Square Garden. But the government and the American public in general paid little attention. On November 24, after having received confirmation from Welles, Wise arranged for press conferences in Washington and New York and made public what he knew. The Associated Press carried the story, which appeared in the *New York Herald Tribune* under the headline: "Wise Says Hitler Has Ordered 4,000,000 Jews Slain in 1942." The publicity was far greater than anything generated previously.

The result of Wise's efforts, as one State Department official soon complained, was "a flood of mail to the President and the State Department aimed at procuring 1) a joint declaration by the United States and the United Kingdom censuring barbarism and promising retribution; 2) opening Palestine to the Jews; 3) removing all barriers to the immigration of Jewish children; and 4) exchanging Jews in occupied Europe for interned Axis nationals." To the further irritation of State Department officials in the European Division, Wise disclosed that he had received the information about the Final Solution through the channels provided by the State Department, and he alluded to State Department confirmation as well. But State Department officials refused to comment on the information and directed all inquiries to Wise.

Wise also obtained an appointment for himself and four other Jewish leaders at the White House on December 8. The Jewish officials gave the President a memorandum entitled "Blue Print [sic] for Extermination" drawn from the Riegner-Lichtheim memorandum to Harrison and from other sources. It included a special section on Hitler's extermination order, which quoted sections of Riegner's telegram and repeated the inaccurate information about Herbert Backe, Hans Frank, and Heinrich Himmler. But the report correctly noted the essential point: for most Jews, deportation was just a euphemism for death.

Did Roosevelt believe the report? There is no record of his thoughts on the matter, so we can only make an informed guess. In September or October 1942 he may have thought the Schulte-Riegner report to be dubious. If Felix Frankfurter could not at first accept the reality of an assembly-line operation to destroy millions of his fellow Jews, Franklin Roosevelt may have reacted in a similar way. But by late November the evidence was overwhelming.

In early November FDR had asked Congress to approve a Third War Powers Bill that included a provision allowing the President to suspend laws hampering "the free movement of persons, property and information into and out of the United States." Assistant Secretary of State Breckinridge Long believed that Roosevelt had no intention of using this power to admit more refugees from Europe to the United States. Some conservatives in Congress and the press, however, thought otherwise. They may have been right.

Two days after Stephen Wise's press conferences Franklin Roosevelt held a meeting with Vice-President Henry Wallace and Sam Rayburn, Speaker of the House. According to Wallace's brief account, the President spoke chiefly about the need for legislation to loosen restrictions on immigration and im-

ports. Rayburn, however, pointed out that there was great con-
gressional opposition to this move, particularly in the Ways
and Means Committee. Roosevelt then appeared to retreat,
stating that this was Congress's responsibility to decide. Did the
President's lobbying have anything to do with the Riegner telegram? He was a master at concealing his true intentions.

In any case, conservative forces in the Ways and Means
Committee first deleted the word "persons" from the provision
and then held up the entire War Powers Bill until it died. Hos-
tility to increased Jewish immigration was a major factor in the
President's defeat. It is not surprising then that FDR was not
particularly eager to wage a major political battle over the desperate plight of European Jews.

Roosevelt was not an unfeeling man, but he carried the
weight of the world on his shoulders. He had decided early on
in the war that the best way to end all the suffering was to
bring the war to a successful conclusion as quickly as possible.
If he gave in to the ever-present requests for special assistance,
there would be no end to them.

Wise appealed to FDR at the December 8 meeting to bring
the extermination program to the world's attention and to
make an effort to stop it. Roosevelt said the government was familiar with most of the facts, but it was hard to find a suitable
course of action. The Allies could not make it appear that the
entire German people were murderers or were in agreement
with Hitler's actions. He agreed to release another statement
denouncing mass killings.

One could think of various extenuating circumstances for
the President's inaction and the State Department's refusal to
give publicity to the tragic fate of European Jewry. FDR's advisers probably told him that too many people in too many
places would object to expressions of Allied solicitude for the
Jews. Any measures to make the facts about the mass murder
known, to slow it down, or to stop it were thought to be politically or militarily inopportune: they would interfere with the
war effort.

And yet, all things considered, these arguments were quite
unconvincing. Roosevelt was a very busy man, but a look at his
calendar during the fall of 1942 shows that not every minute of
his time was devoted to vital and urgent matters of high policy.
He made a speech on September 16 when he presented a submarine chaser to a Norwegian princess; he made speeches to
the International Student Assembly, to doctors, lawyers, fac-

tory workers. He spoke in hospitals, offices, ballrooms, universities, and hotels. Could he not have found half an hour to make one of his famous, powerful speeches about the dreadful fate of the Jews, a speech that would have reverberated around the globe? Did he think that even a gesture would have been too much of a political risk?

In the end, it was left to the British to take the initiative. Winston Churchill had taken a personal interest in the various reports about Nazi extermination policies. The British Cabinet approved the text of a declaration confirming Hitler's intention to exterminate the Jewish people, condemning cold-blooded murder, and promising punishment of those responsible. Foreign Minister Anthony Eden read the Cabinet statement to the House of Commons, whose members stood in silence as a token of respect for the victims. The State Department dragged its feet up to the last moment, but in the end the United States and eleven other nations joined the British government in mid-December in a joint declaration on Nazi killings of Jews.

Rabbi Wise proclaimed that this historic statement "will bring solace to, and hearten Jewish people throughout the world as a reaffirmation of the determination of the free peoples that Axis murderers cannot . . . destroy any race or faith of people."

It had been four and a half months since Eduard Schulte had brought the horrifying news of the Final Solution to Zurich, and three and a half months since Wise had received Riegner's telegram. Schulte had wanted the Allies to attack the death camps; instead they issued a tardy denunciation of Nazi killings. Schulte had to wait until the creation of the United States War Refugee Board in January 1944 to see that his message was not entirely in vain. By that time most of the Jews in Europe were dead.

CHAPTER SEVEN

Enter Mr. Dulles

Eduard Schulte's Switzerland consisted of less than a square mile of Zurich, namely the area on both sides of the Bahnhofstrasse, between the railway station and the lakefront; it also included the Limmatquai and the tree-shaded promenade on the lakeshore, where he took his constitutionals. His work was in the "city"—at the stock exchange, the main banks, and some other business offices that he frequented. He usually had business to transact with the Zurich banks in connection with Giesche's sale of zinc to Switzerland. This was done with the permission of the German government, as part of a wider deal between the two countries. Whether Schulte's frequent trips to Zurich were absolutely necessary for business reasons is doubtful, but he was a persuasive man, and so he got his way.

The other reasons for going to Zurich were more decisive for him. He needed the trips to pass on information and warnings to the Allies, and he wanted to escape the giant prison that the Nazis had made of Germany, to breathe the free air of a neutral country. He enjoyed the fact that in Zurich one could talk freely, at least among friends, and that there were newspapers and books available that did not express an all-pervasive and mendacious propaganda.

Schulte liked to stay in a good hotel where service was excellent and unobtrusive. He wanted to see Doris, of course. He liked to stroll on the Bahnhofstrasse and to window-shop or to walk along one of the quays. But his Switzerland was not that of St. Moritz, Davos, or Pontresina, of winter sports, summer resorts, and beautiful mountain landscapes. He came to Zurich above all because he was a man with a mission. He was perfectly aware that this mission involved enormous risks, that each trip could be his last. The slightest slip, a minor accident, could bring disaster. But he was a brave man convinced of his duty, and so he continued to travel to Zurich every month or two.

Until late 1942 it would have been difficult—and also highly dangerous—for Eduard Schulte to have contacts with Americans in Switzerland. American diplomats had not been trained for intelligence work, nor were they encouraged by their superiors to engage in such activities. Since British intelligence in Switzerland had also been weak, the Allies had relied mainly on information from the Poles, Czechs, and some tidbits from Swiss sources. It was almost a repeat of the First World War: then too the Allies had waked up rather late to the importance of Switzerland.

Then in November 1942 Allen Dulles arrived in Bern. He came on the very last train from Vichy France to Switzerland, a day after the Allied landing in North Africa—only hours before the Germans occupied southern France and cut the rail link. Ostensibly taking up a post as assistant to the American minister in Bern, Dulles's real job was to organize the Office of Strategic Services (OSS) Mission in Switzerland: in other words, to establish an American professional intelligence outpost on Germany's border.

Allen Dulles's background was impressive: he was a Princeton graduate, a partner in a prominent Wall Street law firm, a nephew of former Secretary of State Robert Lansing, and at one time head of the Near Eastern section at the State Department. His last job had been that of director of the New York office of OSS. Dulles was a self-made spymaster, but a quick learner and a "deeply concerned advocate" (to use his own words) of the role of intelligence. He was not a believer in clandestine methods at all costs. He recalled in later years that when he arrived in Bern in November 1942,

> one of the leading Swiss journals produced the story that I was coming there as a secret and special envoy of President Franklin D. Roosevelt. Off hand, one might have thought that this unsought advertisement would have hampered my work. Quite the contrary was the case. Despite my modest but truthful denials of the story, it was generally believed. As a result, to my network flocked a host of informants, some cranks, it is true, but also some exceedingly valuable individuals. If I could not separate the wheat from the chaff with only a reasonable degree of error, then I was not qualified for my job, because the ability to judge is one of the prime qualities of an intelligence officer.

From the day of his arrival, Dulles was on the lookout for reliable helpers and informants on Germany. He quickly recruited Gero von Gaevernitz, the naturalized American citizen living in Ascona who had excellent contacts in Germany. Gaevernitz became his right-hand man and chief adviser on German politics. Gaevernitz moved into the house at Herrengasse 23 in Bern that had become Dulles's residence and office.

Not everyone in his Swiss household was trustworthy. Dulles's security precautions somehow ignored his cook, who was in the pay of the German Legation. The American Legation had even greater security problems: the American military attaché, General Barnwell Legge, unsuspectingly employed a Nazi spy in his office. The legation's codes were regularly broken by the Germans and even by the monitoring services of small nations such as Finland. This was disastrous because Dulles's shortage of staff meant that he had to send some of his own messages through the legation. When in early 1943 he learned from his German contacts about the breaches in security, he persuaded American Minister Leland Harrison to retain the broken codes, lacing bits and pieces of true information with false reports to mislead the Germans. The really important messages were put into new codes.

Dulles got much top-secret intelligence from the very people who had been sent to watch him, the Abwehr, German military intelligence. The Abwehr had been very active in Switzerland even before the war. It knew more or less all it needed about the deployment of the Swiss Army and its defense planning, and it had a good idea what British intelligence was doing in Switzerland. It found not a few collaborators among Swiss citizens. But in 1942 the Abwehr's sources began to dry up, partly because Swiss counterintelligence had improved, partly because the Allied services had become more active.

By this time the anti-Nazi elements inside the Abwehr, led by deputy director Hans Oster, had intensified their activities. Some participated in various plots aimed at a coup against Hitler; others even cooperated with the Allies. Allen Dulles's best source throughout 1943 was a leading member of the Abwehr in Zurich, and this same man was soon to play a crucial role in the life of Eduard Schulte.

Hans Bernd Gisevius was a *Sonderführer** in the Abwehr who was posted to Zurich in October 1940. His official title was vice-consul, but he appeared more often in Abwehr headquarters in Bern than in the consulate general in Zurich. Since he had not belonged to the diplomatic service before the war, it stood to reason that Gisevius was no ordinary diplomat. He made no secret of his real assignment: he first told the Swiss about it, then the British, and later also the Americans. And he further informed them that within the Abwehr he represented the small but determined anti-Nazi opposition. Gisevius's appearance was as stiff as the collar he wore. A man of towering height, he looked like a caricature of a senior Prussian civil servant. He was so ostentatious in his behavior that few chose to believe at first that this strange creature was a bona fide secret agent. Some thought him a buffoon; others, an impostor putting on an elaborate act. Many believed he was a dyed-in-the-wool Nazi trying to hoodwink the Swiss and the Allies. Surely no one in his right mind would talk so openly about secret matters.

Gisevius's background also raised many questions. His

---

* This was a special rank for civilians attached to the Army.

record as a student leader before 1933 had been dubious. He had represented the pro-Nazi wing within the German youth movement. When Hitler came to power in 1933, Gisevius was twenty-nine, a young legal adviser with the Prussian Ministry of the Interior attached to the Prussian police. Yet this very junior official went out of his way to ingratiate himself with leading conservatives. He made influential friends, including Count Wolf Heinrich von Helldorf, chief of the Berlin police, and Arthur Nebe, who became head of the criminal police. He was on the scene when the political police was transformed into the Gestapo. There was reason to assume that the young careerist would soon be among the leading figures in the SS-Gestapo empire. But Gisevius did not become a Nazi Party member, and the Nazis never quite trusted him. When Himmler took over as chief of the German police, Gisevius was transferred from Berlin to some unimportant administrative job in the Interior Ministry in the provinces. The Nazis' suspicions were right. Gisevius was not one of them, and although he had helped to pave the way for Hitler, he was also one of the first to recognize his mistake and join the opposition. He became one of its most active members.

In a memorandum written after the war Gisevius claimed that he and his friends had done all they could to warn Britain and France about Hitler's intention to make war. After the outbreak of the war they had passed on "precise and timely warnings against the countries threatened by Hitlerite invasion such as Norway, Holland, Belgium, Yugoslavia, and even the Soviet Union." After the invasions he had sent further information "to thwart the Hitlerite plans to subjugate Europe and prolong the war."

In several cases in which Germans and other nationals were threatened with arrests as spies, Gisevius and his friends had "obliterated the traces, protecting many Germans and others." They had engaged in various rescue actions helping individuals—these included the Polish military attaché Antoni Szymanski and a group of German Jews. Gisevius was not a man of outstanding modesty and restraint in his actions, speech, or writing: yet the claims he made about himself and his associates were essentially correct.

Gisevius had certain traits that antagonized many of the people he worked with. A friend described him as a gangster fighting for a good cause, an "uncouth scarlet pimpernel." He was very self-centered. A strong proclivity toward conspiracy led him to plot not only against the Nazis but also sometimes against his own side. Very ambitious, he once made it known that he wanted to be chief of police in a post-Nazi government. But he was a man of strong religious convictions, and courageous to the point of recklessness. In the final analysis Gisevius did more against the Nazi regime than many better-known figures of the German resistance. There were certain duties he had to fulfill on behalf of the Abwehr, such as "laundering" German money in Switzerland, so that intelligence operations could be financed; but these activities were of no consequence as far as the German war effort was concerned. He could have defected early on during the war, in which case his conscience would have been pure and his record clear. But for an activist like Gisevius this was quite unthinkable. He would no longer have been of help to the resistance.

When he first ran into this extraordinary character who questioned the sanity of Hitler and "his lackeys and sidekicks," Eduard Schulte did not know what to make of him. He decided to be on his guard, and it was only months later, and after having been reassured by a close friend, that he established contact with Gisevius. This Abwehr official, it appeared, was on intimate terms with Hjalmar Schacht, General Ludwig Beck, and, above all, the heads of the Abwehr, Canaris and Oster. Schulte and Gisevius never became friends, but they regarded themselves as comrades-in-arms.

Gisevius made contact with Dulles earlier than the more cautious Schulte. In February 1943 Gisevius notified Gaevernitz that the American Legation's codes were not secure, earning Dulles's gratitude. Three months later, prompted in part by OSS officials in the United States who knew Schulte personally, Dulles made contact with him, with Chojnacki and Gero von Gaevernitz serving as intermediaries. It turned out that Dulles and Schulte had met once before. Almost fifteen years previously Schulte and Dulles had participated in some business conferences at the offices of Sullivan and Cromwell, Dulles's law firm, which sometimes represented Giesche's partner Anaconda Copper.

The two men met several times over the next few months. Schulte even kept the American advised as to when he expected to return to Switzerland. Dulles, as Schulte saw him, was different from the average American businessmen he had known: educated, polite, politically knowledgeable, and a good listener. Dulles for his part was impressed by Schulte—here was a real captain of industry, a man of formidable presence, with a great deal of knowledge and even a sense of humor. Dulles had come to know all kinds of Germans whose anti-Nazi credentials were not to be doubted. But they were mostly political émigrés, usually acting as diplomatic (or semi-diplomatic) go-betweens, useful people certainly, but not men of substance like Schulte. At first, but only for a short time, Dulles did not fully trust Schulte, regarding him with the same caution he would show toward any new arrival on the scene. Later on, the only real barrier between the two was that of language, for while Dulles had some German, his poor pronunciation made it almost impossible for Schulte to understand him. Schulte's English was even more limited than Dulles's German. But somehow the two managed to get along extremely well, with Gaevernitz acting as interpreter when the going was rough.

At their very first meeting Dulles asked Schulte to prepare a detailed memorandum on present-day conditions in Germany and to include in it his recommendations for the postwar reconstruction of the country: this would be translated and forwarded to the most influential people in Washington. Schulte complied, and the memorandum was promptly sent off. Dulles pressed Washington to respond quickly, so that he could relay American reaction to Schulte during his next visit to Switzerland. Dulles was most eager to promote good relations with Schulte. Using Schulte's code number rather than his name, the OSS official told Washington: "643 is believed to be a most valuable source. . . . He is a prominent businessman who, we feel, can be depended upon to cooperate with us after G's [Germany's] collapse."

Washington was eager to learn of men such as Schulte. OSS headquarters had encouraged its officials abroad to compile a list of Germans who could aid in the rebuilding of a new Germany in the event of the sudden surrender or collapse of Nazi Germany. Dulles gave Schulte a prominent position on his list.

Dulles was eager to cultivate the industrialist both because of his present helpfulness and because of his potential for the future. Schulte had begun to supply the Americans with very useful information. The Allied leaders were exceedingly well informed on certain aspects of German military planning. The fact that the British had broken some of the highest-grade German codes was the best-kept secret of the Second World War, and this gave them insight into the most astounding details of

German operations. But Ultra had narrow limits; it could be
used only for intercepting long-range wireless communications.
German orders sent by special courier or telephone remained
immune to Allied interception, and this included almost all
that happened inside Germany.

On August 25, 1943, OSS Secret Intelligence headquarters
in Washington sent Dulles a priority inquiry. The crack SS
Adolf Hitler Panzer Division was reported to be withdrawn
from Russia for action elsewhere, and Washington was "very
anxious" to learn the whereabouts of this division. Could
Dulles's sources help?

On September 9 Dulles cabled Washington with information from Schulte that there were now fifteen German divisions, including two top Panzer divisions (*Das Reich* and *Adolf
Hitler*), concentrated in Italy or at the Italian border. Ordinar-
ily, such a piece of information would perhaps not be accorded
top priority, but at this time it told the Allied leaders what they
had specifically asked about. Mussolini had just been deposed,
and six days earlier Italian leader Marshal Badoglio had secretly signed an armistice with the Allies. The concentration of
German troops in Italy showed clearly that Hitler did not in-
tend to let his old ally down. Three days later the Duce was
liberated from prison, and German conquest of northern and
central Italy began.

There were few other sources who could give the Allies such
direct insight into Hitler's thinking. On October 1, 1943,
Dulles summarized for Washington the contents of another
conversation with Schulte:

> Lately from the north [,] very competent and
> well informed, 643 said in a conversation that
> East Front developments are no longer receiv-
> ing Hitler's personal interest. General Staff,
> Mannstein [*sic*], Von Kluge, etc. are being left
> with this, while Hitler takes a direct personal in-
> terest in Balkan and Italian campaigns.
> Though, our informant states, Rommel is not
> personally in agreement with Hitler's program
> for defending outposts in Italy and Balkans,
> Hitler's orders are still decisive here. Hitler's in-
> sistence that everything should be held if possi-
> ble is not in accord with Rommel's belief in the

Eduard Schulte around 1930.

Giesche's zinc and lead facilities at Beuthen, on the German side of the German–Polish border.

A main entrance to the Auschwitz camp. The sign reads: 'Labour makes one free.'

Heinrich Himmler (right), head of the SS, with an I. G. Farben official at Auschwitz, July 18, 1942.

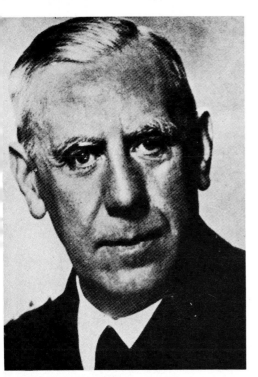

Wilhelm Canaris, head of the Abwehr.

General Hans Oster, another leader of anti-Nazi resistance.

Dr. Eduard Waetjen, whose phone call saved Schulte's life.

Hans Bernd Gisevius, who helped Schulte escape.

By this
Certificate of Service
I record my appreciation of the aid rendered by
Eduard "Hans" Schulte
as a volunteer in the service of the United Nations
for the great cause of Freedom.

B. L. Montgomery

Field Marshal

Date 1st January, 1946. *Commander in Chief, 21st Army Group*

Allen Dulles, U.S. Intelligence chief in Switzerland, later head of the CIA.

Certificate of appreciation from the British Government, signed by Field Marshal Montgomery.

> strategy of withdrawing to lines which are more defensible.

The information that Hitler was pursuing a foolish long-term strategy of trying to hold all positions turned out to be quite accurate.

• • •

During 1943 one problem came to preoccupy Allied intelligence more than any other—the secret or "miracle" weapons the Germans were said to be developing. Hitler himself had made the first reference earlier, dropping dark hints about formidable new weapons that would soon have a decisive impact on the course of the war. And earlier in the war a document had been dropped into the mail box of the British naval attaché in Oslo, Norway, which included a fairly accurate and complete list of new weapons under development in Germany.*

Several reports reached the Allies during 1940 (including one from a source close to the Abwehr) that the Germans were experimenting at Peenemünde, in Pomerania, with a gun of exceptionally long range. The reports got the location right, but not the weapon. Even before the war the Allies knew that German secret rocket research was concentrated in Peenemünde (on the island of Usedom in the Baltic Sea), but this knowledge was of limited use, since neither the British nor the Americans knew much about rockets at the time. Germany had pioneered rocket technology and was many years ahead in this field.

During 1941 and 1942 Allied leaders were inclined to play down the importance of German secret weapons. They were not altogether wrong, because during the early years of the war the Peenemünde rocket wizards suffered several humiliating setbacks. Hitler was not impressed by their work; he had a dream that the rockets would never reach England. Research was not stopped, but the projects had low priority. By late 1942

* The identity of the author of this most astonishing intelligence document of the Second World War is still a secret. Some writers have suggested Hans Heinrich Kummerow, a Berlin chemical engineer; but Professor R. V. Jones, who headed British scientific intelligence during the war, says that Kummerow was not the man. The family of the author of the Oslo document has so far opposed publication of his name, but it seems likely that his identity will become known soon.

London and Washington heard that the Germans had overcome some of the main technical obstacles, and that Hitler had
become less skeptical about the rockets. This information came
from several sources. An engineer from a neutral country visiting Berlin had picked up a conversation between two German
scientists in a Berlin restaurant; two German generals who became prisoners of war were overheard discussing the new weapons; a group of workers in Luxembourg who had done
construction work at Peenemünde smuggled out some technical data that sounded plausible enough.

Despite initial incredulity in the Western capitals, the evidence became so strong by April 1943 that Churchill decided
to give top priority to the collection and evaluation of reports
on the new weapons. His son-in-law Duncan Sandys was appointed to head a special investigation committee that had the
code name Body Line. Concurrently, Washington gave the
subject much higher priority. Allen Dulles was entrusted with
the task of collecting evidence on the rockets and carried it out
so well that at the end of the war he was given a special presidential citation.*

Some of this information about German rockets came from
Eduard Schulte. In part it was conveyed to Dulles directly, but
on other occasions it seems to have reached him by the way of
Chojnacki or Gisevius. Some of Schulte's information was surprisingly accurate. When he reported on September 9, 1943,
that the two recent Allied bombing raids on Peenemünde (August 4 and August 25) had set back production by two months,
this was exactly the estimate of General Walter Dornberger,
the director of the rocket laboratory. It appears from his report
that Schulte knew that some of the main laboratories at Peenemünde were underground, and that not all those above ground
had been destroyed. He virtually urged more such bombing
raids, warning Dulles not to underestimate the seriousness of
the rocket threat. He also reported that the scientists had managed to cut the rockets' margin of error to about a thousand
yards, which was a reasonably accurate account of the stage
they were at.

Gisevius warned Dulles at various times that German mili-

* This citation for Dulles's intelligence work specifically mentioned "the first
reports on the German experimental laboratory at Peenemünde for testing
the rocket bomb." They were not the first; the Allies had known about the
laboratory at Peenemünde even before 1939. Still, Dulles's information was
of very great importance.

tary sources had great confidence that the new rocket would be effective, especially in the bombardment of London. He also passed on a list of factories involved in making parts for the rocket, correctly identifying the name of the rocket program (A-4) and that of its chemical director (Dr. Otto Ambros of I. G. Farben).

On other occasions, information passed to the Allies was contradictory or mistaken, but this was true with regard to all the reports emanating from Peenemünde. Only a very gifted engineer specializing in ballistic missiles could have decided how much of the mass of information from Germany made sense. It was not clear for a long time whether the Germans were producing one "miracle" weapon or several, whether it was a rocket or a pilotless aircraft or a giant gun, what kind of fuel was used, and so on. Some reports belonged to the realm of fantasy: for example, that a super-heavy gun some 130 feet in length had been constructed, or that extensive experiments had been carried out in occupied Russian territory.

Dulles noted on one occasion (May 1943) that he was hesitant to pass on material of this kind because of its contradictory character. But as Washington's interest in the subject was constantly growing, and as the information came from reliable sources such as "512" (Gisevius), "643" (Schulte), "513" (a Polish source), and "680,"* he felt compelled to carry on sending the information, and to see that the British received it too.

What did Allied intelligence headquarters make of the details—true, half-true, and false—that reached them in increasing quantity during July, August, and September 1943? They had to decide whether the weapons were "liquid air bombs on the rocket principle," as some maintained, and whether they carried gas or germs. They had to prepare estimates concerning their range and accuracy, concerning the gap between experiment and operational readiness. Some British scientists still believed that the whole issue was an elaborate hoax—a "mare's nest," as one of them put it. However, by late summer in 1943, the majority had reached the conclusion that a rocket with a range of 130 miles—sufficient to reach London from the Continent—was technically feasible. By September 1943 most of

---

* "680" cannot be identified with absolute certainty. But there is reason to believe that he was a relative of Helmuth James von Moltke, one of the leaders of the German resistance, and worked for one of the biggest German corporations.

those concerned with evaluating the reports were convinced
that the Germans were working on not one but two "flying
bombs," as they were then called—the V-1, a rather primitive
device, a pilotless aircraft, slow and low-flying, and the V-2, a
far more sophisticated missile flying at high altitude and
reaching a speed of 3,600 miles per hour.

These estimates caused considerable apprehension in London. The issues were fully discussed with Washington at the
highest level, and a systematic pooling of intelligence was
agreed upon. Thus, when the German armed forces began to
launch the V-1 against London on June 13, 1944, seven days
after the Allied landing in Normandy, the new weapon did not
come as a surprise. The V-2s were first used in September 1944.
Their military effect was very small, and the losses among the
civilian population, though substantial, were not remotely as
large as had been feared.

But what if the missiles had been ready six months earlier?
What if the Germans had then targeted the sites in southern
England that served as the bases for launching the Allied invasion of the Continent? General Eisenhower, supreme commander of the Allied forces, asked these questions in his
memoirs. He thought that the results would have been very serious indeed. It was a very good thing, then, that Allied bombing attacks delayed the progress of the V-2.

It is also true that General Dornberger, commander of the
Peenemünde installations, expected an Allied attack almost
from the moment in October 1942 when his senior scientists
succeeded in launching experimental long-range missiles. He
reasoned that while it had been easy to conceal work done inside the walls of the laboratory, it would be impossible to hide
missiles traveling long distances. In his memoirs he wrote that
he was surprised the Allies took so many months to put the various bits of information together in order to know where and
what to attack. Given Allied superiority in the air, and the
shortages Germany experienced in certain raw materials, it was
quite certain that the V-2 could not have been a decisive
weapon even if Hitler had given it higher priority. It is certainly true, however, that but for the timely intelligence reports
on German rockets, the war might have lasted longer and taken
an even heavier toll in lives and material. Schulte, Gisevius,
and others had here made a major contribution.

• • •

One day in early September 1943 Gisevius brought Schulte into contact with Eduard Waetjen, a young lawyer who was visiting Zurich on behalf of a large German corporation. Schulte found him a pleasant young man. Since Gisevius talked quite openly to Waetjen, Schulte concluded that the lawyer was also somehow connected with the Abwehr and that he shared Gisevius's anti-Nazi convictions. Schulte met a great many people during his business trips, and under normal circumstances he might well have forgotten Waetjen. He could not have known on that September morning that within a few months he would owe his life to the timely and decisive intervention of Waetjen and Gisevius.

CHAPTER EIGHT

Escape

On the morning of December 2, 1943, Schulte and three of his closest colleagues at Giesche, Albrecht Jung, Lothar Siemon, and Günter von Poseck, drove from Kattowitz to nearby Gleiwitz for a meeting of the Silesian coal syndicate—coal mining was an important sideline for Giesche. Jung, it will be remembered, was the firm's legal adviser; Siemon was Schulte's right-hand man as well as a personal friend. The chain-smoking Poseck, who headed the Kattowitz operation, shared Schulte's passion for hunting. Having read the newspaper over breakfast, the four men discussed the war situation. The Russians had taken Kiev, German troops were retreating in Italy, the Allied bomber offensive against major German cities continued. Hamburg had barely survived a fire storm; now it was Berlin's turn. Heavy attacks were reported almost every night; some ministries had been hit; others were evacuated from the capital. Communications were interrupted. For the first time, business activities in Germany were directly affected by the Allied bombing offensive.

Schulte, usually talkative with this trio, was silent during much of the trip. What he had predicted for so long was now coming true. He had often told his closest aides that one of these days the Russians would reach Silesia "and we shall get our marching orders." They had not contradicted him but had come to regard him as an eccentric and a pessimist. No longer. There was no joy in his heart, however, no desire to say to his colleagues "I told you so." What a price Germany was beginning to pay now, he must have reflected, for the madness of its leaders and for the blind obedience of its people.

The meeting started on time. After an hour one of the secretaries entered the room and whispered in his ear: *"Herr Generaldirektor,* someone from Berlin on the line. He says it is very urgent. Should I tell him to call again?" Schulte went to the phone in the adjacent office.

"Schulte here."

"This is Eduard."

"Eduard who?"

"Surely you remember me, we met a few months ago in Zurich when we had lunch. . . ." It came back in a flash— Eduard Waetjen, who had been present at Schulte's last meeting with Gisevius.

"Yes, I do remember."

"I just had a call from our common friend. He thinks, and I agree with him, that your presence in Zurich is urgently needed. A critical situation has developed in the negotiations and your presence is required."

"What situation?"

"It would take too long to explain."

"Right, so I shall come next week."

"Next week may be too late. You should come now, right away."

Schulte hesitated for a moment. "I understand, I shall come at once."

He returned to the meeting room. They were about to break for coffee. He beckoned Jung, Siemon, and Poseck, who joined him in a corner. "I have to leave immediately for Switzerland. There is an order out for my arrest. Tell them that I had to go abroad suddenly."

"But you have no luggage," Siemon said.

"True," Schulte answered, "but I have my passport; do give me your bag." Siemon had some luggage with him because he was on his way to Breslau and Berlin. Schulte asked one of his colleagues to phone his wife and to reassure her; she should be told that it was probably a misunderstanding connected with some complicated business transaction. It would blow over in a few days. But it was safest to ride out the storm abroad. "I shall phone you after my arrival," he said in parting. It was typically Schulte; he had no doubt that he would be all right.

Siemon, Jung, and Poseck would not see Schulte again until well after the war. They were surprised by his sudden departure but not unduly shocked. Giesche had engaged in trade with neutral countries, and while most of it had been above-board, there were so many wartime regulations that it was easy to violate some of them. They had become accustomed to sudden inspections and threats of arrests. The Gestapo had previously shown interest in Giesche's complicated dealings. And Schulte, with his tendency to criticize the government openly and loudly, was an obvious target. He had done so only in his small circle of friends and colleagues, but perhaps someone had talked out of turn. Schulte was an important man, however, an essential figure in the war effort. Even if he were arrested, a call to some minister would probably get him out, the three men agreed.

Schulte took the train to Breslau from the Gleiwitz station. Far too slowly for him, the train passed through the fertile plains of Silesia, which had produced a good harvest that fall. He was not overcome by the sudden turn of events; he had seen it all coming. Perhaps the only surprise was that there had been sufficient time for his friends to warn him, so that he had a chance to make a getaway.

One evening not long before at Hermann Schulte's home in Berlin the cousins had discussed the supervision of border control, one of the functions of Hermann's Abwehr department. Hermann had mentioned in passing that the police bureaucracy was by no means as speedy and efficient as the public assumed. Each order for an arrest had to be processed and confirmed by several offices, and then it usually took another day or two until border police got instructions. In the case of some minor border crossings it might take a week or even longer.

Schulte changed trains in Breslau. He studied the small, well-thumbed railway directory that he always carried with him. It was of limited use in wartime, with all the dislocations and cancellations. Then it suddenly occurred to him that he ought to go first to Berlin to consult his friends. Perhaps he should not take this warning so seriously. Leaving Germany in a hurry would be an admission of guilt; the road back would be closed to him. And even if his friends in Berlin advised him to escape, the trip via the capital would mean a delay of only a few hours. If the Gestapo was already looking for him, he would be as safe in Berlin as elsewhere.

By this time it was evening, and the train to Berlin was almost empty. A great many people were leaving the German capital by the end of 1943; few went there except on urgent business. When the train pulled into the city, Schulte saw why.

He had stayed in Berlin for long periods during the war, and had seen the terrible damage caused by the heaviest air raid so far, the one on August 23, 1943, when large parts of the Friedrichstrasse and the Wilhelmstrasse had been destroyed, including some of the ministries, hotels, department stores, and other landmarks. Then there had been a lull in the bombing, but then on November 18 the raids had resumed. Since then there had been hardly a quiet night. Schulte was not prepared for the havoc caused by these most recent air raids. He had no idea whether his hotel, the Coburger Hof, was still standing, nor did he want to find out. He decided to stay with friends in Charlottenburg. But it took a long time to find a taxi and even longer to make his way to the west end. Traffic was constantly detoured. Schulte saw that some of the most elegant neighborhoods, such as the Tauentzienstrasse, were in ruins.

He phoned his cousin, and they agreed to meet the next afternoon. When they met and Hermann heard about the warning, he became alarmed. He would try to find out more, but it would not be easy. He had no direct channel to the Gestapo, and what with the general confusion caused by the bombings, it could take days. And it was not certain whether he would get a conclusive answer, if indeed he got one at all. Would it not be advisable for Eduard to go on a business trip to Switzerland in any case? Within a few days one might know more.

It was now too late to resume the journey, and Eduard Schulte was very tired. Before the cousins parted, Hermann promised to call on General Erich Fellgiebel, who was in charge of army communications. Fellgiebel was a cautious, reticent person, but those near him also knew that he was one of the best-informed people in the country and a bitter opponent of the regime.

Schulte made his way back to the friends with whom he was staying and had dinner with them. Then the air-raid sirens sounded. After a few minutes one could hear the heavy bombers approaching, and then the bombs fell. When the all clear was given about two hours later, and they came up from the shelter, Schulte's mood was somber. It was the first major raid he had experienced. It was not the fear of the bombs that agitated him: rather the feeling that he was caught in a trap, that he would no longer be able to escape.

Early next morning, December 4, Hermann came to see him. He had tried to phone, but the lines were out of order, and the electricity supply had also been interrupted. General Fellgiebel was not in Berlin; it was pointless to wait any longer. The official morning broadcast did not sound good: the Anglo-American air raids continued to terrorize the civilian population. According to the broadcast, fifty-three planes had been shot down, but hospitals, churches, schools, and historical monuments had been hit. It seemed unlikely that railway traffic would be resumed for a day or two, but Schulte was willing to try anyway. They managed to get a private car that took him to the Anhalt station. He was lucky; it was one of the few stations in Berlin operating that morning.

After waiting for several hours in the morning cold, he got a seat on a train leaving for Leipzig or Dresden. It did not really matter. Once he left Berlin, he would somehow make his way to south Germany.

Schulte had stood in the crowd in front of the Anhalter Bahnhof when Hitler had arrived there after his greatest victory three and a half years earlier. Hitler had told the enthusiastic crowd more than once that ten years hence they would not be able to recognize the capital. The prophecy was coming true sooner than anyone had expected. How quickly had the elation of 1940 given way to the dejection of late 1943. Schulte bought a sandwich at the railway kiosk; the days of the luxury railway cars and dining cars had gone long ago. There had been several police checks, but no one seemed to take an interest in him. A middle-aged man with a game leg was not likely to be suspected of being a deserter from the Army; and his passport and other identification papers were in good order, and he was a leading industrialist, a big wheel in the German war effort. Should he head for a minor border crossing? He considered the idea, then dismissed it. It would only attract attention if someone like him tried his luck in a place meant to serve only the local population. In a little out-of-the-way village, police knew all the locals; a stranger would be suspect. No, it was to be either the train to Zurich via Konstanz, or to Basel via Freiburg. In the past Schulte had much more often taken the Konstanz train. This time, he opted for the longer route to Basel. Perhaps he thought that if the Gestapo knew his habits, they would be waiting for him in Konstanz.

He traveled through Saxony by night. There were long delays, presumably because of a heavy attack on Leipzig; parts of the city had been destroyed. In the early hours of the morning the train reached Hof, the entrance to Bavaria, then crossed the Fichtel mountains and stopped at Marktredwitz, the great railway junction.

Schulte had spent a considerable part of his life on trains. Usually he had a book with him, or business correspondence to study in preparation for a meeting. This time he had nothing to read apart from some magazines he had bought at the station in Berlin, but he would have found it difficult to concentrate in any case. After he had finished glancing at the magazines, he took out his wallet and counted his money. There was enough to last him for a week or two in Switzerland, and he had an account in a Swiss bank. He checked his passport; it was lucky that his Swiss visa had just been renewed.

He unfolded the letter that he always carried with him and which he had read many times. It was from his elder son, Wolfgang. Written while he was serving on the eastern front, it was dated January 12, 1943.

> DEAR PAPA!
> I am leaving this letter with Dr. Siemon in case you get an official message that something has happened to me. You should then know that I shall no longer be alive, irrespective of how this message will be phrased. Confronting an enemy like this there is no other way out; there always should be one last bullet. Please inform Marie-Luise Weber, since I intend to write only one letter of this kind. I had wanted to propose to her during my next stay. My stamp collection should be given to Ruprecht's

future son once he is old enough to appreciate
it. Everything else should be left to Ruprecht. I
face my fate calmly and in the conviction that it
was necessary to give everything in this struggle.
You will have to support Mother more than
ever, so that she will get over this blow; she will
find support in Ruprecht—and perhaps one
day in his children. My last thoughts will be
with you and Marluis [Marie-Luise].
Your son
WOLFGANG

The letter had originally passed into Lothar Siemon's
keeping, as Wolfgang had intended, though how it had gotten
to Siemon can only be guessed at. Wolfchen, as he was called in
the family and by his friends, most likely gave it to an injured
fellow officer about to be flown out of the Stalingrad area.
Wolfgang did not make it; less than three weeks after his letter
was written the German units under Field Marshal Friedrich
von Paulus surrendered. The official message that his son was
missing in action reached Schulte in Breslau in February 1943.
Wolfgang's letter, which Siemon gave to him soon after, must
have softened the blow slightly.*

It had indeed been a severe blow for Schulte, and Clara
had been distraught for many months. In fact, she was never
quite the same again; she had been particularly close to her
elder son. Wolfgang should have studied law in Germany and
abroad; he should have seen foreign countries and enjoyed
himself. Instead, he had been called up to the army in 1937, at
age eighteen, and war had broken out in the summer of 1939.
Just when he was about to be released, he had served in a signal
unit virtually without interruption from the Polish campaign
on. Since the invasion of the Soviet Union he had been home
only a few times.

Wolfgang had taken the war in his stride. Like everyone
else's children he had belonged to the Hitler Youth, but he had
never been a fanatical Nazi. He regarded the fighting as something inevitable, of the same order as a natural disaster. But on
each visit home after June 1941 he appeared more pes-

---

* Wolfgang Schulte was not killed in action. He died in Betekowka, a POW
camp. But this became known only years after the end of the war when German prisoners began to return from Soviet captivity.

simistic about the outcome and about his own chances of survival.

Ruprecht was called up following the Polish campaign, serving first in a signal unit and later in a tank division. He had been wounded several times and had been decorated. The two brothers had met on the eastern front a few times: Wolfgang had a motorcycle and came to visit Ruprecht when they were stationed not far from each other.

Eduard Schulte abominated the Nazi regime but was in some ways proud that his sons were serving as officers. They had achieved what he had failed to do because of his severe leg injury. He had always known that the Third Reich would cause untold suffering, but somehow he had never imagined that he and his family would be affected. He had felt sure his sons would survive the senseless slaughter. Few human beings are able to accept the certainty of death; it is only natural to ignore it as long as possible. Schulte was a great realist, but as far as the life and death of those close to him were concerned, he behaved like most other people.

As in so many other German homes, 1943 had not been a happy year in the house of Schulte. Eduard had his work to distract him, but there was no such escape for his wife. Clara's depressions became more frequent. There was little comfort Schulte could offer her.

•   •   •

Schulte returned to his present predicament: what if he were arrested at the border or even before? He was not a fearful man, but the possibility of falling into the hands of the Gestapo was disquieting, to say the least. Everyone knew they had ways to extract confessions. Most of the Gestapo types he had known were rather stupid; perhaps he would be able to talk his way out. But he would have such a chance only if he knew what proof they had against him. Schulte was a man of considerable ingenuity and self-confidence. It was his firm belief that there was a way out of almost any difficulty. His main obstacle as he saw it was that he had to fight against an invisible enemy.

The train crossed the hills of the Swabian forest. It was getting dark when it descended into the Neckar valley. In Stuttgart Schulte changed to another train; but then shortly before it was due to arrive in Freiburg, the new train came to a halt. No reason was given; someone thought that perhaps there had been an air raid and the railway line had been hit, which could mean a very long stay in the middle of the forest. Schulte had been traveling for more than twenty-four hours and everything until this holdup had gone smoothly. He was now very near the Swiss border. How ironic if his escape should fail because of some stupid accident that no one could have foreseen. For the first time during this long trip doubts beset him: should he leave the train, make his way to the nearest town, hire a car, and head for the Swiss border? He rejected the idea: he did not know how close he was to any town, hiring a car would be next to impossible, and even if he succeeded he was bound to attract dangerous attention. A full hour was to go by before the waiting ended.

Schulte was not a patient man at the best of times, nor was he much prone to anxiety or fear. Now the peril grew with every minute that passed. In later years Schulte would tell his friends that this hour in a stationary train close to the Swiss border—so near and yet so far—had been one of the most trying in his life. But then, suddenly, the train began to move again. Border control was in a place called Mühlheim. He produced his passport, which had been renewed in Breslau only a few months before. He had a valid Swiss visa. He was a *Generaldirektor*. From the many stamps in his passport the officials gathered that he had frequently been to Switzerland, and for lengthy periods. They consulted their list of wanted persons in a perfunctory way. Generaldirektor Dr. Eduard Schulte was not among those wanted. They wished him a good night. Schulte re-entered his compartment and the train began to move again. He was safe. The journey continued for a few minutes on German territory. There were several tunnels, and then in the darkness he saw the Rhine, split up at that place into several branches. A few minutes later there was Basel: Swiss border control. When the Swiss officials too saw from the passport that he had often been to Switzerland, they lost interest in him.

Schulte went to a hotel near the main railway station. It was not quite up to the standard he was accustomed to, but he was very tired. They looked at him distrustfully because he had so little luggage. But he did not care; nor did he regret that it was too late for a meal, too late even for phoning friends. He was safe.

"Welcome," Gisevius said when Schulte phoned him early the next morning, adding that Schulte was a very lucky man indeed to have made it in time. They agreed that Schulte would come to Zurich as soon as possible and see Gisevius in his apartment.

He took a train to Zurich and checked in at the Baur-au-Lac. They were very friendly as usual, found him a good room, and got him a new shirt and a pair of pajamas within the hour. He had his first proper meal in three days and then walked over to see Gisevius, who lived in a small hotel in the Nüschelerstrasse.

Gisevius was waiting in high spirits, obviously pleased with himself. "You ought to fire your Swiss secretary," he said. "Better yet, strangle or poison her. But you can't, at least not for the time being."

Schulte asked him to start from the beginning. Gisevius replied by asking Schulte when he had first seen Allen Dulles. Schulte said he had met him that May in the company of Chojnacki. At a late hour they had visited Dulles at his home in the Herrengasse. Dulles had asked Schulte to write a detailed memorandum about the situation in Germany and his suggestions for the future. Schulte had dictated it to a secretary who had been recommended to him as absolutely reliable.

Gisevius then explained that not all the carbon paper had been destroyed, and that another typist working in the same office had fished a carbon out of the wastebasket and had taken it home. She had shown it to her German lover, who happened to be a member of the SS attached to the German Consulate General in Zurich.

The SS man did not know what to do with this material. He should have passed it on to Sturmbannführer Hans-Christian Daufeldt, who was the senior representative of the SD (the SS intelligence service). But the German diplomats in Switzerland did not like outsiders in their midst; they always caused problems with the host country. They had been reluctant to extend diplomatic cover to Abwehr representatives in 1940. They had even refused to give a desk to Gisevius when he had first arrived in Zurich. After applying much pressure, the SD had at last succeeded in getting Daufeldt appointed to Switzerland and attached to the consulate general, but the minister had quickly gotten him out of the way. Daufeldt was sent to Lausanne, where, it was thought, he could do the least damage. And so, in the absence of a senior SD official in Zurich, the SS man had taken the carbon paper to the consulate, and it had landed on Gisevius's desk. Gisevius's office

was on the first floor of the consulate at Kirchgasse 48, a historic old building with a small medieval entrance and numerous bay windows. (Next door Zwingli, Gottfried Keller, and
other prominent citizens of Zurich had once lived.)

Gisevius, a man of considerable *sang-froid,* had praised the
SS man for his find. He had explained that this was a matter of
such great importance that no one else must be told for the
time being. But there was also another reason for keeping the
discovery truly secret; Köcher, the German minister in Bern,
had just solemnly promised the Swiss government that there
would be no more intelligence operations on Swiss soil directed
against Swiss interests or involving Swiss citizens. The Swiss
had become very indignant in recent months, and many German agents had been arrested. Gisevius explained to the SS
man that if it became known that a Swiss secretary employed
in a Swiss office had passed on secret information to the Germans, this would certainly lead to her arrest and to her lover's
expulsion from the country. The SS man had not considered
the possibility that his patriotic duty might cost him his girl
friend and his comfortable apartment in affluent and peaceful
Zurich; he might then be asked to show his devotion to his
country as a combatant on the eastern front. He hastily assured
Gisevius that he would do as he was told, and that so too would
his girl friend.

But Gisevius did not trust the SS man. He informed Allen
Dulles, who told him that Schulte ought to be warned of the
great danger facing him.* Next, Gisevius told the story to Balsiger, the quiet but powerful head of the Swiss police, and
Heinrich Rothmund, the feared chief of the police department
that dealt with aliens in Switzerland. He was on friendly terms
with these two. Balsiger and Rothmund pondered the Schulte
affair and then told Gisevius that it was in everybody's interest
to ignore it for the time being. Gisevius's own position at the
embassy would be in danger if the Swiss arrested the secretary
and the SS man. It was best therefore to leave them alone. But

---

* There are discrepancies between Allen Dulles's version of this episode and
the version given by Gisevius and Waetjen. According to Dulles, the report of
the SS man was intercepted *before* it reached the Gestapo. According to Gisevius, the Gestapo had already been informed and he had to engage in *Un-
terschlagung und gefälschte Berichte* (the suppression and forging of reports) to
save Schulte. There is reason to believe that the Gisevius version is the correct
one; Dulles's knowledge of the affair was secondhand.

the two would be kept under observation. After the war they would be confronted with the evidence in a court of law and, if found guilty, would get their deserved punishment.*

Balsiger told Gisevius that he felt under an obligation to consult with von Steiger, the Swiss minister of justice and police. For if something should go wrong with the police's handling of the carbon paper affair, it might be construed as interference with the administration of justice.

Eduard von Steiger, the scion of an old Bern family, was a leading Swiss politician during the war, and a consummate one at that. The line he had taken during the first years of the war had been dubious to say the least. The slogan "the boat is full" was his, and he had been the driving force behind the decision to throw out illegal Jewish immigrants who had already reached Swiss soil in 1942. He had also favored strong censorship so as not to offend the Nazis. But when after the war a *post mortem* of Swiss policy was carried out, it appeared that von Steiger had left few traces. What had gone wrong was mostly the fault of colleagues such as Marcel Pilet, head of the political department, or of subordinates such as Rothmund, who, not altogether without reason, became the chief scapegoat. Rothmund was demoted after 1945; von Steiger became president of the Swiss Confederation.

In the Schulte case von Steiger was willing to stretch a point. There was a Swiss interest in this German industrialist who had been of great help to them in the past. Since no clear evidence of a crime had been brought before him, von Steiger agreed with the chief of police that the SS man and his girl friend should not be charged for the time being.

But there were further complications. The SS man did not keep his word to Gisevius; he talked to at least one person in the German secret service, Gisevius learned—and possibly to others. Gisevius was not certain whether it was Hans Meisner, the head of the Abwehr branch in Bern, whom the SS man contacted, or Major von Pescatore, who was in charge of coun-

---

* Justice finally caught up with the secretary and the SS man. The trial that the Swiss had saved up for them took place in June 1945, with Schulte as a witness. The two were found guilty and were sentenced to relatively short prison terms. The SS man apparently made violent threats against Schulte in the course of the trial.

The proceedings of the trial are still secret. Only after they are made accessible will it be possible to establish with certainty whether the secretary and the SS man "stumbled" on the memorandum to Dulles or whether Schulte was already under observation by the German security services.

terespionage. A report of sorts had been sent to Berlin and had reached the Gestapo. It was badly written, and full of inconsistencies. As a result, there were queries from Berlin to Zurich. This was how Gisevius discovered that something had gone wrong.

Not for nothing had Gisevius once worked for the police. He used all the tricks known among bureaucrats. He delayed his answer; he omitted to send on documents pertaining to the case that had been requested; he summarized others in such a way that even greater confusion was spread; and he provided a great deal of irrelevant material. He mentioned the possibility that since Allen Dulles's assignment was essentially economic in character, and since Giesche had negotiated for years with American corporations, the background of the affair was perhaps economic rather than political. He believed that in any case further investigation was needed.* But of course Gisevius realized that with such maneuvers he could at best only delay further action on the part of the Gestapo. Once a major investigation had begun, it could not be stopped.

He decided therefore to take up the matter with Canaris the next time he went back to Berlin. By the fall of 1943 the Abwehr was fighting a losing battle for its survival. The stubbornly dedicated anti-Nazi Hans Oster had already been removed; others were under investigation, some for "treasonable activities," others merely for incompetence. Canaris had become lethargic, quite incapable of fighting back. Gisevius had every reason not to return to Germany at all. On his last visit he had been threatened with arrest by an investigating judge. If his connection with Allen Dulles had come to light, he would have been arrested on the spot. But Gisevius also knew that if he did not go back, he would cut himself off from the resistance, from those senior men inexperienced in the art of conspiracy, who, he was convinced, would never take action without constant encouragement and support on the part of people like Oster and himself.

At Abwehr headquarters they had more urgent preoccupations than the Schulte affair. Gisevius nevertheless succeeded in talking to Canaris. In between discussion of two other items of business, he mentioned Schulte. Unlike Oster, Canaris

---

* For a long time the fact that Allen Dulles represented the OSS in Switzerland was not believed in Berlin; rather it was assumed that the assignment of this Wall Street lawyer was to conduct economic warfare against Germany or to initiate postwar economic planning.

was not an admirer of Gisevius. He thought of him as a perpetual schemer and intriguer, lacking a sense of political realities, in short, an adventurer. But he also knew that Gisevius had his qualities, and when he heard the name Schulte he seemed to remember something and said that one ought to help to get Schulte out of trouble. He suggested that Gisevius should take it up with Bentivegni, one of the three Abwehr section chiefs. Canaris was the epitome of the noncommittal man: Gisevius knew that his cryptic comment meant that something ought to be done immediately, because the case could cause further damage to the Abwehr. It also meant that Canaris did not want to be involved.

Colonel Egbert von Bentivegni was the head of Abwehr III, the section engaged in counterespionage. He came from an old family of army officers. His father had been killed in action in the First World War. A small man of dark complexion, he wore a monocle and affected an aggressively Prussian manner, possibly to compensate for the Italian origin of the family. He knew Gisevius and received him politely. But his department was the main target of the SS campaign; he could do little for others. He had in fact been dismissed a few months earlier; Canaris had only been able to recall him because his successor had been incapacitated by a grave accident.

When Gisevius mentioned the name Schulte, Bentivegni told him that, while he knew no details, the SS security service strongly suspected this man, though as yet it had no firm proof. Gisevius then tried to find out whether the Gestapo was listening to Schulte's phone calls. Apparently they were. It was then that Gisevius asked Waetjen to call Schulte to warn him.

After Gisevius had recounted all this to Schulte, he returned to present matters. If he were Schulte, he would sit out the war in Switzerland. In any case, Schulte should wait until he was absolutely certain that the Gestapo had nothing against him.

Schulte was certainly lucky to have gotten out of Germany. There were many decisions he now had to take. He was still in danger, but as far as could be established, the Gestapo had received conflicting messages about him. In the circumstances it would be best to stick to the story that this was an ordinary business trip taken on very short notice. How would he explain the delay in his return? On some occasions in the past he had been away for several months. Those who knew him had be-

come accustomed to his prolonged absences. But there had
been plausible arguments on past occasions, such as the need to
negotiate with Anaconda, and this was no longer true in December 1943. Some new arguments were needed in order to
dispel suspicion, for he wanted Clara to join him in Switzerland, and he was anxious not to endanger Ruprecht, still serving in the Army. He also wished to avoid harming his friends
and the firm.

Eduard Schulte was quite widely known. He could not
suddenly disappear without a trace. A faked death perhaps?
This was the stuff detective stories were made of; such things
did not occur in real life. Perhaps he could suddenly fall victim
to a serious disease that would make it impossible for him to
return soon. He could not spin this out indefinitely, but he
would gain a few weeks' breathing space, perhaps a few
months', and then he would think of something else.

Later that evening Schulte told Doris that it had been necessary for him to get out of Germany in a hurry, and that it was
doubtful whether he would be able to return before the end of
the war. He did not give her any details of his escape, and he
implored her to keep the whole affair utterly secret. He had defected, but it must not be known that he would not return. He
had come on a regular business trip and had suddenly fallen ill.
Did she know a doctor who could be trusted and who might be
of help? Schulte enjoyed good health. His artificial leg had to
be adjusted from time to time, and he was slightly neurotic
about his teeth. But in all these years in Zurich he had not
needed a doctor except for some minor complaints. Doris did
know one, Dr. Semyon Polishuk, a physician of East European
origin who had studied in Switzerland and then stayed on to
work in Zurich. Like all foreign-born doctors, Polishuk was not
permitted to have a private practice in Switzerland, but he was
a trustworthy man and could refer Schulte, if necessary, to a
Swiss colleague.

They contacted Polishuk and told him that it was an emergency. He saw Schulte the next morning. Schulte understood
that he had to take a risk and so told the doctor most of the
truth. Polishuk made a few notes and then examined the "patient." He measured Schulte's pulse, took his blood pressure,
listened to his heart and lungs with a stethoscope, and checked
his reflexes. This took about half an hour; he then summarized
his findings. For a man of Schulte's age, with his condition—he
pointed to Schulte's artificial leg—he was in good shape. True,

he was overweight, which was a risk factor, and if one strained one's ears, there was a slight heart murmur. Schulte would not die from it, but then the heart was the least predictable of organs. He must have been out of breath at one time or another, felt a missed heartbeat or some pain in the left shoulder? Schulte agreed that he had indeed experienced these and other sensations on rare occasions, whereupon Polishuk said that in this case angina pectoris could never be ruled out. But a diagnosis by a leading cardiologist would still be needed. It was an unusual case, it would be expensive; most probably it would be necessary to keep him for observation in a hospital for a while. Schulte said that he could afford the cost of the treatment; it was indeed a matter of life and death. Being an active man, the idea of being confined to bed in a little room was abhorrent to him. But he grudgingly accepted that unless he stuck to the rules of the game, his story would not be credible. Polishuk said that he would discuss the case with a distinguished colleague, and that Schulte need not fear—he would be in good hands.

Later that day Schulte had a call from the secretary of Dr. Haemmerli-Schindler. He was told to go to the doctor's consulting rooms in the Hohenbuhlstrasse. What passed on this occasion is not known. Probably there was another examination. Schulte left the doctor's office with a letter to the effect that Herr Dr. Eduard Schulte, general manager of Giesche, at present living in the Hotel Baur-au-Lac, had been treated on a previous occasion in July 1943 for angina pectoris. The patient had suffered today, December 10, another acute attack and needed hospitalization at the Hirslanden Klinik. There he would be subjected to a course of injections, which in all probability would take several weeks. In the meantime, he was incapable of traveling. The doctor suggested to the Swiss authorities concerned that they grant a prolongation of Schulte's stay so that he could undergo full clinical treatment. Haemmerli-Schindler was not only the leading cardiologist of the day; he belonged to two of Zurich's leading families. A medical report issued by him could not easily be dismissed.

Schulte then went shopping: he bought another pair of pajamas, a pair of slippers, and some other essentials, as well as stationery and a few books. The next morning he checked in at the Hirslanden Klinik, the best-known and biggest private clinic in Zurich. They gave him a room where he was undisturbed, and he even had a radio at his disposal. Doris came

once a day to see him; so did Trentini, Giesche's local representative. Otherwise he had few visitors. He was given some injections, vitamins probably or some other harmless substance, to
enhance his general well-being.

Despite the calm atmosphere of the well-ordered clinic,
there was much to worry about. Sooner or later the Gestapo
would find out about him, and then his family, his friends, and
he himself would be in acute danger. What could be done to
forestall it? Above all, his status in Switzerland had to be regularized.

Before entering the clinic he had gone to the head office of
the Union Bank and seen his old friend Dr. Schaefer. He had
explained that this was no ordinary visit to Switzerland, that
he had been forced to escape from Germany, but that the fact
must not become known; for the time being he was "very ill."
Could Schaefer talk to his contacts in the government?
Schaefer promised to help; the fact that Schulte had been of
assistance to the Swiss authorities in the past would surely
count in his favor. But it would take time. Meanwhile they had
better make a few copies of the doctor's certificate. In the event,
Schulte's request for political asylum was granted quite speed-
ily. What is more, the Swiss agreed to Schulte's request that the
fact of his having received asylum at all be kept secret; and it
remained a secret almost up to the end of the war.

Schulte stayed in the clinic for two weeks. It was a new,
rather impersonal building a few hundred yards south of the
lake, in a quiet neighborhood. The doctors were polite; the
nurses spoiled him. He read and reread old business correspondence, and dictated letters to a secretary. In no time at all he
became bored and restless. He considered giving up the Hotel
Baur-au-Lac, much as he liked it; he was not a poor man by
any standards, but he would have to husband his means, at
least until the war was over. He knew the Eden-au-Lac and the
Bellerive, somewhat smaller hotels with imposing baroque
fronts, side by side on the lakeshore. He asked his Zurich office
to reserve a room for him in one of them after his discharge
from the clinic.

The day his "treatment" ended he went to the offices of
Erzag, a joint venture of Giesche and La Roche, in the midst of
Zurich's financial district, not far from the central railway sta-
tion. Schulte called Kattowitz and reached Albrecht Jung.

"I'm glad to hear your voice," said Jung. "Do you feel a little better? Are you allowed to leave your bed?"

"Don't worry, I'm fine," Schulte said, much to Jung's consternation, since Jung knew that foreign telephone calls were monitored. They chatted for a few minutes and then Schulte said, "By the way, could you send Jeschke to Zurich? There is some urgent business we have to attend to." Jung, a little puzzled, said they would try.

Jeschke was a pleasant man in his forties, an accountant by profession who had tried for years with some success to bring order into the complicated foreign currency dealings of the firm. He was one of Giesche's most trusted employees, even though not a member of the top staff. He was a steadfast, utterly reliable person. His very appearance exuded confidence.

Jeschke had no valid passport, but people at Giesche pulled a few strings, stressing the company's contribution to the war effort, and after a few days he was on his way to Zurich. Schulte told the accountant on his arrival that for various reasons he had found it necessary to stay on in Zurich, probably for a long period. The discreet Jeschke refrained from asking any awkward questions. Schulte went on to say that his wife was in very poor health; their elder son was missing in action. He did not want to leave her alone at a time like this; she ought to join him. It was not easy in wartime to get permission, but Schulte thought it could be arranged. Clara had been very ill with typhoid fever in 1941, and upon her recovery she had been permitted to go for a few weeks to the Swiss Alpine resort of Pontresina, so there was a precedent. Jeschke was instructed to go to Berlin to look up cousin Hermann, who had many useful connections in government offices.

Jeschke duly made his way to Berlin, and there he arranged certain phone calls. Some money and several boxes of fine cigars seem to have changed hands. All this was highly irregular, of course, not at all in the German tradition. But this late in the war, the standards of the bureaucracy were not quite what they used to be. Having received a German passport and a Swiss visa, Clara Schulte arrived in Zurich on January 7, 1944. Her husband was waiting for her at the railway station, and he took her to their new home in the Hotel Bellerive-au-Lac.*

---

* The official who had issued her passport was dismissed later. Jeschke also went to see Oskar, Schulte's younger brother, working then as a forester in a little place in Westphalia. He told the brother that Eduard had fled, but the reason he gave for the sudden escape was less than the whole truth: Schulte, he said, had criticized the Nazi leaders at a public meeting and for this reason the Gestapo was after him.

A few days later Clara sent a postcard to Ruprecht, on which she indicated that Eduard was as well as could be expected. Ruprecht had been allowed to go home on leave when he learned of the sudden grave illness of his father. His parents had been able to take virtually nothing to Switzerland. He went down to the well-stocked wine cellar, which had been kept mainly for the benefit of guests. The longer Ruprecht stayed in the solitary house, the more he recognized that this might well be his last visit, that this phase of the Schulte family's life was over. And so he closed the front door, left the keys with the family's friend Dr. Siemon, and rejoined his battalion.

Eduard Schulte continued to live the life of a German businessman in Zurich. He kept in touch with Gaevernitz, and also Gisevius. When he saw Waetjen, whose phone call had saved his life, he warmly embraced him. He met with Allen Dulles, who asked him to prepare a more detailed paper containing his ideas for the reconstruction of a democratic postwar Germany. But all of this happened in secrecy. In theory, he was still a German citizen of good reputation, and he wanted to maintain the fiction as long as possible, so as not to endanger his son.

But one day in spring 1944 Schulte received a communication to the effect that he had been awarded the Kriegsverdienstkreuz, the War Cross of Merit, a high decoration for civilians who had made extraordinary contributions to the war effort. As far as the Nazi authorities were concerned, he was apparently still in good standing; his past services were appreciated.

Could it be that Waetjen's warning had been a false alarm, that the damning evidence of the carbon paper from his memorandum to Dulles had been forgotten? The award proved that he was in the clear; and as spring turned into summer in Zurich, Schulte, we can be sure, often felt the urge to return to Germany. But instincts warned him against returning. He was held back by an uneasy feeling that all was not well, that his time was up as far as the Nazis were concerned.

And he was right. The alarm triggered by the Zurich secretary had been a great blessing in disguise. It had saved his life, for if he had stayed in Germany, he would almost certainly have been arrested and executed. Part of the story he was to learn from the Americans during the last few months of the war; most of it became known only years later.

.   .   .

Ever since 1940 German signal intelligence stations had monitored Polish radio broadcasts from Bern to London, but they had been unable to solve the code. In June 1943 there was a breakthrough, apparently connected with the Gestapo's arrest in Toulouse, France, of a Polish army captain who headed an espionage network based in the city.* For the first time the German authorities could read the accumulated messages transmitted by Chojnacki and his assistants. It gradually emerged that this network had no fewer than two hundred informants in France and Belgium and was probably the biggest anti-Nazi information-gathering group in continental Europe at the time. Its code name was Jerzy.

The information that had been collected and stored and was now decoded concerned concentrations of the German Army, Navy, and Air Force; transport by land and sea; lists of ammunition dumps; coastal fortifications, especially in France; selection of targets for air attacks; and so on. The Polish underground watched rail traffic at Trier, Aachen, Saarbrücken, Strassburg, and in the Ruhr; it observed the Rhine crossings at Duisburg, Cologne, Düsseldorf, Mannheim, and Ludwigshafen. Later on there was also information about the development of German secret weapons. According to one German official involved in the investigation, the Chojnacki network had sent to London in the spring of 1943 the complete German operational plan of the Battle of Kursk—one of the great battles of the Second World War—three months before the actual attack was launched. This specific assertion has not been confirmed by other sources; given the state of Soviet-Polish relations, it is doubtful anyway whether the Poles would have informed the Russians—who in any case had advance knowledge about this critical battle from Communist sources and

* Toulouse was one of the centers for Allied espionage. The Polish network there, headed by Captain Gustav Firla, apparently found it difficult to send all its information to London. Geological conditions and atmospheric disturbances impaired its radio transmissions. Even more important, the longer the Polish radio operator stayed on the air, the easier it would be for the Gestapo's unmarked radio-detecting vans to pinpoint the location of the transmitter and arrest the operator. The result was that the Toulouse group maintained contact with Polish operatives in safer locations, such as Spain and Switzerland, from where radio messages could be sent more easily.

In June 1943 Firla was arrested by the Gestapo. This arrest and the seizure of Polish coding materials seems to have given the German cryptographers enough information to break the Polish code. The connection between events in Toulouse and the deciphering of Chojnacki's codes was made in a postwar affidavit by a senior Gestapo official, Walter Huppenkothen.

their own aerial reconnaissance, radio reconnaissance, and from German deserters.

But it is certainly true that Jerzy provided information of exceptional importance, also including a list of factories producing oil and rubber. One German intelligence analyst said that Polish intelligence "outshone the British Secret Service as the sun outshone the moon." When the Polish transmissions from Bern were deciphered and sent on to Berlin, German authorities were stunned.

The transmissions revealed that valuable material was provided by "509," Chojnacki's most cherished source, whom he described in his signals as having access to Hitler's headquarters. Who was this elusive 509? Hitler and Himmler personally ordered a priority search.

In the early years of the war Gestapo control had been well-nigh complete in Germany and most of the occupied territories, but this was no longer the case in 1943 and even less so the following year. As the tide of the war turned, the opposition against Nazism grew in Germany and outside, and as heavier and more frequent air raids caused disruptions, control became far more difficult. During the last two years of the war the Gestapo was fully occupied with hunting down the "enemy from within"; its resources were stretched to the breaking point. It was asked to take over most of the functions of the Abwehr, which made its burden even heavier. As a result of Allied air raids, regional Gestapo headquarters were hit, communications were interrupted, and files were destroyed.

The normal reaction of a bureaucratic organization in these circumstances is to pass some priority items to subordinates. Josef Häusler was made head of a *Sonderkommando* (special command group) for this case, and he was assisted by Obersturmführer Karl Heller. Once the matter had been referred to the middle echelons of the Gestapo, it became more likely that little progress would be made in investigating this case.

The people dealing with "509" were neither fanatical Nazis nor very knowledgeable. Most of them had served in the police force of the Weimar Republic, which had been less Nazi-infested than the judiciary or other parts of the state bureaucracy. Häusler, for instance, was a practicing Catholic from Bavaria who had joined the Nazi Party only in 1937 (as did his boss Friedrich Panziger), when every state official had to become a member of the party, following the promulgation of a new law. These were conscientious policemen, willing to serve any political system. They might have behaved decently in a democracy; they were capable of committing almost any atrocity in the service of a dictatorship such as Nazism.

But the whole affair was somewhat above their heads. These were people of lower-middle-class background, without higher education, who had not seen much of the world, and lacked knowledge of foreign languages and conditions outside Germany. Their training and experience had prepared them to deal with Communist organizers inside their own country. But they did not have the sophistication to deal with foreign affairs (which until 1942 had been the province of the Abwehr), let alone with the world of international business and finance. The two heads of the special command group were colorless people who had served in counterespionage units in Eastern Europe and were transferred, no doubt much to their relief, back to Berlin. Häusler's personnel file said that he was "always convinced of the importance and results of his work," which was probably another way of saying that he was a man very full of himself.

What could these people make of Jerzy and, above all, of "509"? With the help of the German security forces in France, after twelve months of methodical work they arrested many of the people connected with this network, about three hundred of them. But the order was given only on June 30, 1944, and the arrests were carried out only on July 13, which is to say, well after the Allied landing in France and only six weeks prior to the liberation of Paris. These arrests, in which Klaus Barbie, the butcher of Lyon, played a role, were tragic, but they came too late to have even the slightest effect on the course of the war.

Schulte was bound to appear in the Gestapo's list of German suspects, simply because he was so often in Zurich, but so were other German travelers. The fact that "509's" information seems to have come from several German sources, one located in southern Germany, another in northern Italy, further confused the Gestapo. The facts did not fit Schulte.

Sometime in 1943 the Gestapo investigators seem to have established a link between Chojnacki and certain individuals in Basel, whence much of the important intelligence concerning Germany originated, and this led them to Koppelmann. It was not difficult to find out that Schulte had close business ties with Koppelmann. Thus, the Gestapo had more and more material against Schulte, not altogether conclusive perhaps, but enough to call him in for a long and hard investigation. They hesitated, apparently assuming (and not without reason) that Schulte's arrest would serve as a signal to his sources.

In September 1943 the Germans obtained more incriminating evidence against Schulte. When Dulles contacted Washington with information from "643" (i.e., Schulte), Dulles added that "643" had also met with agent "497," who was not an American. In all likelihood, "497" was either a French or a Polish agent. Dulles simply wanted to alert Washington that it would probably get the same information through another channel. It is unlikely that the Germans deciphered this message or that they could identify "643." But "497's" communications with London were not secure. When "497" foolishly radioed Schulte's real name to London, the Germans picked it up. They now had a good case against Schulte.

Patience is a policeman's chief virtue, but they waited too long. When the Gestapo informed the Abwehr counterintelligence, the latter, through Gisevius and Waetjen, warned the prospective victim.

But even after Schulte's defection in December 1943, the Gestapo could not have been certain that he was their man, or, at any rate, the only culprit. How to explain otherwise that no urgent message went out to the German police that Schulte was wanted for espionage, that his wife was allowed to join him in Zurich, and that no sanctions were taken against close friends and relatives who might have been instrumental in supplying him with information? And how to explain that he was not deprived of his citizenship, as was customary in such cases, but that, on the contrary, the War Cross of Merit (First Class) was bestowed upon him six months after he had left the country?

There are several possible explanations. The fact that the Gestapo *Sonderkommando* knew about Schulte, or at least strongly suspected him, does not mean that those who gave his wife permission to leave Germany knew about him—any more than did the authorities who gave him the War Cross of Merit. On the other hand, it is possible that the Gestapo wanted to lure him back to Germany, by making him believe that there was no evidence against him; any hasty move on their part would, of course, have frightened him off. Schulte himself, writing after the war, thought that he had been given the War Cross of Merit with precisely this intention, and his suspicion may have been well founded. From secret German police files discovered after the war, it appears that at this very time the

Gestapo tried to lure back an Abwehr employee named Bo-
binger stationed in Switzerland, whom they suspected of having passed information to the British.

Lastly, it is possible that the Gestapo was not aware of the
full extent of Schulte's involvement up to the very end. His
name had appeared in one or two enemy signals, but this did
not necessarily mean that he was actively involved in spying.
Many German industrialists visited Switzerland and talked out
of turn, and their stories were picked up by the Allies without
them even knowing it. Many such indiscretions were known to
the Gestapo. Schulte was, after all, a most unlikely enemy of
the regime, a man without an anti-Nazi past, or at any rate
without any record of one, and with no obvious contacts who
might have enabled him to obtain access to state secrets, except
perhaps in the economic sphere.

Many people have consistently overrated the astuteness
and efficiency of the Gestapo. The Gestapo had not the slightest inkling of the highly amateurish officers' plot against Hitler
in July 1944, which involved hundreds of conspirators and had
been planned for years. The Gestapo was neither omniscient
nor omnipotent; it is not surprising that a single individual
acting with great circumspection could have escaped it. Karl
Heller, one of the heads of the *Sonderkommando,* lost his home in
one of the massive raids on Berlin and had to take his family to
the country. Another Gestapo official was involved, on top of
his many official duties, in explaining to the senior SS leadership why his young wife (he had married a secretary aged
twenty-one early during the war) had not yet conceived and
what he was going to do about it. In short, the Gestapo was
never as busy as in 1944.

Whatever the Gestapo may have been thinking, Allen
Dulles did not doubt that Schulte was in danger. Shortly after
Schulte's move to Switzerland Dulles cabled Washington that
Schulte's contacts with agent "497," and possibly also his contact with Dulles himself, had been exposed. Schulte, Dulles
said, had arrived in Switzerland "barely before Jerry [the Ger-
mans]. It does not appear impossible that the BKRZLC [inde-
cipherable code word] communication system from this end
may be prejudiced. This arrival may possess . . . great importance."

As we have seen, Schulte was genuinely afraid that the Gestapo would hunt him down, kill, or abduct him, even in Switzerland. But it acted in a curiously lethargic way. It put him on

a postal censorship list, and it dissolved the *Sonderkommando* and transferred the Schulte file to another department in the State Security Main Office. No new initiatives were taken, however, as some of the top SS leaders began to play with the idea of ingratiating themselves with the Allies in order to save their own skins.

And so the Nazis' file on Schulte was never closed. Schulte could have enjoyed his lakeside walks in Zurich with relative peace of mind, but, of course, he had no way of knowing this.

CHAPTER NINE

The End of
the War

Life in Zurich during the last year of the war was one long agony of waiting. The weeks and months passed with unbearable slowness as fall turned into winter, and winter into spring. In early June 1944 the Allies took Rome; two days later they landed in France. On August 25 Charles de Gaulle returned to Paris. In September, Finland and Rumania signed armistices with the Soviet Union. And yet the German armies fought on, even though the Luftwaffe had virtually ceased to exist, and German cities were being laid waste by Allied air attacks. Inside the Reich, the forces eager to end the war were not strong enough to overthrow the Nazi regime. The officers' plot against Hitler failed on July 20, 1944, and the war went on to the bitter end.

For Schulte, watching the last acts of the protracted trag-

edy from abroad was difficult. It was obvious to him that with
each day of the war the devastation was spreading further, and
postwar reconstruction becoming more difficult. This was of no
concern to Hitler and his paladins, who knew that there was to
be no future for them. A few fanatical believers—not many
were left by late 1944—hoped that Hitler's miracle weapon
would turn the tide of the war, or at least bring about a stale-
mate. But for the great majority of thoughtful Germans, there
was no longer any doubt about the final outcome. The only
question that remained was how Germany would be divided
between the Soviet Union and the Western powers.

Eduard Schulte should have felt reasonably secure in his
Swiss refuge, but he was far from happy. Living in a hotel
could not possibly replace the comforts of his large home in
Breslau or his estate in Pomerania, but that was of little importance. His wife disliked Switzerland. Everything was too orderly, too neat and clean. At a time when most of the world was
in flames she watched the conflagration from a safe point, and
she did not like the experience. Outwardly, she bore up quite
well, but her bouts of depression became more frequent. She
still hoped against hope that Wolfgang was alive and would
come back one day. But in her heart she must have known he
would never return. She corresponded with Wolfgang's fiancée,
Marie-Luise, and the two women drew closer in their mutual
sorrow.

Eduard saw Doris fairly regularly, and this was no secret to
Clara. She gradually persuaded herself that her situation in
Zurich was altogether intolerable. It was not right that life
should go on normally, as it were, while her own world was
collapsing.

There was only infrequent news from Ruprecht, who was
not having an easy time. He had been wounded four times
during the war, and was in constant danger from the Gestapo.
For these were the days of *Sippenhaft* (blood purges), when
whole families were punished for an individual's political
wrongdoing. As Himmler, the great Nazi genetics enthusiast,
had said of the Stauffenbergs, theirs was a case of "bad blood."
It was not enough to execute the man who had attempted to as-
sassinate Hitler—the whole Stauffenberg clan was eradicated.

As long as Ruprecht served on the eastern front, he was
physically beyond the Gestapo's reach, but in 1944 he was
transferred to France, where the Gestapo was active. Eduard
Schulte, who did not rule out Nazi attempts to kidnap or assas-

sinate him in Zurich, also feared that Ruprecht might be taken
hostage. By this time Schulte knew that a member of his junior
staff at Giesche had told the Gestapo that the *Generaldirektor* had
always been an enemy of the Third Reich, that he had tried to
sabotage the Nazi regime in various ways. There was every reason for concern.

The last year of the war must have been intensely anxious
for Schulte. His defection to Switzerland had in fact ruined an
elaborate OSS plan, drawn up by one of his business associates,
Irving Sherman, to put Giesche's Magdeburg zinc refinery out
of commission. Sherman, a New York banker, had gone to
work in the New York office of the OSS. He had formed a high
opinion of Schulte as an anti-Nazi, remembering him in later
years as a real "two-fisted hombre."

Sherman was convinced that the loss of Giesche's electrolytic zinc refinery would be a major blow to the German war
economy. Would Schulte help bring this off? Some senior OSS
officials, such as John C. Hughes, head of the New York office,
and General John Magruder, deputy director of intelligence,
liked Sherman's plan, whereas Major Otto Doering, William
Donovan's assistant and law partner, apparently had reservations about it.

What Sherman specifically suggested was that the United
States government offer Schulte a *quid pro quo*—namely their
approval of a complicated business deal. In 1941 Schulte's business associate Jacques Rosenstein had tried unsuccessfully to
arrange for a Swiss consortium's purchase of all the shares of
the Silesian-American Corporation (Polish Giesche)—German
Giesche's 49 percent and the 51 percent owned by Anaconda
and Harriman. The United States Treasury Department, suspicious that the Swiss were acting as a front for German interests and that the deal would benefit Germany, had rejected the
proposal. After war broke out between Germany and the
United States, Schulte secretly went ahead and transferred
Giesche's stock to the Swiss consortium anyway. Even in 1943
the Swiss consortium was still willing to purchase the Ameri-
can-held shares to gain control of the company. Sherman proposed that the Treasury Department approve the transaction
in return for Schulte's cooperation in incapacitating the refinery. The Treasury officials in the Foreign Funds Control Division were not at all enthusiastic, but Sherman claimed to have
the backing of the Joint Chiefs of Staff.

The Magdeburg refinery was Schulte's brainchild. He

wanted to bring about the downfall of the Nazi regime, but he would just as soon have injured a member of his own family as helped to sabotage this plant. Perhaps it was just as well that Schulte escaped to Switzerland before the American authorities could reach agreement. He would have had to face an uncomfortable choice.

Meanwhile, there were some constructive things Schulte could do in Switzerland while he awaited the war's end. In mid-1943 Allen Dulles had asked Schulte to put on paper some of his thoughts about the future of Germany. Then, after his flight to Switzerland, OSS headquarters encouraged him to prepare a long memorandum on the industrial and business reorganization of Germany. Schulte responded with alacrity, and not only because he had time on his hands (a luxury he had seldom if ever experienced in the past). He had demons to exorcise. This was a chance to reflect on the recent history of his country and Western civilization and to diagnose the fundamental problems that had permitted the rise of Hitler and the establishment of his barbaric regime. He had lived close to the epicenter of the earthquake, and had ideas about causes and consequences, punishment and prevention. Eduard Schulte wrote on and on, mixing economics, politics, philosophy, and sociology with broad strokes. It was unlike anything he had ever done before. Within six months he turned out a moderately polished 150-odd-page manuscript, which reflected his humanistic values more than any specific business perspective. Perhaps he wrote in part to convince himself that what he had done for the Allies was proper and necessary. Certainly there was not a trace of softness toward the Nazi leaders or the German business elite in the manuscript. Schulte had compassion for the German people, but not for those who had led Germany into a course of aggression, nihilism, and wanton destruction.

Nazism, he wrote, was a product of the economic problems and social tension in Germany that had followed the First World War. One factor was the hasty dismantling of economic controls soon after the war and the lifting of restrictions on foreign currency transactions. Although businessmen had vehemently criticized what they regarded as government interference and excessive bureaucracy, the German economy was not then ready for a quick return to the free market. Hyperinflation, excessive reliance on foreign loans, and ultimately depression punctuated the brief life of the Weimar Republic.

Nazism's early followers came from the uprooted, impoverished, and economically endangered elements who rejected the new democratic political order. Schulte stressed the role of German youth, estranged by the lack of economic opportunities after the war.

Furthermore, most Germans were preoccupied with their own affairs—the state was "they," not "we." The Germans had grown up politically under a powerful semiautocratic government headed by an emperor, and they had had little experience of participation in self-government. What they saw of the Weimar Republic did not encourage them to change their minds. The fundamental reason for the failure of the republic was that Germany had not broken completely with its feudal past.

Under severe economic pressure during the Depression, and facing demands from labor, the coal and steel executives decided to attack the "Marxist" trade unions, a decision that led some businessmen to back the Nazis financially. The National People's Party (DNVP), the party that many industrialists supported, opted for collaboration with the Nazis. Some older conservative leaders in the DNVP, who recognized the danger, were outvoted. Non-Nazi experts acceptable to the DNVP were appointed to the Economics Ministry and the Finance Ministry in Hitler's Cabinet. But the non-Nazis were quickly tamed or gradually eliminated, and within a year it appeared that heavy industry had lost its gamble and its influence. Even after Hitler had wrested all power for himself, many of the business executives continued to support the regime, mainly because the economic recovery had gained strength and rearmament meant large government contracts for heavy industry. The workers received jobs, wages, and heavily advertised social programs. Other groups also benefited from the upsurge. Hitler seemed to be the strong man whom Germany needed.

Some Germans after 1933 held out against the allurement of Nazism: these were people who still adhered to a belief in the rule of law and the need to respect individual rights. They were found among former trade-union members, high-level bureaucrats instilled with the positive features of the Prussian tradition, Christian believers of every persuasion, and sections of the educated middle class. One of the first tasks for an Allied military occupation government, Schulte wrote, would be to sepa-

rate the innocent from the potentially dangerous elements.
Some sort of classification and detention system would be necessary.

The Allies, Schulte thought, had to move swiftly and mer-
cilessly against the active Nazi leaders and bearers of Nazi ide-
ology. It was not merely a question of locating the thousands
who had committed war crimes. The whole Nazi leadership
corps, numbering tens of thousands, had to be deprived of all
future influence. Many others, of course, were also guilty, albeit
to a lesser degree.

Schulte believed that the Allies should expropriate the
wealth of those individuals who had personally profited from
Nazi rule. The Allies would not foster respect for the law
among the defeated Germans by protecting all private property, irrespective of how it was acquired. All Germans should
be *compelled* to inform the authorities of what they knew of Nazi
crimes and even threatened with punishment for withholding
such information.

With shortages of essential goods likely, it would not be
possible to rely on a free market economy. One possibility was
state socialism. Whether such a move would benefit German
consumers was questionable. Instead, Schulte recommended
the establishment of a joint national board representing pro-
ducers, consumers, and distributors. This corporatist organization, functioning like a cooperative, would determine which
goods were most needed and would arrange for production and
delivery throughout the country. It would make use of existing
sales channels, but should not be limited to them. This was in
essence a scheme for a "mixed" economy.

Schulte favored a direct government role in certain key
areas of the economy—transportation, public utilities, defense
industries, basic products used in defense industries (e.g., steel),
and synthetic raw materials. In all sectors, he wrote, the Allies
should appoint commissioners to take immediate control. Except for defense, the commissioners would gradually turn over
control to new public agencies.

Schulte conceded that there was a more general danger in-
herent in the German economy. Germany suffered from "industrial hypertrophy," and its dependence on foreign markets
had tempted some Germans to consider conquest as a solution.
Unless drastic action was taken, this temptation would persist,
regardless of the political system. Schulte favored an effort to
intensify German agriculture and make the economy less de-

pendent upon industrial exports. Germans returning from abroad as well as those leaving overcrowded cities could be transformed into independent farmers. The country's small-scale crafts also might be revived with some state assistance. Schulte considered it essential to preserve a middle class independent of big business.

But he rejected the idea of turning Germany into an agrarian country by removing industrial facilities or prohibiting industrial exports. Such a policy would only damage the European and world economies, and restart the cycle of problems that had contributed to the war. Schulte thus rejected the concept of "pastoralization" embodied in Treasury Secretary Henry Morgenthau's plan of 1944, which had briefly been considered by Roosevelt and Churchill.

What was needed instead, Schulte argued, was some way of integrating Germany more closely into the world economy. Solving the economic problems of Germany would go a long way toward healing Europe's social and economic tensions, and would prevent a new war.

Schulte dismissed the idea that whatever was good for business was good for the country and the continent. Europe could not afford to leave international economic relations to private enterprise. The best course was multinational economic planning. Private business would remain intact, but general decisions about production, investment, and employment goals could be made collectively by a multinational economic board, thus reducing economic friction among nations to a minimum.

In formulating his proposals Schulte had drawn on his own experience of running a multinational corporation. Economic cooperation among nations was needed to give meaning to the United Nations organization. Perhaps he hoped to fire the imagination of President Roosevelt, who had no great love for big corporations. Another factor that strongly influenced him was the extent of wartime destruction. Little of the world order was left; it seemed pointless to re-establish the old economic system. Like many other businessmen and economists at the time, Schulte felt that *laissez-faire* capitalism had had its day.

He consulted two like-minded individuals in Switzerland when preparing his blueprint. One was Dr. Andreae, a brother-in-law of Walther Rathenau, the Jewish German foreign minister who had been killed in 1922 by a gang of right-wing terrorists. Andreae was about twenty years older than Schulte and had been one of the pillars of the banking and industrial establishment in Berlin, chairman of the board of the Dresdner Bank, and deputy of AEG, the giant electrical corporation. With his wife, Edith, and his four daughters, he had moved to Switzerland soon after the outbreak of the war.

Schulte had known Andreae when Andreae worked for a while in the German Ministry of Economics. He had visited the Andreae villa in the Grunewald, where bankers and industrialists mingled with leading academics and artistic figures such as Max Reinhardt. Andreae was a profoundly decent man who loathed Nazism. He was highly cultured, an expert on Goethe and a friend of Hofmannsthal's. But he combined the native caution of the banker with the circumspection of an elderly man who continued to receive his pension from Berlin. He would talk quite openly with Schulte on almost any subject. But like many people of his generation he had an instinctive aversion to politics, and he did not want his name to be associated with any manifesto or memorandum, even a private and confidential one. Some of Rathenau's ideas on planning can be discovered in Schulte's memorandum, but when it appeared, Andreae's name was missing and Schulte figured as the sole author.

The other collaborator was Eduard Waetjen, the man whose timely phone call probably saved Schulte's life. By this time Waetjen too had moved to Switzerland and established good ties with Dulles, who gave him the code name Gorter. Waetjen's path to anti-Nazi resistance had been a somewhat complicated one.

His mother was American, and the family had other ties with America. His father had represented the Morgan Guaranty Trust in Germany; his sister had married Sterling Rockefeller. Waetjen was a product of one of Germany's progressive schools, Salem, founded by Kurt Hahn. He had also been (much to Hahn's dismay) one of the few Salem graduates to join the Nazi Party as a student, though well before 1933. When Joseph Goebbels had organized a demonstration on the Kurfürstendamm on the occasion of the premiere of the American-made film *All Quiet on the Western Front*, Waetjen had been among those who took part. But his enthusiasm did not last long, and he dropped out of the party before it came to power.

He married into the well-connected Sarre family of Berlin, and worked in a highly respectable Berlin law firm. He also became friendly with some of the main figures of the Kreisau

Circle, one of the main groups of the German opposition. Meanwhile, he took a position in the Abwehr. His dislike of the Nazis finally got him into trouble; after a close friend denounced him to the Gestapo in a letter, Waetjen was in grave danger. By a stroke of luck, the case against him wasn't pursued, but there was always the danger that one day it would resurface.*

Waetjen reached the sensible conclusion that he would be better off if protected by the Abwehr with long stays abroad. He was repeatedly sent to Turkey and also to Switzerland. His cover was that of a representative of a major German corporation. It was more than a cover, though: Waetjen did in fact do some business on behalf of a large German firm.

Waetjen knew Oster well and he had had dealings with Gisevius even before the war. Toward the end of 1943 he was warned that the old case was likely to come up again, and he requested a permanent assignment abroad. The Abwehr was no longer then in Berlin, Oster had been removed, and Canaris had lost much of his authority. The organization was run by Colonel Hansen, who was willing to give Waetjen Gisevius's old job in Zurich. But Waetjen wanted to take with him his wife, his aging mother, and his children, and this could no longer be arranged by the Abwehr. In order to achieve this— though in what way his family was to be involved was wholly obscure—he had to convince Walter Schellenberg of the SD that he had a wonderful scheme to instigate an anti-Allied Muslim rebellion in Afghanistan, the Maghreb, or some other suitable place, with the help of Nuri, a Turk who was the brother of Enver Pasha, the Turkish military leader of First World War fame. The SS was almost always open to innovative ideas, however harebrained, and even though Göring refused to put a plane at his disposal to carry out his promising project, Waetjen left Germany with all his clan in January 1944.

Allen Dulles found Waetjen congenial. His English was very good, he was a fellow lawyer, a pleasant conversationalist, and willing to cooperate with the OSS. He and Gisevius kept Dulles extremely well informed as early as January 1944 about the resistance's plans for a coup against the Nazi regime.

---

* The letter to the Gestapo began with the words, "Though Mr. W. is my best friend, I feel obliged . . ." This letter fell into the hands of a bureaucrat of the old Prussian school who concluded that a man who informed on his best friend was himself suspect. He decided therefore to bury the file.

Waetjen was also preoccupied with postwar issues—like
Schulte and Andreae. When the Nazis began their investigations after the failure of the July 20 plot, Waetjen's involvement in the conspiracy emerged, and he was placed on the
Gestapo's wanted list. He knew of course that he had to remain
in Switzerland; and hearing of a house that was available, the
Casa Rossa in Ascona; he took the lease, and in fact stayed
there for the rest of the war, translating Homer into German.

Although Schulte consulted Andreae and Waetjen in
drawing up his economic blueprint, the ideas and the formula-
tion were his own. In retrospect, it has to be said that he ex-
ceeded his mandate and perhaps also his competence.
Economic planning, while useful, was no panacea. Experience
would teach that referring problems to higher and larger agencies did not necessarily overcome parochialism. Even a more
limited economic and political venture such as the Common
Market would take decades to evolve into a functioning entity.
Postwar Germany needed more immediate solutions. Nonetheless, certain proposals that Schulte made in his work and in
other memoranda seemed attractive to Allen Dulles. Schulte
argued that the German Labor Front and the Reich Agricultural Estate established by the Nazis should be maintained
during a transitional period and used to safeguard the rights of
workers and farmers. The fact that the Nazis had employed
these organizations for corrupt purposes did not make them
any less useful in principle. Schulte also suggested that the
Allies establish an advisory committee of Germans to help on
personnel decisions at the end of the war.

Dulles was impressed by Schulte's recognition of the need
to separate and punish Nazi criminals and his acceptance of a
long Allied occupation of Germany. In August 1944 Dulles radioed his superiors in Washington:

> I have been constantly in touch with 643 since
> he fled from [to] here last December.... 643
> has been engaged in drawing up plans for post-
> war Germany of an economic and industrial
> nature. I believe that he is anti-Nazi and en-
> tirely trustworthy, he is one of the few techni-
> cally able and up-to-date persons who could be
> of service to our army of occupation following
> the collapse of Germany. In addition, I trust his
> judgement on anti-Nazi groups who might be

relied upon to work with us. . . . I would like to
be advised whether we can give some encouragement to men like 643. . . . There will not be
many Germans of his kind that we will be able
to locate. . . .

OSS headquarters asked Dulles to let them have a summary of
Schulte's postwar plans, as the whole memorandum was far too
long to cable. They were reassuring:

In our opinion he ought to be encouraged by
you in this work. When the frontier opens
[Switzerland was of course still cut off] you will
be in a position to forward these proposals to
London, where they can be properly evaluated. . . . We feel that you ought to get together
a proposed group of reliable, willing Germans
since such a band cannot be organized by official action.

That was at least a tentative endorsement of a postwar role for
prominent anti-Nazi Germans such as Schulte.

· · ·

In the fall of 1944 Eduard Schulte caught pneumonia and
almost died. In spite of an otherwise robust constitution he was
prone to respiratory infections. The doctors in the Hirslanden
Klinik, to which he was admitted once again, this time as a
genuine patient, were worried. Gaevernitz was informed, and
with the help of Allen Dulles, Schulte's doctors obtained peni-
cillin, then in very short supply, from American military
sources. The drug probably saved Schulte's life. It took him
many weeks to recover and regain his strength.

While recuperating, Schulte felt sorely isolated from his
business and his friends. Gisevius had gone back to Germany
for the July 20 conspiracy to overthrow the Nazi regime. When
it failed, he had to go underground, and he succeeded in
reaching Switzerland again only in January 1945. Waetjen had
retired to Ascona. One day in January 1945 Riegner came to
Zurich with another leading official of the World Jewish Congress, and both men paid their respects to Schulte. This was the
first time that Riegner had actually met the man who in 1942
had given Koppelmann the dreadful information about the
Final Solution. They made small talk; Schulte answered with
"Yes" and "No." Riegner had the impression, as they parted,

that this man did not want to talk about his tragic mission of
July 1942, nor about Germany past or present.

During the last months of the war, Schulte's isolation was
eased by a new friendship. He found a kindred spirit in Emmy
Rado, a Swiss-American woman who arrived in Bern wearing a
major's uniform. Born near St. Gallen, Switzerland, she had
studied in Berlin in the 1920s and met her second husband
there. Sandor Rado was a Hungarian Jew and a Freudian psy-
choanalyst of international repute. He was invited to come to
America and eventually became a professor at Columbia University. When war broke out, the now very Americanized
Emmy offered her services to the American intelligence community and began work in New York debriefing new arrivals
from Europe and North Africa, and compiling biographical information on important Nazis.

When the Allied invasion of France opened up the routes to
Switzerland, Emmy Rado persuaded the OSS to send her to
Bern to help Allen Dulles: after all, there were not many OSS
officials fluent in Schwyzerdeutsch, the Swiss-German dialect.
A strong-willed, passionate woman, she pursued two major
projects in Switzerland. Although a non-practicing Christian
herself, she argued that religious institutions would have to
play a substantial role in re-educating the German people at
the end of the war. The Allies had neglected to develop Protes-
tant contacts, and she set about remedying this. Her second
specialty was to cultivate the "crown jewels," Allen Dulles's pet
term for trustworthy democratic Germans such as Schulte. She
interviewed Schulte repeatedly, and the two came to like and
respect each other. For Schulte, she was a godsend, for here was
another OSS official, besides the busy Gaevernitz, whom he
could talk to in German.

As the war entered its final phase Schulte received occasional news from his office in Breslau and the works in Upper
Silesia, where more than twenty thousand Giesche employees
were located. He knew that it was only a question of time before this region was occupied by the Russians. In early January
1945 the Soviets launched a major new offensive. By January
19 the industrial region was cut off, and five days later
Giesche's offices and mines in Kattowitz were closed. Some of
the senior staff members made their way to Czechoslovakia, as
yet unoccupied; others reached Breslau, which held out to the
last day of the war. Some were killed during the fighting; the
rest were taken prisoner. Lothar Siemon, however, managed to

reach Berlin, carrying with him a small quantity of platinum.
But there was no demand for this rare metal during the last
days of the Third Reich. Eventually, on April 25, Siemon arrived in Hamburg, which was in British hands.

.   .   .

On April 30, 1945—just days before Germany's unconditional surrender—Schulte received word from the Hotel Bellerive telephone operator that there was a long-distance call for
him. He picked up the receiver, and immediately an immense
burden fell from his heart. It was his son Ruprecht calling from
Lucerne, the last person he expected to hear from. For many
months, as the slaughter continued on the eastern and western
fronts, both parents had doubted whether they would ever see
their younger son again. Now he was safe in Switzerland—interned by the Swiss, to be sure, but safe nonetheless. Later that
memorable day, Swiss radio announced that Hitler had committed suicide. Like millions of Europeans, the Schultes celebrated the Führer's death that evening, but they had an
additional personal reason to be happy.

The next day they went to Lucerne. After receiving the necessary permit to visit the prisoner, they were allowed to enter
the building. They found Ruprecht haggard and suffering
from stress, but otherwise in good health. They were eager to
hear how he had reached Switzerland, but did not press him at
their first meeting in almost two years. Gradually, the full story
emerged.

After being transferred from the Russian front to the west,
Ruprecht was placed in charge of a forward supply unit. By
late February 1945, British forces had reached the Rhine at
Kalkar, north of Cologne, and on March 5 the Americans took
Cologne itself. Following the use of strong parachute forces
(Operation Varsity), the Allied troops crossed the Rhine on a
wide front. Ruprecht, who had already had more than his
share of frontline fighting in the east, was now made head of a
battalion whose regular commander and staff had been killed
in the bombing of a small railroad station. To make matters
worse, the remnants of the battalion were given a suicide mission—in soldiers' German, they were a *Himmelfahrt* (heaven-
bound) commando. Confronting many American divisions,
First Lieutenant Schulte's task was to counterattack the
bridgehead which had already been established at Remagen.
But when his and some other small units reached the Remagen

area, the bridgehead was at least three miles deep, and antiair-craft cover in place. The German units made an attempt to penetrate the bridgehead at night, but it failed. The following evening Ruprecht was wounded again (his fifth time), but not seriously, by a shell that killed the radio operator next to him. He was sent back to his supply unit to recuperate.

During the following days he heard rumors that the officers in charge of the failed counterattack had been arrested and were to be court-martialed, possibly shot. The information turned out to be wrong; only the officers responsible for letting the Americans capture the bridge intact were in fact court-martialed. But for Lieutenant Schulte the rumors were the last straw. Quite apart from this last incident, he knew he was in constant danger of arrest (and worse) because of the flight of his parents to Switzerland. Together with two other soldiers, he commandeered a car and headed for the Swiss border. The distance was considerable, and the trip took several weeks. Nor was it an easy one. In the final period of the war, every two-bit local Nazi leader with a few armed thugs at his disposal could arrest and execute officers and soldiers caught where they had no right to be. But Ruprecht Schulte was a highly decorated officer, and he and his comrades bluffed their way through to the Swiss border at Waldshut in Baden. They even managed to get fuel along the way, which was virtually unobtainable in those days, and some food.

By late April, SS units were in charge of the sector near the Swiss border. They had begun to pull back, leaving a strip of no-man's-land. Ruprecht's two companions decided not to risk being shot and took their chances with the advancing French troops. Ruprecht had had enough. On April 25 he crossed into Switzerland in broad daylight. He was not sure whether the SS troops would shoot, but after five years of war, he was past caring. No shots rang out—the sentries too must have known that it was all over. Perhaps they even envied Ruprecht. He reported to the Swiss border guard and asked for asylum. The same evening he was taken to Lucerne. Ten days later, after some strings had been pulled, he was released and taken to a private clinic. He eventually received a permit to stay in Switzerland, specifically to study agriculture at the Zurich Polytechnical Institute.

. . .

When the war ended, Eduard Schulte wanted to return to his country. In early August 1945 the OSS Mission for Germany drew up a list of Germans qualified to fill positions in a German central government to be established by the Allies. The hundred-odd names, sent to Berlin to an Interdivision Coordinating Committee on German Government Personnel, were divided into two categories: those qualified to serve as heads of ministries and those more suited to direct subdivisions of ministries. Schulte was one of the few placed in the first category. The brief OSS biographical statement added luster:

> Leading industrialist in heavy industries, especially mining, transportation, and coal. Persecuted by Gestapo. Throughout the war in close contact with Allies. Came to Switzerland under great personal risk. One of the few German leading industrialists who never compromised with Nazi Party. Fair English.

Only the last statement was exaggerated. Encouraged by Allen Dulles, Gaevernitz, and Emmy Rado, Eduard Schulte left Zurich at the first opportunity that came. Not that he needed any encouragement; he was full of ideas and enthusiasm for doing his share in the rebuilding of Germany. Sadly, his hopes in that regard were very soon to be frustrated.

CHAPTER TEN

A Postwar Nightmare

Schulte's aircraft landed at Tempelhof in the American
sector of Berlin early one afternoon in August 1945. He
had traveled from Munich on a military plane; there was no
regular civilian transport in those days. It was a homecoming
of sorts for him; almost two years had passed since his flight
from Germany.

The main thoroughfares had been cleared of debris, and as
the aircraft circled down he had recognized the Kurfürstendamm and some other streets without difficulty. A great many
landmarks were missing and whole quarters were obviously
badly damaged, but in the summer sunshine and from a considerable height the destruction had seemed less extensive than
he had feared. Later, however, when exploring the streets by
car and on foot, Schulte realized with a shock that only the

shell of the city remained, in the form of the outer walls of railway stations, castles, churches, theaters, and museums; behind
these façades there were giant heaps of masonry, collapsed
beams and pillars, and rubble in every shape and form—the
whole city a study in various shades of gray, a grim chaos of
ruined and half-ruined buildings.

At Tempelhof a military car waited for him, and he was
whisked through passport control, which was run by the military, and driven to an address in the Dahlem section of Berlin.

The drive from the airport took a long time and led
through quarters that he would have sworn he had never
seen—though he must have known them well. The farther
away they went from the city center, the more buildings were
intact. The car came to a halt in front of a complex of buildings
that had been taken over by the Americans. There was an
American flag, and GIs on guard duty. He discovered afterward that the barracks had belonged to the German Air Force.

A young officer welcomed Schulte. The officer had received
a cable stating that Dr. Schulte would serve as adviser to the
military government, with a status somewhere between that of
a German civilian and an Allied official. This was an interim
period; no hard-and-fast rules had been established, and there
would be anomalies and hardships, which Schulte would have
to put up with. His superior would probably be Colonel James
Boyd, but in the meantime he should report to Lieutenant Colonel Howard Jones, who was in charge of the selection of German nationals to be employed by military authorities. They
had some guest rooms where Schulte could stay for the first few
days, but they expected visitors from the States, and he ought
to look for accommodations elsewhere. Surely he must have
friends and acquaintances in the city who could put him up?
American headquarters were concentrated in Dahlem, and
Schulte would be well advised to look for lodgings near his future place of work, for public transport was as yet unreliable,
and army vehicles too few and far between. It shouldn't be too
difficult to find such lodgings, since many civilians had left
Berlin and the southwest part of the city was in relatively good
shape, much better preserved than the French or the Russian
sectors. Beyond this the captain could give Schulte no useful
information, having himself arrived only two weeks earlier.

Then Schulte was invited to dinner, which was being
served in a nearby hall. They crossed a little bridge, and
Schulte found himself in a building that seemed vaguely famil-

iar. When he saw the place again in daytime, he realized that it
was the Harnack house, the building that had once housed the
German Academy of Sciences. There was plenty of food,
though it looked unexciting, to say the least, and Schulte had
to queue with a few dozen others. He had never before had to
stand in line for food. With his leg beginning to hurt, this was
an inauspicious start for his new life in Berlin. Not for many
years had he been accustomed to being told by others what to
do.

Having learned how bad conditions were in Berlin at the
end of the war, he had sent food parcels to some of his friends in
the city as soon as it was possible to do so. He had used private
messengers, since there was at that time no regular postal communication between Germany and outside countries (it was
not to be restored for another year). And now on his return he
had taken care to bring some food parcels with him, and other
useful items. He had experienced rationing in the First World
War, and he well remembered how grateful people could be for
a piece of soap or a couple of cigars: such things, once taken for
granted, had become luxuries.

He found a room first with friends named Spielhagen in
Zehlendorf, later with the Morgensterns in Wannsee—the suburb where Reinhard Heydrich unfolded the Final Solution of
the Jewish Question to assorted government and party experts
in January 1942. Zehlendorf, a residential suburb with an
abundance of gardens and trees, had emerged from the war
relatively unscathed, and many fine villas in Wannsee were
also undamaged. Life was still a long way from the comforts of
Breslau or Zurich, but this was not what mainly bothered him.
Considering the general suffering and the shortages, he was
certainly among those who were well-off. Schulte was a dynamic, restless man, and what irked him above all was that he,
a born organizer and doer, seemed to have been consigned to a
state of limbo. Yes, he was told, he was wanted for a responsible
and important job. But no, not quite yet. The wheels of bureaucracy turned at an agonizingly slow pace, and he was
forced to sit around with little or nothing to do.

Schulte used his involuntary leisure to locate old friends
and acquaintances and to get his bearings in what had been
until recently the capital of a united Germany. He had known
three different Berlins since he first arrived in the city thirty-
two years ago: Imperial Berlin, Republican Berlin, and, of
course, Nazi Berlin. Now he would experience yet another Ber-

lin—a city destroyed, occupied, and quartered. Whatever the differences in its three previous phases, the physical shape of the city had never changed very much. Unter den Linden, Friedrichstrasse, and Wilhelmstrasse had been the heart of the city, the Tiergarten—a vast park—the lungs. Working-class Berlin included "red" Wedding and the area around Alexanderplatz, which had left an imprint upon German literature just as much as the coffeehouses and the cabarets along the Kurfürstendamm. Despite all the political and social earthquakes, the popular songs had declared that *"Berlin bleibt doch Berlin"* ("Berlin Still Remains Berlin") and *"Durch Berlin fliesst immer noch die Spree"* ("The Spree River Still Flows Through Berlin")—in short, that Berlin would always stay much the same.

Now the heart of the city had been destroyed together with its lungs and other vital organs. Only rubble remained, ruins as far as the eye could see. Harry Hopkins, Roosevelt's emissary and confidant, had called it "a second Carthage." Schulte had never been an uncritical admirer of this city and its atmosphere, the famous *Berliner Luft*. It was not exactly beautiful, and its vulgarity had sometimes repelled him. But he had always been attracted by its dynamism, the pulsating life, the dry humor of the Berliners. It had been the capital of the Nazi Reich, but of all the major German cities it had perhaps been the least affected by Nazism.

To explore the remnants of this city, the fourth Berlin, was like exploring a new country, and a desolate one at that. From Schulte's base in the suburbs it was not at all easy to reach the former heart of the metropolis. Berlin these days was a city mainly of women, old people, and children, though most of the younger ones had been sent to the countryside in the last phase of the war as the air raids had gotten progressively worse. The majority of the men had been fighting and were now in prison camps. If the main thoroughfares of Berlin were cleared, it was mainly thanks to the women of the city. But an estimated 55 million cubic meters of rubble remained, and the experts were saying that at the present rate of clearing it would take between fifty and one hundred years to return to normal conditions.

The first schools were reopened in October. In the meantime the children played hide-and-seek in half-destroyed houses and among large heaps of rubble—an exciting new game, no doubt, but a dangerous one too. From time to time one of the walls would collapse, or an unexploded shell would go off.

Some of the cinemas had reopened and were showing Russian films. Of the cabarets, the old Femina and Rio Rita had miraculously survived, so there was already a night life of sorts. *Neues Deutschland,* a daily newspaper sponsored by the Russians, began to appear almost immediately after the war. In late September *Der Tagesspiegel* followed; it was published in the Western zone. The main source of information, including the all-important announcements of the Kommandatura, the executive committee of the four occupying powers, was the radio. But the supply of electricity was limited to a few hours a day, and life was more or less regulated according to those hours.

As Schulte walked through the streets of the city, he gathered a great deal of useful information. Food, of course, was rationed. In principle, everyone was entitled to about one thousand calories a day. Unfortunately, the food was not always available. Some people had even resorted to eating grass, acorns, stinging nettles, and the bark of trees, to eke out their miserable supply of proper food.

More than once he was accosted by people who asked whether he had any cigarettes to sell—some of them said he looked like a smoker. But he had never smoked cigarettes, and he began to equip himself with a modest supply of Lucky Strikes and Chesterfields only because these had become the new universal currency, a development his economics professors at Erlangen before the First World War had never anticipated. The black market fascinated Schulte. What laws of supply and demand decided that a Leica could be obtained for a dozen packs of Camels, and a valuable Persian carpet for a sausage of dubious origin and equally dubious contents, plus a dozen eggs of uncertain age? It did not take Schulte long to master the basic principles, and he reckoned that if he addressed his business acumen to this crazy new economy, he could be a very rich man within a few weeks. But he was already rich, and he had not returned to Germany to make a fortune from the misery of millions. He had volunteered to work for the Americans for no salary.

The little story of the miner and his hen that was going the rounds in Berlin at this time, and which several people he met had made a point of telling him, neatly epitomized the state of things. The miner's weekly wage was 60 marks; the hen laid five eggs a week, one eaten by him or his family, the other four

exchanged on the black market for twenty cigarettes, which
could be sold for 160 marks. Thus the hen earned almost three
times as much as the miner! The story (which later made its
way into textbooks of modern economic history) illustrated an
absurd situation, and Schulte knew from long experience that
absurd situations do not last very long. He saw it as his task,
with others, to persuade the Americans to adopt a more sensible policy.

To locate people was an almost full-time occupation in
those days. Many of Schulte's friends had left Berlin months
earlier, either because their offices had been removed or because they wanted to escape from the concentrated Allied
bombing, which reached a crescendo in early 1945. There was
no regular mail service, and telephone connections existed only
to and from offices providing vital services. Former government
officials and senior army officers had disappeared; they were
either in captivity or had moved to western Germany. Old
business contacts he spoke to seemed more than a little uneasy:
Was there a future for them in Berlin? Was there a future for
them anywhere?

There were a few inveterate optimists, but among most
people Schulte found an overwhelming sense of despair and
self-pity, from which they were distracted only by the daily
struggle to survive, or to obtain the bare minimum of food,
fuel, and other essentials. The street scene was dominated by
people walking around with rucksacks, pushing carts such as
those once used by street vendors. The fortunate ones riding
bicycles were the new aristocracy, and everyone was in search
of something to purchase or exchange. The centers of the black
market were in the now desolate area in front of the old
Reichstag building and at the Alexanderplatz, or what remained of it. "Black market" was a misnomer in more ways
than one, for the authorities tolerated it as essential to keep the
country going. It was in fact the primary market.

The common Berliners had kept some of their sense of
humor, a very black humor by then. But among those who had
only recently been in leading economic positions, a mood of
stark hopelessness prevailed. The situation was terrible in itself,
but also there seemed to be no prospect of any improvement.
The Allies were dismantling what remained of German industry. It seemed they had decided that Germany should never
again be an industrial power, for without an industrial base, it
would be in no position to threaten its neighbors again.

As a business leader and economist, Schulte knew that while Allied anger and revenge were to be expected, they were not a sound basis for the conduct of policy—not in the long run, and perhaps not even in the short run. Sixty-five million Germans had to be fed, and since the country did not produce enough food, the Allies would have to bring in additional supplies if they did not want mass starvation on their hands. They would either have to feed Germany indefinitely or they would have to permit it to export industrial goods to pay for food imports. Earlier than others, Schulte realized that the Allies would have to allow German industrial production to resume.

To make matters worse, the Americans and the British barred all but the most essential contact between the occupying forces and the German population. One American colonel, trying to explain the policy of nonfraternization to his men, said that fraternization "was when you stay for breakfast." But at the same time that they were to avoid fraternization, the Allies had to re-educate Germans toward democracy. Where were the instructors in political retraining to come from, and how could Germans learn about democracy except from American and British soldiers? Moreover, neither Western power had the desire to rule Germany directly for an extended period. Yet they tried to avoid giving Germans positions of importance in the administration. In short, Allied policies rested on basic contradictions. One could even say that, in the beginning, there was no American or British policy for Germany.

In October the American military government apparatus in Berlin began to take shape. Dwight D. Eisenhower's deputy for military government, General Lucius Clay, established an Office of Military Government (United States), which became known as OMGUS. Colonel James Boyd became the chief of the Industry Branch of the Economics Division, and it was in this new arrangement that Schulte was finally given a function, and an office to go with it. The office was adequate—a plain rectangular one, off a long corridor, in what was known as Building C, a large L-shaped structure.

At first he was listed as a consultant; later, he was promoted to a position described as chief of the office of consultants to German industry. He was able to assemble a staff that began to prepare reports on the condition and prospects of various industries. His superiors assured him that this was only a prelude to something bigger. But it is unclear whether they had any definite plans for more than a few weeks ahead.

Schulte seems to have made a good impression on Colonel Boyd; his deputy, Colonel Scharff; and the chief legal adviser, Major Demuth. He had given them copies of his 1944 study of what should be done in postwar Germany, and they liked what they read. Fred Gaethke, an Anaconda executive who had known him for twenty years through Giesche of Poland, and who was now chief of the coal and nonmetallic mining section in the Economics Division, also spoke highly of Schulte.

Colonel Boyd's memorandum summarizing Schulte's qualifications described him as "a man of outstanding character and ability . . . entirely honest, very energetic, and intelligent."

Boyd selected Schulte and four other Germans—Walter Schreiber, Ferdinand Friedensburg, Konrad Mommsen, and Otto Heinz von der Gablentz—as candidates for top positions in the proposed central German departments for industry. (Schreiber had been Prussian minister of finance in the Weimar Republic. Friedensburg and von der Gablentz were professors; the former had been a leading liberal in the republic and served as deputy mayor of Berlin after 1945. Mommsen, a descendant of the great historian Theodor Mommsen, was an industrialist who would resume his career after 1948.) These central departments were supposed to administer all four zones of occupation. Schulte would have been, in effect, one of several German economic and financial executives (*Staatssekretäre*), a deputy minister in an appointed German government subject only to an Allied Control Council.

There were obstacles. The French, only recently admitted to the status of occupying power, fought vehemently against the central German agencies, which they feared would become a central German government. General Clay recognized obstructionism when he saw it and asked Washington for permission to proceed with the establishment of central agencies for the three remaining zones of occupation. Washington was amenable, but the Russians were not. They had already begun to make appointments within their own zone. It became increasingly evident that the Russians would accept central agencies only on their own terms. Clay did not give up on the idea of central departments, but he began to construct separate administrative and political machinery within the American zone.

Meanwhile, a new development affected Schulte's promotion—the American policy for the denazification of Germany. Back across the Atlantic a great many Americans felt that it was high time to oust those responsible for the Nazi system and all its crimes. A good many voices demanded a purge of anti-democratic elements to prepare the foundation for a new and peaceful spirit in the country. Both as punishment and as prevention, denazification seemed imperative, and the American government and military authorities agreed.

What was admirable in theory turned out to be difficult in practice. The military authorities needed trained German administrators to help re-establish order, but most were compromised by service in the Third Reich. General Clay laid down the law to his division directors: the military government would denazify all areas of German life, the private sector as well as the public one. A business enterprise would have to certify that it had no Nazis in high positions. Anyone who had been a member of the Nazi Party (there had been twelve million) had to prove to the military government that he or she had not been active, in order to escape the new ban. One complication was that every German state employee, however humble his position, had automatically become a member of the Nazi Party under a law promulgated in 1937. At the same time, some of the worst culprits, including people responsible for the murder of thousands in concentration camps, had not belonged to the party.

Nazi Germany had been a jungle of overlapping and competing party, government, and military organizations. There was no simple way to figure out who had been responsible for what. The number of American experts who really understood how the Nazi political system had worked could gather in a small room. And it took a great deal of time and effort to locate the relevant documentary material and to make sense of it.

The scale of the denazification process matched its complexity: thirteen million Germans in the American zone had to fill out the official questionnaire, whose 131 questions minutely probed a person's background, political activities, and organizational affiliations. People who had not joined the Nazi Party were not necessarily in the clear; those categorized as militarists and prominent supporters of the regime, even if they had not been party members, were also to be removed or barred from significant future roles in the country. The burden of decision in these matters fell on the Division of Public Safety, which, through its Special Branch subsections, had to plow through all the paper and carry out the sometimes impossible task of separating the dishonest replies from the truthful ones.

The somewhat daunting character of the denazification procedure is conveyed by the instructions issued to the Special Branch subsections:

> In order to accomplish its mission, the flow of Fragebogen [questionnaires] and Work Sheets must be handled as on a production line, with each unit and each person within the individual units specializing in the accomplishment of his small part in the task. The rate of flow will be set by the number of Fragebogen which the Evaluation Unit can analyze each day. The numbers employed in the Civil Service Records Unit, the Police Records Unit, the Counter-Intelligence Unit, and the Index and Files Unit must be gauged by their ability to handle the output of the Evaluation Unit without a bottle-neck which will slow down the output. For example, Monday's evaluations of Fragebogen must be cleared through the Civil Service Records Unit by Tuesday, the Police Records Unit by Wednesday, the Counter-Intelligence Liaison Unit by Thursday, and the Index and Files Unit by Friday.

From the end of the war until mid-March 1946 the Special Branch subsections processed more than one and a quarter million of these sets of documents. Even if all the American officials had been knowledgeable and competent, the assembly line, confronting this torrent of paper, was bound to make many mistakes. Moreover, there was constant reshuffling of personnel in 1945 and 1946, and many an official dealing with German affairs had minimal knowledge of the situation. The safest course for such a bureaucrat was to suspect everybody.

One of OMGUS's first tasks was to see which Germans could safely be employed by the American military government. Reviewing the files, officials sorted out people according to five categories: 1) Mandatory Removal; 2) Discretionary Removal, Adverse Recommendation (i.e., removal recommended); 3) Discretionary Removal, No Adverse Recommendation; 4) No Evidence of Nazi Activity; and 5) Evidence of Anti-Nazi Activity. Groups 3–5 were to provide recruits for the new German government and key positions in the private sector. For OMGUS officials drawing up their charts and statistics for Washington, it was important to show that they had not retained or employed any German in the two unfavorable categories.

Schulte had always been careful to keep his activities in support of the Allies secret, but this policy now created a problem for him. If one looked hard enough there was an apparent stain on his record. The American forces had issued an order on July 7, 1945, specifying who was to be removed and/or excluded from public office: in all, 136 groups were listed, and No. 104 was "*Wehrwirtschaftsführer* (defense economy leader)." Because he had been awarded this purely honorary title under the Nazis, Schulte automatically fell into the category of Germans debarred from public service. When in September he learned that this was the case, he reluctantly came to the conclusion that he would, after all, have to break his own rule and submit some evidence of his work for the Allies. He sought help from Allen Dulles.

Dulles wrote two letters for Schulte. The first was a brief, somewhat high-flown commendation. Schulte, it read, had cooperated with Dulles during 1943 and 1944 and had "rendered most valuable services to the cause of the United Nations, motivated solely by his hatred of the Nazi system. . . ." He had "uniformly stood for the ideals and principles of liberty and democracy and has always made himself available to promote those principles in his own country, Germany." The second letter, addressed to Lieutenant Colonel Howard Jones, head of an interagency personnel board in Berlin, dealt directly with the problem of Schulte's disqualification. Dulles confirmed that Schulte's title of *Wehrwirtschaftsführer* had been purely honorary and had entailed no duties. When Schulte had received it, he was actually assisting the Allies. For Schulte to have rejected the award would have been risky; it would have made him suspect to the Nazis and ended his usefulness to the Allies. Dulles asked Jones to remove Schulte's "technical disqualification" for Allied service. That explanation was more than enough for Colonel Boyd and his staff, who expected Schulte to be cleared shortly.

In the fall of 1945 Lieutenant Colonel Joseph W. Darling took on the job of clearing German consultants for employment with the Industry Branch. Darling recognized that Schulte was an unusual person and that the standard bureaucratic rules and procedures should not apply to him. He not only cleared Schulte; he came to be friendly with him—his office was down the hall from Schulte's. The two men were in frequent contact, since Darling had to clear the other Germans hired by Schulte in his capacity as chief of German consultants to industry. How many industrialists, Darling must have wondered, would have volunteered to serve in government without salary?

Darling's early clearance of Schulte was effective only for the Industry Branch. The Schulte file subsequently went to the Public Safety Branch in Berlin, which was not aware of his wartime activities. There he earned the designation "No Evidence of Nazi Activity" (rather than "Evidence of Anti-Nazi Activity"). Because of his *Wehrwirtschaftsführer* title he was still in the mandatory "remove/exclude" category. Until he was cleared through a more formal bureaucratic procedure, he would remain ineligible for employment as state secretary for industry, the position for which he had earlier been selected as a candidate. An official in such a position would have to have a spotless record, vouched for not only by the Americans, but also by the other three occupying powers.

In December 1945 Schulte's agency had submitted a memorandum to the Denazification Policy Board endorsing the punishment of those businessmen who had contributed substantially to the support of the Nazi regime, even if they had had no formal ties with the party. (Schulte himself had probably had a hand in this memorandum.) But the Industry Branch also recommended that lists of businessmen who had held positions in Nazi governmental or quasi-governmental agencies should not be used inflexibly. For example, the prohibition on the employment of a former *Wehrwirtschaftsführer* "should be limited to those persons receiving the honor on or after 10 April 1942." Schulte had been designated *Wehrwirtschaftsführer* in April 1941 and probably knew very well that only during 1942 had the Nazi Party taken direct control of the nomination procedure.

This suggestion made too much sense to be accepted. But Schulte would not have been in the clear even if it had been. Someone had supplied the OMGUS Office of the Director of Intelligence with the inaccurate information—one of many mistakes—that Schulte had been appointed *Wehrwirtschaftsführer* in the summer of 1943—which meant that there was all the more reason to examine his case with a magnifying glass. So the intelligence officials began a long investigation of a man who had prominent American backers, but who had also raised doubts in some quarters.

The political climate in Berlin was laden with suspicion. There were already complaints in the American press—and in internal OMGUS memoranda—that the United States had done little to prosecute German business executives. Only one industrialist was among the major war criminals on trial at Nuremberg—the senior Krupp, who was soon deemed mentally incompetent and unable to stand trial. Some of those who had profited most during the Nazi years had gone scot-free. In March 1946 the Office of the U.S. Chief of Counsel at Nuremberg drew up a list of eighty-five prominent German businessmen and requested from other government agencies evidence connecting any of them with war crimes. Schulte's name was not on this list, but several other bona fide anti-Nazis were. Even General Clay expressed a desire to do more about punishing industrialists who may not have been members of the Nazi Party but who were implicated in war crimes. American officials preparing evidence for war crimes trials assessed the businessmen who had been named *Wehrwirtschaftsführer* as follows: "Only men regarded by the party as trustworthy pillars of the system could receive such appointments after the beginning of the year 1938, while earlier appointees owed their appointment to a special distinguishment in the cause of rearmament." This quite inaccurate judgment meant that anyone who appeared on the list of *Wehrwirtschaftsführer* was forced to undergo minute examination.

And so it was decided that before Eduard Schulte could be appointed to one of the highest positions in the new Germany, he would have to pass the most rigorous inspection. One office involved in the investigation was the Evaluation Section of the Personnel Office (later part of the Civil Administration Division). Most of the officials were well meaning but inexperienced, and they found themselves making important decisions quickly, based on little information. On one occasion General Clay himself had ordered a report on a German banker recommended by the Swedish naval attaché to General Eisenhower; Eisenhower and Clay wanted a report within twenty-four hours. The official in charge, Lieutenant Thomas B. Stauffer, told Clay that he could not turn in a report until he had something solid to go on. After some digging, Stauffer discovered that the "innocent" banker had been in charge of all the property stolen by the Nazis from Austrian Jews. General Clay then thanked Stauffer for doing his investigation with his usual care, thereby sparing OMGUS great embarrassment.

Stauffer and his colleagues drew the logical conclusion: the worst mistake they could make was to clear a real Nazi. They nicknamed their unit the "skunk works," for they dealt with plenty of German nominees whose past had an evil smell.

When Stauffer looked at the Schulte file, he saw reason for concern. Schulte had slipped into American employment in the weeks soon after the end of the war, when procedures were still informal. He was said to be an anti-Nazi, but he certainly had a curious record for one—the German War Cross of Merit and *Wehrwirtschaftsführer*. Schulte (accurately) claimed that he had been appointed *Wehrwirtschaftsführer* in 1941—without his knowledge—and that the War Cross of Merit, First Class, was a Gestapo lure to induce him to return to Germany in 1944. Both statements seemed unconvincing to Stauffer.

Thomas B. Stauffer was then twenty-nine years old. His family was of German ancestry, but they had never idealized their country of origin. The Stauffers had moved from Wisconsin to Chicago, and Thomas Stauffer had graduated from the University of Chicago. He had then done graduate work at Chicago and Princeton in political philosophy, picking up some German along the way. After several years in the army, he arrived in Berlin in July 1945 and ended up in the Evaluation Section. Four men in the section were Jewish, and Stauffer himself later married a Jew.

In the spring of 1946 Schulte limped into the offices of the Evaluation Section, then located in a house on Saargemünderstrasse in Berlin-Dahlem, not too far from the large Berlin forest. According to Stauffer, he was most cordial and cooperative. At the same time, he knew what he wanted: to satisfy the requirements of any regulations quickly in order to please the petty officials. He gave Stauffer the impression that "we men of the world" were really above all that. His presence evoked the word "sovereign." He commented with pleasure on Stauffer's knowledge of German culture. On one level Stauffer was impressed—this was a man of great power and subtlety. Yet Stauffer was not quite at ease: Schulte clearly was not telling him everything. Schulte would make a delightful friend, but a redoubtable enemy. Stauffer decided to make sure that someone else was present as a witness during his meetings with Schulte. Although Stauffer became very friendly with Ferdinand Friedensburg, another German nominated for high office, he could not bridge the gap with Schulte. And given his experience with Germans who had skeletons in the closet, he decided to suspend approval until his doubts were removed. In fact, he wrote in an official memorandum that without convincing testimony from the American intelligence agency, Schulte "will be considered an active Nazi."

There was little that Schulte could do to hasten the process. He rewrote his curriculum vitae in English, putting in additional details about his intelligence work during the war. He reluctantly gave OMGUS copies of his citations from the Polish, French, and British governments. Koppelmann, with close links to Polish and British intelligence, had insisted that the British give Schulte some kind of certificate of merit signed by a high-level authority. When the certificate arrived, it was signed by none other than Field Marshal Bernard Montgomery: "By this Certificate of Service I record my appreciation of the aid rendered by Eduard "Hans" [his British code name] Schulte as a volunteer in the service of the United Nations for the great cause of Freedom."

By midsummer of 1946 there had still been no progress, and Schulte left Berlin for Switzerland. He had no difficulty in getting permission to travel. His artificial limb needed repair, and his gall bladder was infected. Medical treatment was better in Switzerland and he knew the doctors there. Besides, he had business to attend to. If OMGUS did not need him, he would take his time in Switzerland. He might even go to the U.S. for business conferences with Anaconda. He arrived in Zurich on July 19 and, after completing his hospital stay, moved into the Hotel Bellerive-au-Lac.

He soon wrote Colonel Wilkinson, the chief of the Industry Branch, formally asking for an extension of his leave until the end of January. He explained that Anaconda and La Roche officials wanted to confer with him at length, and that there seemed to be no urgent need for him in Berlin. Wilkinson complied with the request.

That same month (September) he wrote to his secretary and friend Elisabeth Urbig in Berlin expressing his annoyance at the ridiculous fact that for him a "denazification," even though only a so-called "technical" one, was necessary at all.

Schulte now documented some tracks that he had once worked hard to cover. He expanded a short summary of his activities during the war, adding some details about his escape to Switzerland. He appended copies of his citations from the British, French, Polish, and American governments, and had the whole package notarized in Zurich on November 1. He must

have wondered whether any of the bureaucrats who investi-
gated him could boast of having served four Allied governments and risked their lives in the process.

He still thought there was a chance that the whole affair
was the result of a misunderstanding or lack of knowledge,
rather than malice. He wrote Lothar Siemon in January 1947:

> ... some of the officers higher up are well in-
> formed, but the many subordinate ones cannot
> and do not know anything, and it would not be
> suitable to tell them all the details, because cer-
> tain allied authorities higher up don't want to
> keep everybody informed about matters which
> they wish to be treated confidentially ...

As Allen Dulles explained to Richard Helms—at the time, July
1946, a junior intelligence official in Germany—Eduard
Schulte was a man capable of great stoicism. But there were
limits, and Dulles observed that Schulte and an unnamed anti-
Nazi German "would be good choices for high level jobs under
military government unless they have been kicked around to a
point where they have become embittered." By late 1946
Schulte had every reason to be embittered.

Even if Schulte had been classed as "denazified," it is probable that the important job he had hoped for in the reconstruction of Germany would not have materialized. By late
1945, it was already clear that Berlin was not where the main
action would be: Schulte was in the wrong place. The American military government established a Regional Government
Coordination Office, mainly concerned with the economy, with
its seat in Stuttgart, in the villa of the former Gauleiter. Berlin
had merely a branch of this organization.

Eventually the Americans transferred power to elected
German officials. Schulte could have played a central role in
the new German government only if he had joined one of the
political parties and had been nominated as one of its representatives—like Konrad Adenauer and the other leaders of postwar Germany. It is doubtful whether Schulte, who had
abstained from party politics all his life, would have opted for
such a career at this stage. Though he would have made an excellent minister of economics, he would not have wanted to
campaign for the post.

There were other Germans, such as Ludwig Erhard, later
economics minister in Konrad Adenauer's government, equally

capable of steering the economy through the shoals of the post-war period to a new prosperity. One cannot really claim that Schulte's disqualification represented a historic misfortune for Germany. Nor could it be accounted a personal disaster, for Schulte was a wealthy man and thus not interested in the material rewards, which in any case were meager. Yet it did represent a loss for his country that a man of his caliber was not given the opportunity to put his talent at its service.

The fate of the other three "musketeers" in Switzerland—Gaevernitz, Waetjen, and Gisevius—followed a similar pattern. All had performed outstanding services for the Allies at considerable personal risk during the Second World War, and all were sharply criticized, even "punished," by authorities after the war. The bureaucrats who appeared on the scene found (as one of them later wrote in a memo) that though these anti-Nazis had "allegedly" been of help during the war, they had suspicious ties or contacts—they had served more than one master. As the vetting continued, all kinds of rumors and insinuations that had crept into the files over the years resurfaced. Even Gaevernitz, a naturalized American citizen, found himself under attack. Was it not true that he had helped transfer a Finnish ship in the harbor of Lisbon into Swiss registry? And wasn't he close to Hugo Stinnes, Jr., a notorious Nazi sympathizer? Gaevernitz's relationship to the Stinnes family was through Edmund Stinnes, his brother-in-law. The bureaucrats neglected to consider that Edmund Stinnes was not on speaking terms with the rest of the family in Germany, that he had left the country as a political refugee, and that he had taught at Haverford College in Pennsylvania during the war.

In two sharp exchanges with officials of the American Legation in Bern, Allen Dulles was forced to come to the defense of anti-Nazi Germans, including Gaevernitz, his own right-hand man. Legation officials had heard from other Germans who were interrogated (such as a former consul) that these men were unregenerate German nationalists, and they proposed to notify Washington of this adverse characterization. Said Dulles:

> You [the legation officials] and I do not agree about these things or people. You condemn men who got out and at great risks to themselves did valuable things for us: and on what grounds? The gossipy statements of other Ger-

mans who were too afraid to do other than sit on the fence and draw their pay. You know that it was Gisevius who told me that the Germans knew your code—which you then stopped using. He told me in advance about the 20th of July incident [the assassination attempt on Hitler]. It was through his contact that we learned about Peenemünde. I could tell you a lot about these people, but you [the legation] don't want to believe me. . . .

I think that it is an outrage that the testimony of Germans should be used to damn a patriotic American (v. G.) [von Gaevernitz]. Krauel [the German consul] was just jealous because we ignored him. I never trusted him. How does he know that Canaris instructed his agents to get in touch with v. G., and through him with the Americans? Do you know that some of your people are trying to "get" v. G.? This will just serve to damn the man. . . .

When I get to Washington I am going to report on everything and I'll cover this then. . . . Why do you want to send the thing [the despatch] anyway? I wouldn't even use it; it is not complete enough.

But Dulles's remarks fell on deaf ears, and the legation sent off its sanctimonious nonsense to Washington.

Gisevius did not fare any better. Swiss authorities opened legal proceedings against him after the war, and most of his Allied friends did not lift a finger to help him. It was unlikely that Gisevius could have remained in Switzerland during the war if he had engaged exclusively in anti-Nazi activities. Still, his work for the Allies was of infinitely greater importance than whatever services he performed for the Abwehr. Gisevius refuted the charges against him in a long memorandum. But he preferred, perhaps rightly, not to put all his trust in the forces of logic and justice. Gisevius also used a little blackmail; if the Swiss dared to take him to court, they would regret the day they opened proceedings. Gisevius knew too much, so the Swiss authorities shelved the charges.

Gisevius became a key witness at the Nuremberg trial of the major war criminals. Gaevernitz and Waetjen also emerged from the cloud of suspicion. But all three felt bitter—as did Schulte. They had deserved better.

Why did they become suspect? Ignorance explains a great deal, and it is also true that once the denazification machinery had been installed, everyone who had survived the Nazi regime automatically became suspect, including those who had escaped. Americans had no political experience with resistance to Nazism. And so, quite frequently, the wrong people were promoted, and those who had resisted Hitler fell under suspicion. It would be invidious to single out particular officials; it was the fault of the system.

• • •

Schulte left Berlin almost exactly a year after he had arrived. He may not as yet have given up entirely the idea of serving his country—his official resignation from OMGUS came only in January 1947. But he must have known that he was in Zurich for more than a short stay and that under present conditions there was little room for him in Germany. What irony—his prospects would have been brighter if he had sat out the war quietly somewhere in Switzerland or Latin America, if he had never passed on his warnings and information to the Allies.

Schulte's postwar nightmare did not end with his departure from Berlin. His corporate empire was under attack by Communists, capitalists, and the United States government alike. The Russians dismantled Giesche's refineries and plants in the eastern zone of Germany and transferred the machinery and equipment to the Soviet Union as part of their share of reparations. The Polish Communists nationalized many large enterprises. German property was a particular target, but even other foreign-owned corporations were offered only the possibility of future compensation. Schulte was a realist, and these developments in Eastern Europe did not surprise him.

The American attitude was more difficult to understand. Schulte had kept his corporate allies in the U.S. as well as the American government apprised of his business strategy. He thought they realized that he had tried to operate in their interest also, and he expected their maximum support at the end of the war. But Schulte was too optimistic.

Before the United States entered the war he had tried to arrange Swiss purchase of all the shares and bonds of the Silesian-American Corporation—the holding company for the Pol-

ish Giesche properties—which were 49 percent owned by German Giesche, 51 percent held by the Anaconda Copper Company and Harriman and Company through a holding
company. If this deal had gone through, it would have protected the Americans against German seizure of American
property. It would also have protected German Giesche against
seizure of its shares of Silesian-American by the American government. But the United States Treasury Department had
foolishly blocked the transaction as "of potential benefit" to
Germany. The immediate result was the collapse of the Silesian-American Corporation. Schulte's company was unable to
get money to the United States, therefore unable to pay interest on its loans from Silesian-American. The Delaware company, in turn, could not pay interest to its bondholders.
Because of the barriers between Germany and the United
States, Silesian-American was in default—its stockholders and
bondholders in jeopardy of losing everything.

Schulte then tried another approach. In August 1942, in
return for additional loans, he irrevocably transferred ownership of Giesche's Silesian-American shares to Erzag, a Swiss
firm controlled by his Swiss financial backers (La Roche). With
that the Silesian-American shares became Swiss property, although Schulte was an officer of the Swiss corporation too. He
knew very well that he was playing a dangerous game. While
he turned German assets into Swiss assets, he was telling the
Nazi government that his aim was to reunify the whole Giesche
enterprise under German hands. He could not possibly have
explained how transferring Silesian-American shares to Swiss
ownership could aid his stated goal of making the whole
Giesche empire German again. He had to keep the whole plan
secret—his life depended on Berlin not learning about it. Fortunately, his friends at La Roche were entirely trustworthy and
discreet.

Schulte even obtained the Nazi government's permission to
export zinc, an essential war commodity, to Switzerland. This
was necessary, he said, to help finance the Swiss purchase of the
American shares and bonds of Silesian-American. Thus
Schulte not only deprived the Nazi war economy of an important raw material, but also of the export profits. The revenue
from the zinc sales stayed in Swiss banks, allegedly to be used
in the stock and bond deal. At this stage the whole deal became
utterly confusing, impossible for an outsider to understand,
and this may have been Schulte's intention all along. That

Schulte could persuade German officials to go along with him says a great deal for his persuasiveness and skill at manipulation.

Almost a year after Germany declared war on the U.S., the United States Justice Department took over the Giesche shares of Silesian-American Corporation as enemy-owned property. Since the stock certificates themselves were in Europe, Justice got a court order to cancel the shares and issue new ones. The Alien Property Custodian of the Justice Department became trustee. Perhaps Justice Department officials thought that they had struck a blow against a large and powerful German corporation. What they had actually done was to seize shares that Schulte had just secretly transferred to Swiss interests—at great risk. The Justice Department's paper holdings would not be worth much unless whoever controlled the property at the end of the war recognized them. For the duration of the war German Giesche controlled its sister corporation, because Germany controlled Poland, and because Schulte succeeded in warding off a take-over by the Hermann Göring Werke.

At the end of the war there were, in effect, two parties claiming the rights to the 49 percent of Silesian-American stock. The Justice Department had no intention of returning its stock to a German corporation. On the other hand, the Swiss banking consortium claimed that it had acquired the Silesian-American shares in 1942, prior to the Justice Department's action, and that the Justice Department had no right to the shares. It was a conflict over who was going to claim compensation from Poles for nationalized property—the Justice Department or the Swiss.

The first Swiss attempt to wrest legal control of the shares from the Justice Department failed. A suit was lodged charging that Justice had illegally seized the Silesian-American shares in the first place. In September 1945 the Southern District Court in New York ruled on behalf of the government, and the Circuit Court upheld the verdict upon appeal. The Supreme Court refused to review the case late in 1946. But there were more legal proceedings to come over the rival claims between Justice and the Swiss investors.

There was only one person who knew exactly what had happened and when and why—and where all the assets were. This was Eduard Schulte. Far from expressing gratitude to Schulte for what he had done during the war, the Justice Department now became his antagonist, convinced that Schulte sided with the Swiss in the Giesche litigation. All of his claims were treated with suspicion.

The State Department began an investigation of Schulte's business arrangements during the war. Again Allen Dulles and another OSS official who had dealt with Schulte wrote positive recommendations for him, but the investigators also turned up German Economics Ministry documents that they regarded as suspicious. In their report dated July 23, 1946, the State Department's investigators called for documentary proof of Schulte's anti-Nazi activities and additional interrogation of Schulte about his correspondence and contacts with Nazi authorities.

By then Schulte was in Zurich trying to reconcile his obligations to his Swiss bankers and to his American partners, and to make a strong case for getting compensation from Poland for nationalized property. The Poles, who had the bulk of Giesche's properties, were more likely to pay off Swiss investors than the American government. Schulte had to explain the whole situation to Anaconda executives and to work out a common stance that could be presented to the American government.

On October 7 he applied to the American Consulate in Zurich for a nonimmigrant visa that would allow him to visit the U.S. for about two months. Cautious officials in the consulate cabled Washington, where the Visa Division asked in return for a report on the Schulte case. Schulte's application was sent to the American Legation in Bern, where Germans of every type were suspect. The legation made new inquiries. An official representing the Polish government-in-exile in Switzerland backed Schulte, but one of Allen Dulles's successors in Switzerland, who was not familiar with the whole affair, gave him only a lukewarm recommendation. The July 1946 report on Schulte by the State Department Division of Economic Security Controls was damaging.

The Office of the Political Adviser for Germany then contacted the American Legation in Bern to warn that whatever Schulte had done for the Allies during the war, "he has served several masters." It was an interesting turn of phrase that cannot be explained solely by bureaucratic idiocy. There must have been an element of malice. Someone concluded that Schulte's company had contributed to the German war economy, and he had done too well for himself to be regarded with favor. Now he wanted to go to the U.S., at a time when travel permits and visas were scarce, obviously to add to his profits. Bern responded by advising the consulate general in Zurich to withhold action on the visa.

By this time Schulte had spent more than a year answering the same questions and documenting the same activities. Whenever the investigators came up with favorable information about him, they ignored it. His associate at Giesche, Lothar Siemon, told OMGUS officials that Schulte had emphatically refused to join the Nazi Party and that he had many Jewish friends.

Schulte's former secretary Hella Jerchel had for years regularly taken dictation from him at the Breslau headquarters. She recalled that during these sessions, whenever he heard anything about Nazi activities, he blew up and "shouted that those fellows would cause heaps of ruin larger than [anyone had] ever seen in the world."

Günter von Poseck, who managed the Polish Giesche operations during the war, declared that he had known few Germans whose hatred of National Socialism had been as fervent and uncompromising as Schulte's, or who had displayed such strength of inner conviction. Schulte considered National Socialism to be the greatest possible disaster for Germany and the world. Unfortunately, German witnesses for their fellow countryman were not given much weight.

There was one person in a position to wage bureaucratic war successfully for Schulte. Although Allen Dulles had returned to private law practice, he did not hesitate to wield his remaining influence on Schulte's behalf. Learning that Schulte's case had reached Undersecretary of State Will Clayton's office, Dulles wrote to Clayton, who happened to be a friend. Dulles explained that he had no professional interest in the matter and no knowledge of Schulte's business affairs.

Consequently, Dulles could not judge whether Schulte's business was so important that he deserved to get a visa to the United States. But the former OSS official could testify to Schulte's character, and he could evaluate better than almost anyone Schulte's past services to the United States. Without going into specifics on Schulte's intelligence activities, which both men thought should be kept as quiet as possible, Dulles made it clear to Clayton how important and how courageous this industrialist was. Schulte, Dulles wrote, was one of the decent Germans who could form a nucleus to build up something better in postwar Germany. He had been anti-Nazi when most

Germans were not, and when much of the world was appeasing Hitler. He remained totally opposed to the Nazis throughout the war. To deny such a man a visa now would be rank ingratitude, and it would tarnish the record of a great democracy. Dulles was not overstating the case.

Allen Dulles still had considerable influence. On January 7, 1947 Undersecretary Clayton responded that the State Department had concluded that Schulte's visit to the United States would be in the national interest. On January 22, 1947, the Visa Division cabled Zurich that it had no objection to Eduard Schulte receiving a visa. That was as far as the department usually went, because technically the final decision on individual applications remained with the consul on the scene.

Two days later Schulte took a step he had long been contemplating. OMGUS had made the choice for him, having refused to clear him for a high government position and treating him as a subversive. He sent in his resignation.

But the battle for the American visa was by no means over. The Justice Department sent a team of three men to Berlin, who discovered that during the war Schulte had signed letters to Nazi ministries with "Heil Hitler." Anyone with even a modest knowledge of conditions in Nazi Germany could have told them there was no way to avoid using the dreadful salute when dealing with a state or party institution, whether in speech or in writing. The investigators either did not know this basic fact or did not want to know it, and they thought that at long last they had found the evidence they needed of Schulte's Nazi sympathies.

A protracted bureaucratic battle ensued. The Justice Department brought pressure on the State Department to refuse a visa to Schulte, and when that failed, it contacted the Immigration and Naturalization Service. The Justice Department was anxious to interrogate Schulte in connection with the Giesche litigation, but it wanted to talk to him in Berlin rather than in New York. At one stage a Major Hess of the OMGUS intelligence branch even discovered a dangerous plot—obviously some highly placed American OMGUS officials had conspired with Schulte. These people should now be kept under surveillance; "surreptitious entry" into their residences was recommended as well as telephone and postal censorship.

This particular turn of events in the anti-Schulte campaign began to worry some people high up in Army intelligence. To accuse a suspect German was one thing; to implicate highly placed American citizens in some sort of conspiracy was not only seriously incorrect but also politically dangerous. So they refused to cooperate, and the Justice Department lost its battle. Schulte did talk to the investigators for eleven days in Zurich. The Justice Department realized that he would be a key witness for the Swiss in the forthcoming trial over the conflicting claims to Giesche's Polish assets, and therefore tried to blacken his image.

He got his visa at long last but was again subpoenaed and interrogated in New York in February and March 1948. Justice still wanted to prove that he had been a Nazi, but the only evidence the officials were able to find supported Schulte's claim that he had deceived the Nazi government all along. This was the last thing that the Department of Justice wanted to hear.

In May 1951 Schulte received a letter at his hotel from Thomas B. Stauffer. Five years earlier Stauffer had expressed reservations about denazifying Schulte and had held up his clearance for a major government post, but Schulte had never learned what took place behind the scenes. Now Stauffer, who had become a Foreign Service officer, was in trouble himself. A former official from the Labor Division of OMGUS had accused him of being "soft" on Communism and Communists. There was really no evidence for the charge. Shortly after the war Stauffer had said that he did not favor the U.S. going on to fight the Soviet Union, but that was established American policy. Another factor may have weighed against Stauffer: during the war he had worked under Jürgen Kuczynski on the United States Strategic Bombing Survey, and after the fighting stopped Kuczynski had worked briefly for OMGUS. It later became known that Kuczynski was a committed Marxist whose sister was a KGB agent. At the time of Senator Joseph McCarthy's witchhunts for Communists, Stauffer now found his career in jeopardy. The State Department abruptly recalled him to Washington and subjected him to a loyalty hearing. Stauffer needed to prove that he was no Communist or Communist sympathizer, and Schulte was one of those he contacted to ask for help.

The irony was exquisite. Schulte had failed to satisfy American officials in Germany that he was not a Nazi. Now he responded to Stauffer with an allusion to his own experience: "It is not so easy to prove anything negative, nevertheless I have prepared a statement that I hope should help you to overcome the trouble if such a paper can help." Schulte enclosed a notarized statement clearing Stauffer of even the "tiniest sign" of sympathy for the Soviet system. Schulte wrote that he had looked upon Stauffer as a man of "absolutely bourgeois origin" at the beginning of a promising career in public service.* It was a typically generous gesture.

In 1960 the United States government reached an agreement with Poland over claims by American citizens whose property had been seized by Poland. The Polish government agreed to pay two million dollars a year for twenty years as settlement of all American claims, which had totaled several hundred million dollars. In the end, compensation for the Silesian-American Corporation property amounted to a few hundred thousand dollars per year for twenty years, divided among the Swiss, Anaconda, Harriman, and the United States Treasury. But by 1960 Eduard Schulte's service to the U.S. had been long forgotten.

. . .

Aristotle noted that nothing grows old as quickly as gratitude. Students of history and human nature should not be particularly surprised by the treatment meted out by American officials to Eduard Schulte. Bureaucracies frequently engage in perfectly senseless activities, simply because those they employ have to be kept busy. But it is also true that some activities are more ludicrous than others.

When Washington bureaucrats engaged in their campaign against Schulte, they were facing urgent major challenges, such as a need to build a new democratic order in Germany and to devise a concomitant program for economic assistance. Quite a few notorious war criminals were still at large or had not yet been brought to trial. Yet American officials devoted a considerable amount of time and effort to the persecution of a dedicated anti-Nazi, Eduard Schulte, a campaign that—quite apart from all ingratitude—was an act of truly monumental stupidity. It was bound to fail, and no benefit could possibly have accrued from it to the American treasury. The postwar treatment of Schulte ought to be included in textbooks as a near-perfect illustration of a runaway bureaucracy.

---

* Stauffer was eventually cleared of the charges, but his Foreign Service career ended for unrelated reasons not long after the hearings.

CHAPTER ELEVEN

Epilogue

Eduard Schulte was in his middle fifties when he returned to Switzerland in 1946, and he was to spend the rest of his life there. At first he seemed to be still full of ideas and energy, and his decision to settle in Zurich rather than Hamburg, Frankfurt, or Munich must have come as a surprise to his friends. If the Americans did not want him and if a political career was not to his taste, he could still have played a major role in private industry or banking.* There were few men with such vision, experience, and connections. It was of course at Giesche that he had learned almost everything he knew, but

---

* Schulte's company, Giesche, did not survive as a major corporation after 1945. Silesia was turned over to Poland, and with it went most of Giesche's assets. The Russians pulled down what was left of Giesche's zinc refinery in Magdeburg and carted it off to the Soviet Union.

the transition to some other industrial enterprise would not
have been too difficult. His expertise was, after all, not in mining per se, but in big business, in high finance, in running a
major organization. He was adaptable; in some respects he was
a forerunner of the builders of modern corporations with their
diversified operations. True, these were not yet the years of the
economic miracle; Germany was still a desperately poor country, and working and living conditions were difficult, to say the
least. But this would not have deterred Schulte; it might even
have served as a challenge.

The reasons he did not return were in part political. While
he still had many close friends in Germany, there were also
those whose pro-Nazi past he could not forgive. They might not
have forgiven him either, if they learned what he had done.
Then there was Doris, the woman whom he had known since
before the war, and whom he would marry in 1956, after
Clara's death the previous year. Doris had no wish to live in
Germany, not least because she was Jewish.

Schulte still found it difficult to settle down, and sometimes, at very short notice, he would go on a business trip—not
because his presence in Frankfurt or Stuttgart was absolutely
necessary, but because he missed the movement and the action.

But after a while it became clear that some of the ambition
of old had left him. For weeks he would be quite happy to prepare the balance sheets in Doris's small boutique. His old
friends who had known him as an entrepreneur on the grand
scale were stunned and a little saddened. Some poked fun at
him. Was it possible that this captain of industry had found
fulfillment in doing a job of a junior accountant? At other
times he would be seen window-shopping in the Bahnhofstrasse, or walking on the fashionable lakeside promenade
known in Zurich as the "gold coast." He became a familiar figure among those strolling on the terraces and quays designed
by Buerkli, the city's architect of the last century, watching the
little steamers plying the lake, or, if he turned around, the river
Limmat and the old city of Zurich. It was the part of town he
liked best, the buildings in imposing Biedermeier style, such as
his favorite Baur-au-Lac. Sometimes he would take the tram
and the funicular and go up to the Dolder and walk in the forest, listening to the blackbirds and the woodpeckers. He had always liked the sights and smells of the forest, even if his hunting
days were now over.

He still had a desk in Jacques Rosenstein's Zurich office.

People would call on him and ask for his advice. He became interested in various projects submitted to him. The American ships that brought grain to Europe under the Marshall Plan returned empty, and it occurred to Schulte that it might be a good idea to load them with peat, which was in demand in America. Nothing seems to have come of this project. He was involved in the building of power plants in southwest Germany and the Saar, and in the design of a revolutionary new cigarette filter. But this latter project, too, was less than a full success. Schulte had an interest in the production of rayon and cellulose and cooperated with the Clavels of Basel. He worked on some occasions with Arthur Burkhardt, who had for a time been a valued associate at Giesche and who had become director of the Württemberg Metal Factories, an important corporation. On other occasions he collaborated with Zurich and Basel financiers.

Some of these ventures prospered; a power plant he helped to build in the early 1960s was one of the biggest (220 megawatts) and most expensive at the time. He was also involved in the development of two new concepts in postwar Germany—shopping centers and motels. Other ventures were failures. The single-minded concentration, the tremendous drive he had once possessed, were no longer there. He was cautious, investing only a modest part of his capital in these speculative ventures, like a highly disciplined gambler who never exceeds a certain ceiling in his stakes. Schulte was rich enough to have lived comfortably without lifting a finger. But he needed the stimulus of dealing with others, the excitement of the business trips and the conferences, as a kind of occupational therapy against boredom.

With all this, he was not bitter or disappointed. Günter Schwerin, a young German-American businessman, a native of Breslau and a grandson of the scientist Paul Ehrlich, saw him occasionally in Zurich during this period. Schwerin described him later as a happy man, an amusing conversationalist, an extrovert with a great zest for life. Another old friend who came to see him on business from time to time was Gottfried Treviranus, who had been a Cabinet Minister in the Brüning government in 1930; like Schulte, he had had to escape from Nazi Germany.

Was he afraid of returning to Germany, apprehensive that his pro-Allied activities would be held against him? The idea probably crossed his mind, but it cannot have been a decisive consideration; after all, Giesche's legal counsel in the postwar period was Paul Leverkühn, who had been the most prominent defector to the Americans from the Abwehr during the Second World War.

Schulte continued to dabble in various business ventures until well after his seventieth birthday; then, in a letter to his son, Ruprecht, he announced that he would gradually disengage himself.

Schulte's first marriage had come to an end when he decided to return to Berlin after the end of the war. Clara chose to go back to West Germany in 1946, rather than stay on in Zurich. She had lived a withdrawn life for a long time. After the death of her elder son her depression had deepened, and her dependence on sleeping pills and other drugs had grown more pronounced. On her return to Germany she moved first to Munich and later lived with the family of a Breslau physician, Dr. Nissen. She was aware of her husband's relationship with Doris, but even this was apparently not the main motive when she decided that the time had come for a parting of the ways. There was no showdown, no scenes, no bitter recrimination. It was a case of two human beings very different in character who had drifted apart over the years. Schulte continued to take care of Clara's business affairs up to the time of her death in November 1955.

Without informing his family and friends, Schulte married Doris in 1956. They moved into an apartment in the Alfred Escher Strasse, not far from the lake and his favorite promenade, where he was to spend the last decade of his life.* Ruprecht had left for the United States in 1950 after graduating from Zurich Polytechnic. A few months after the end of the war he had met Hazel, an American girl, a native of Connecticut, who worked at the U.S. Consulate General in Zurich. After a short courtship they got married in the city. Schulte's first two grandchildren were born in Zurich. But after Ruprecht and Hazel emigrated to America in 1950, he was not to see his grandchildren again.

---

* Alfred Escher was the greatest entrepreneur in the history of Zurich. There is a statue commemorating him in front of the main railway station. Some curious parallels are to be found between him and Schulte. Escher's achievements were enormous. He founded one of the greatest Swiss banks, and it was owing to him more than anyone else that the St. Gotthard tunnel was built. But as a result of political quarrels with his fellow citizens, he found himself removed from all major political positions toward the end of his life, and when the St. Gotthard tunnel was inaugurated, he was not even invited to the ceremony.

Schulte's life in Zurich followed a well-defined routine, including daily constitutionals. It was only after his seventy-first birthday in 1962 that Schulte really began to slow down. Walking became more difficult, and he would grumble about his health, which he had seldom done before. Doris persuaded him to take holiday in Flims, Schulz Tarasp, and other such places. He accompanied her without enthusiasm; he had never liked the idleness of a stay at a resort. In the summer of 1965 Ruprecht came for a visit, the first meeting between father and son in fifteen years. Eduard no longer took walks. Instead, he discussed the problems of hotel management with the local dignitaries and offered them free advice.

For some time he suffered from stomach pains. Following exploratory surgery in 1965, the doctors found an inoperable cancer of the stomach. Schulte died in Zurich in January 1966, two days after his seventy-fifth birthday. There was a short, private ceremony on January 10 at the Zurich crematorium. Another small gathering took place a few days later when he was buried in the family vault in Düsseldorf. The sun was shining, and an icy cold wind was blowing, when some of his close relatives and friends came to pay him their last respects.

There was one short death announcement in the newspaper. As far as the media were concerned, Schulte had not been an important man. His widow received letters of condolence from Sagalowitz and Riegner recalling his stand for the cause of freedom and humanity and praising the great courage he had shown. And that was all. There were no messages from the Allied governments or from Bonn, no wreaths from the Swiss or from Jewish organizations. Only a handful of people had ever known about Schulte's wartime activities. Some of these had died; others had forgotten or were no longer in positions of influence. Schulte, in any case, had not wanted much fuss to be made of what he had done.

· · ·

Twenty years have passed since the death of Eduard Schulte and more than forty since the end of the Second World War. For new generations Nazism and the war belong to the distant past, even though they tend to come up frequently in books, movies, and television programs, a mysterious subject of horrible fascination.

Zurich, where Schulte lived for the last two decades of his life, is still half village, half metropolitan center. The Bahnhofstrasse is still the same; shops there seldom change hands. The bank managers complain about bad debts and the world situation in general, but there is reason to believe that they are doing at least as well as in the past. The Baur-au-Lac looks as prosperous as ever. On sunny afternoons many couples can be seen having their tea on the lawn in front of the hotel. The head porter is busy welcoming new arrivals, his uniform unchanged since the days when he welcomed Schulte.

The same statues stand on the lakeside promenade, and there are still boats on the lake, mountains in the distance, and white birds circling over the Limmat. Time seems to have stood still since Eduard Schulte used to stroll there.

Zurich is no longer an island of peace in a world at war. Peace has now prevailed in Europe for more consecutive decades than ever before in its troubled history. Conflicts among the governments now concern the price of cheese and quotas for steel production. The borders once so strictly guarded hardly exist anymore. The traveler is whisked through controls by impatient customs and frontier police who have better things to do than take an interest in his passport.

Two new German states have come into being and two new societies. They are so different from the Nazi regime that Germans who did not live through the dark era find it extremely difficult to understand the events that took place in their country in the 1930s and 1940s. Europe is no longer the political and cultural center of the world. It has almost miraculously recovered from the ravages of the war, but the political center of gravity has moved elsewhere.

The Jews have disappeared from Germany, except for a few thousand who returned after the war. The same is true with regard to Poland, Czechoslovakia, Austria, Hungary, and most other European countries except France and Britain. There are now museums in Auschwitz, Dachau, and Bergen-Belsen. Historians debate why Schulte's message was ignored, and how many Jews could have been saved if someone had paid attention to it. The obtuseness and indifference of 1942 remain riddles despite all the political and psychological explanations.

Katowice and Breslau (now Wroclaw), where in the latter city Schulte had his headquarters for many years, have been rebuilt. They are now purely Polish cities. The coal and zinc mines that once belonged to Giesche still operate. There is in fact considerable demand for the output of the coal mines be-

cause of the low sulfuric content of this coal. The new bosses
have serious labor problems. Both Katowice and Wroclaw are
hotbeds of Solidarity, the Polish workers' union. The workers at
the former Giesche plants have manifested their discontent in
various ways, including even a strike.

Schulte's house in the fashionable southern suburb of Breslau no longer exists. The whole southern part of the city was destroyed in the fighting during the last months of the war. Once
a name to reckon with, Giesche is now known only to some retired managers. All that remains of the old empire is a little factory somewhere in West Germany producing window frames.
Like most German corporations operating in the east before
1945, Giesche did not make the transition after 1945: the losses
it suffered were too great.

Recently, on a bitterly cold and dark January morning, we
went to East Berlin in the steps of Eduard Schulte. In the
Georgenstrasse we looked in vain for the Coburger Hof, the
hotel that had been Schulte's headquarters for many years. But
there were no old buildings left except for a ruin or two. Only a
few new houses have been built since the war. Passersby expressed astonishment; what was there to photograph in this
unremarkable street?

Friedrichstrasse has been widened, and a sign informed us
that Friedrich Engels lived there in 1841 and 1842, when he did
his military service. We passed the House of (East) German
Journalists and the "Press Café" and turned into Unter den
Linden where new linden trees have been planted in rows of
four. It will be a long time before they reach the size of the old
trees. The former German Bank, where Schulte spent many
hours in search of loans, is now the East German Ministry of
the Interior. The famous military museum, the Zeughaus,
serves now as the Museum of German History. The State
Opera continues to function, and even the Opera Café has
been revived. There is an interesting mix of statues—Sophocles
and Aristophanes in front of the opera house, Gneisenau and
Yorck, the heroes of the patriotic war of 1813, in front of the
café: something for everyone, as the theater director says (freely
translated) in the prologue to Goethe's *Faust*.

The Soviet Embassy with its various branches, such as In-
tourist, Aeroflot, and Novosti, the news agency, looms large.
The Brandenburg Gate, sixty-five meters wide, has again become a major tourist attraction. For years it was considered to
be a symbol of Prussian militarism, but more recently the East

Germans have discovered that those who built it in the late eighteenth century wanted it as a memorial to peace. And it is certainly the case that the famous chariot on top of the gate is the chariot of the goddess of peace, drawn by cherubim and preceded by allegorical figures representing wisdom, harmony, heroism, and other unexceptionable themes.

Has peace come? In the Bendlerstrasse, the former Ministry of War and armed forces headquarters, where Schulte's cousin Hermann of the Abwehr worked, they now make perfumes, though not of the highest quality. But it is also true that many of the people seen in the streets are in uniform. It is hard to imagine that this general neighborhood was once the very heart of one of the largest and most important cities in the world, that there were crowds in these streets at almost any time of day and night.

The Anhalter Bahnhof is just inside the Western sector, but here no train has arrived or departed for decades: grass and shrubs grow on the tracks, birds nest in the waiting rooms, an echo of rural pleasures in the middle of the big city. It was from the Anhalt station that Schulte left Berlin in December 1943, a few steps ahead of the Gestapo. Nearby is the Chancellery, where, in the famous Bunker, Hitler committed suicide in April 1945. The visitor will look for the Bunker in vain. It has not been kept as a tourist attraction; every trace has been obliterated.

Germany is now better off than ever before, but a terrible price is still being paid, as Schulte foresaw, for the mad policies of the Nazis. The eastern territories have been lost, one thousand years of German history have been unmade, and the rest of the country has been divided. Will the division ever be overcome? Perhaps, but certainly not in the foreseeable future.

It has been easy to do away with the physical remains of Nazi rule, but far more difficult to come to terms with some of the indirect, less tangible consequences of that era. The country had to be denazified. There were no precedents in history for a process of this kind, and it was perhaps not surprising that Allied policy was inconsistent and often ineffective. Once denazification had ended, many problems still remained relating to the Third Reich. Some of these questions were moral or political, others financial or administrative. Should former Nazis receive state pensions guaranteed to civil servants according to the law (Paragraph 131 of the Basic Law)? What was to become of the property of Nazi leaders; were those who had lost all or most of their property as a result of the war entitled to restitution (*Lastenausgleich*)?

General laws can never do justice to the merits of individual cases. The German courts made a genuine attempt in most cases to reach an equitable solution. Sometimes their objectivity was a little suspect, and in other cases their verdicts were unjust. According to the law, everyone who had held office on May 8, 1945, was entitled to a pension; so were his (or her) heirs. But this means that Gestapo officials were also entitled, whereupon it was hastily decided to exempt them. But the widow of Reinhard Heydrich, the man who had been the head of the Main State Security Office, and thus in charge of the Gestapo, managed to get her pension.

Anyone lucky enough to be transferred in time from the Gestapo to another, less notorious employer had his service in the Gestapo taken into account "if he behaved correctly." How did one behave correctly in the service of the Gestapo? The West German legislature gave no clear guidance to the courts. Some of the leading Nazis or their widows (such as Mrs. Göring) got pensions.

Some anti-Nazis who had been arrested for actively opposing Hitler got nothing, but deputy ministers or generals who had blindly obeyed Hitler to the very end received substantial pensions. It was not that the judges in postwar Germany wanted to punish the anti-Nazis and reward Hitler's followers—though some such instances did occur—it was rather a case of justice meted out by a bureaucracy that disregarded the fact that something extraordinary and unprecedented had taken place in Germany. In that situation, obedience to authority and simple performance of duties were no longer virtues.

In December 1970, Ruprecht and Doris Schulte applied to a Berlin court for certain benefits under the regulations as the heirs of someone who had suffered losses in the eastern territories. Their application entailed a re-examination of Schulte's wartime activities. The court's verdict is of interest not for its legal merit, but because of its political arguments. The court said that by passing on information to the Allies, Eduard Schulte had committed a crime "punishable according to the law of every country." Furthermore, such action in no way manifested opposition to the Nazi regime.

Even if the motive for acting as an agent had
been a hostile attitude to Nazism, it would not
have been a political deed. Only such a deed
could be interpreted as opposition to Nazism.
Schulte's flight in 1943 was therefore not a political escape but the act of an agent who
wanted to escape arrest and punishment.

The judges expressed indignation at Schulte's activities, which
they said had contributed to one outcome of the war—the expulsion of Germans from eastern Germany—and caused damage to those Germans as a result. Schulte had committed
criminal acts and succeeded in escaping punishment; his heirs
certainly were not entitled to any benefits under the law. The
application was dismissed.

How difficult was it until quite recently for many Germans
to come to terms with the past of their country! For some, the
actions of a man such as Schulte are a problem to this very day.
A man who risked his life to warn Hitler's victims is regarded
by some as a criminal, as an enemy of the nation, who must
bear part of the responsibility for the expulsion of the Germans
from the territories occupied by the Poles. The answer to accu-
sations of this kind is only too obvious. If there had been more
people like Schulte, if more had shown such courage, there
would have been no war, or it would have been considerably
shorter. Then there would have been no expulsion of Germans
from the east, and Breslau, Stettin, and Königsberg would still
be German cities.

·   ·   ·

Among the very few documents found in Schulte's papers
after his death was the copy of an article published on November 20, 1952, in the *Deutsche Juristenzeitung*, the main organ of
the legal profession in Germany. It concerned the men and
women of the German resistance: were they heroes or traitors?
The article had been provoked by the trial of a former Nazi officer, Otto Remer, who had publicly attacked the men of July
20, 1944, as criminals and traitors. He was brought to trial for
slander.

Remer, though only a major in 1944, had been in charge of
a guard battalion in Berlin and thus in a strategic position. For
a few decisive minutes he played a role of historical impor-

tance. Soon after the attempt against Hitler's life, Dr. Goebbels asked Remer to arrest the leaders of the coup. He obeyed the Nazi minister of propaganda rather than his own superiors, who were participants in the plot. Major Remer thus helped to prolong the war by almost a year, for which service Hitler made him a general. As a result, hundreds of thousands of Germans died, and it is difficult even to estimate the extent of damage that was caused. After the war Remer became the leader of a neo-Nazi party. Later he vanished in an Arab country. He re-emerged in the early 1980s in West Germany, this time as an advocate of a German alliance with the Soviet Union.

The legal commentator was not so much interested in Major Remer as in the Brunswick judges who had passed judgment on him. Remer's lawyers had argued that while the men of July 20, 1944, had not been criminals, those few among them who had been in contact with the enemy had certainly committed a crime. This argument was in part accepted by the court. The legal commentator rightly noted that the court's attitude was dangerous, for it cast doubts on the legitimacy of the democratic order that had been built on the ruins of the Third Reich.

This was not, of course, an issue for a court to decide. Judges deal with legal issues, whereas the attempt to overthrow the Nazi regime was not a legal but a political matter, and thus beyond the competence of jurists. The judges in Brunswick were not neo-Nazis, nor were those who issued the verdict on the Schultes' claims for reparations in Berlin in 1970. They simply found it difficult to accept that men such as Schulte had acted as true patriots, and that those who had obeyed the Nazi leaders had betrayed their country. They could not admit that the great majority had been wrong, that the deaths of so many fathers, brothers, and sons had been in vain. It is exceedingly difficult to accept that the supreme sacrifice of millions might have been unnecessary—or worse, in the service of a bad cause.

What could and should a young German have done in 1940—for example, someone like Wolfgang Schulte? He was not a fanatic, not a member of the Nazi Party, nor particularly well informed—the Nazi propaganda machine saw to that. His dreams were not about a Germany dominating the European Continent and about the extermination of "inferior races." He would have been horrified if he had known the full truth. He was just doing his duty, obeying orders, as soldiers do. His dreams were about his personal future, his girl friend, traveling abroad, perhaps rowing down a river on a Sunday afternoon. He fought because everyone else did, because one could not let down one's own comrades. Should he have surrendered without a struggle? This would have been cowardly, and furthermore it is not always that easy to surrender. In short, young Germans were trapped.

It is not difficult to find mitigating circumstances for this generation. It is more difficult to find excuses for their elders and betters, the German elite, the generals and diplomats, the economic and cultural leaders. They failed to resist when resistance had a chance of success.

Even the German resistance failed for the most part to grasp the situation properly. Most of its members were preoccupied with discussing the future of post-Nazi Germany. Only a few, such as Oster or Stauffenberg, tackled the basic question of how to remove the dictator and his henchmen. Those in the resistance recognized a responsibility to Europe, to mankind, to universal human values. But for too many of them, this responsibility clashed with a reluctance to "inform," and thus to harm Germany. How anyone could have done more harm to Germany than Hitler is hard to imagine. But even among the German resistance there was a sort of code of honor, a loyalty to Germany. It was, of course, totally out of place in a confrontation with gangsters. Except for a few, those in the German resistance failed to understand that in fighting a ruthless tyranny, they were justified in using any means at their disposal. Schulte was one of those few who saw that there was a chance to overthrow Hitler only with outside help, and that cooperation with the Allies might present aesthetic or psychological problems, but that it was certainly no moral dilemma.

• • •

A few of the main figures in the story of Dr. Eduard Schulte survive. Doris, Schulte's second wife, lives in a hotel on a mountain overlooking Zurich; she seldom leaves her room these days. Ruprecht Schulte has now reached retirement and recently achieved an old dream—to build a house according to his own design in one of the most attractive small towns in the mountains of southern California. His children and grandchildren (Eduard Schulte's great-grandchildren) are dispersed all over the English-speaking world—from Alaska to a farm in

Shropshire, England. In a charming small town in Westphalia lives Schulte's younger brother, Oskar; it happens to be the town in which Gisevius was born. He is now well into his nineties but speaks of his older brother, whom he felt very close to, with great fondness. He remembers many details about their parental home in Düsseldorf, their common joys and sorrows in childhood and later years. He was the regional chief forester, and this vigorous old man worries about the sad fate of the German forests as deeply as the young German ecologists many decades his junior.

Unless he is traveling, Gerhart Riegner can still be found in his office in Geneva, working on his memoirs. He is retired but in fact as busy as ever before. Sagalowitz, Rosenstein, Koppelmann, as well as most of the German industrialists and generals of Schulte's generation, passed away long ago. Of his closest collaborators, Dr. Albrecht Jung, formerly the legal adviser of Giesche, makes his home in Bad Homburg, near Frankfurt. We went to see Dr. Arthur Burkhardt (known at one time as the "Zinc Pope" of Germany), once Schulte's aide, in his apartment in a beautiful suburb of Stuttgart. Both gentlemen remember Schulte well and speak of him with admiration. We talked to Dr. Alfred Schaefer, who was one of Schulte's main Swiss contacts, at his house on the shores of Lake Zurich. Not far from him on a fine estate lives Dr. Messner, the Swiss industrialist and metallurgist who helped to solve the Schulte mystery. Dr. Eduard Waetjen, who saved Schulte by warning him with a phone call, lives in a house on the slopes of Monte Verita in Ascona, Switzerland, not far from the Italian border. Ascona, once a picturesque, dreamy fishing village, has changed its character: it now resembles St. Tropez or Monte Carlo. In wartime Waetjen had translated Homer as an act of mental hygiene. He is now at work on a book on Heraclitus, the ancient Greek philosopher.

The last days of Hanke, the Breslau Gauleiter, are shrouded in mystery. Fortress Breslau was the one major German city that did not surrender before V-E Day. A few days earlier Hanke seized the personal helicopter of the general commanding Breslau's defense and disappeared. Some claim that he was killed by Czech partisans while he was on his way to one of the few German Army groups still intact. But it is also possible that he ended his days under an assumed identity somewhere, perhaps in Paraguay or Bolivia. He certainly lived up to Hitler's praise—"the very best of our Gauleiters."

Hanke's friend Otto Fitzner, also Schulte's close colleague and political antipode, was captured by the Poles at the end of the war. They remembered his role during the occupation and sent him to work in a coal mine. This he probably minded less—it was after all his chosen profession—than the fact that the Poles whom he despised were now the masters. He could not accept the new situation, he called the new masters "pigs," and they beat him to death in one of the mines. Hermann Schulte, Eduard's cousin, close friend, and major source of information, was arrested by the Allies after the war but was released within a few months. He died not long ago, in his nineties, in Düsseldorf.

So much then for the fate of those who were involved at one stage or another in the case of Eduard Schulte. But what about the deeper issues of loyalty and treason and civic courage? They will of course be discussed long after the last individual who appeared in this story has passed away. Eduard Schulte was not a man in the saintly mold. In his strength and weaknesses he was all too human. He was a businessman and manager of genius, but this alone would hardly have been sufficient reason to tell the story of his life, for such talents occur in any age and society. He did possess that lonely kind of courage which is rare in any age and which (as William James once observed) is the kind of valor to which the monuments of nations should most of all be reared.*

---

* William James, "Oration at the Exercises in the Boston Music Hall, May 31, 1897, Upon the Unveiling of the [Robert Gould] Shaw Monument," in *Memories and Studies* (New York, 1911), 57.

Afterword

PART I by Walter Laqueur

Why wasn't the identity of the mysterious messenger discovered before? And how was it eventually unveiled? Although the identity remained for many years one of the best-kept secrets of the Second World War, certain details were made public while Schulte was still in Germany. The *Congress Weekly*, a publication of the American Jewish Congress, reported in its issue of December 4, 1942, that the information about the mass murder of the Jews had been communicated by a German with excellent connections with the top Nazi leadership, and that it had emanated from Switzerland. The same report also said that this German source had previously provided correct information on military matters. This should have been enough to alarm the Gestapo, but Gestapo officials were apparently not in the habit of reading foreign Jewish newspapers in a systematic way. There is no evidence that a search for the leak was initiated. Even after the Nazi authorities became suspicious of Schulte, they did not learn of his humanitarian initiative to save Europe's remaining Jews.

After 1945 the identity of the mysterious messenger remained unknown. As the full extent of the Holocaust became widely known, the fact that six million Jews had been murdered had a shocking, then numbing, effect. In Germany most people preferred to avoid the subject. Even in the West there was little inclination in the early postwar period to inquire whether there had been early warnings about the catastrophe, and whether anyone had paid attention to them.

On several occasions Riegner's telegram to Rabbi Stephen Wise was mentioned. In his diaries, excerpts of which were

published in 1947, former Secretary of the Treasury Henry
Morgenthau, Jr., highlighted the significance of Riegner's message in mobilizing American Jewish leaders to press the United
States government to take action against Nazi killings. That
telegram had revealed that the report about the Final Solution
came from someone with connections with highest German authorities. Stephen Wise mentioned the telegram and the anti-
Nazi industrialist in his memoirs. But there were no further
clues to his identity or his sources of information. The episode
did not come up in the Nuremberg trials or the Eichmann trial
in Israel more than a decade later.

In the 1950s systematic study of the mass murder began.
The first works to become accepted as standard, Gerald Reit-
linger's *The Final Solution* and Raul Hilberg's massive *The Destruction of the European Jews,* did not expand what already had
been known about the anti-Nazi industrialist. They were, after
all, concerned with those who had decided upon and carried
out the killing, not with those who had tried to prevent it. In
the 1960s Arthur Morse, a journalist, became interested in why
the United States had not done more to stop the Holocaust or
rescue those who could be saved. Morse got access to previously
classified State Department files and to Sumner Welles's private papers, which include a letter from Leland Harrison to
Welles about the German industrialist—but no name. Morse
also interviewed Riegner himself, but Riegner had given his
word of honor not to reveal the man's name. (He continues to this day to refuse to name his source.) First in a
1967 article in *Look* magazine and then in his book *While
Six Million Died* (1968), Morse revealed that Riegner had given
Leland Harrison the industrialist's name in a sealed envelope.
But Morse did not find the envelope or solve the mystery.
He did, however, establish that the industrialist's firm had
employed at least thirty thousand people—a major German
corporation.

After Morse's detailed account of some of the key events,
other historians besieged Riegner for the name. Was it not time
to honor the courage of a great humanitarian? It was to no
avail. The other men who might have identified Schulte as the
mysterious messenger—Koppelmann, Sagalowitz, Lichtheim,
and Leland Harrison—had all died by then. The messenger's
name seemed destined to fade into the crevices of the past.

In the late 1970s I gave a lecture in New York on how the
facts about the Holocaust first became known outside Ger-

many. The Nazis had treated the Final Solution as a state secret of the highest order, and the story of how and when the secret leaked out seemed both fascinating and significant. The
lecture soon became a book. In the course of this research I too
interviewed Riegner, who, as on previous occasions, was extremely helpful—except on one matter, the name of the mysterious messenger. I was intrigued. If Riegner's word of honor
was the only reason why the man's name still should be kept
secret, there might be other ways of solving the mystery and
honoring a historical figure.

A first search of the State Department records in the National Archives produced no results because Harrison had not
forwarded the name to Washington. But the once-sealed envelope with the name was also missing from Harrison's personal
papers, kept in the Library of Congress, but not yet cataloged.
Perhaps the name was passed on to OSS in 1942—many of the
OSS records remained classified. Or perhaps it had been lost or
destroyed. There was no quick solution in Washington.

It was no easy matter to find out which of the major German industrialists had visited Switzerland during the war. A
study of the list of visas granted by Swiss authorities in 1942
might have produced a clue, but I was told in the Swiss National Archives in Bern that the visa records maintained by the
Swiss Legation in Berlin and the Swiss border police either no
longer existed or were not accessible.

This greatly complicated the search. Many of the major industrialists of that period were no longer alive. And even if it
could be shown that a certain industrialist had been in Switzerland in July 1942, it did not follow that the traveler had
been in a position to know state secrets of the highest order, had
been in contact with Jewish representatives, and had actually
passed on the information to Jewish friends. Even the least
likely candidate on the list might have had a good friend or a
close relative in a key position in the party or the government,
but this could not be proved.

I also had to consider the possibility that the term "industrialist" was a cover used to mislead the Nazis in case the information leaked out. Perhaps the messenger was really a
journalist specializing in business affairs, or a diplomat, or
some other official German emissary engaged in trade or financial negotiations. There were a great many such people who
had visited Switzerland during the war. Many of them had
talked to Swiss acquaintances about conditions in Germany.

More than a few people in Switzerland whom I consulted believed that the source was either a renegade diplomat or a composite figure—that the Riegner telegram was based on a digest of information from several sources. My search in the German archives produced an almost endless list of possibilities.

Through an accident I established that the man's name began with the letter *S*. At the time, this did not help very much, for *S* is the most common initial for German last names. A great many Schmidts, Schoellers, Strausses, and Stumms had been to Basel, Zurich, and Bern during the war. I inquired among surviving German and Swiss industrialists whether they could give me any clues. I wrote dozens of letters and made scores of phone calls but without results.

Meanwhile, some other historians had reached the conclusion that Arthur Sommer was the mysterious messenger. Sommer was a German economist who had belonged to the circle of admirers of the German poet Stefan George. Another member of this circle was Count Claus von Stauffenberg, the brave officer who almost killed Hitler on July 20, 1944. Sommer served as an officer in the German Army and frequently visited Switzerland as a member of the permanent Swiss-German economic commission. He was not a Nazi, and from time to time he met with Jewish friends in Switzerland, including Professor Edgar Salin, a native of Frankfurt who taught economics in Basel. According to postwar evidence provided by Salin, Sommer sent Salin a letter in 1942 to the effect that extermination camps had been established in Eastern Europe to kill all European Jews (and also most Russian prisoners) by means of poison gas. Sommer requested that the information be relayed directly to Churchill and Roosevelt and suggested that the British Broadcasting Corporation should transmit daily warnings about the plan. Salin did not know how to reach Churchill or Roosevelt, but he contacted Thomas McKittrick, the American president of the Bank for International Settlements, which was located in Basel. McKittrick was in close contact with Leland Harrison and also passed information occasionally to OSS. But to this day no one has found a document indicating that McKittrick made use of the information from Salin. Nothing in Harrison's cables and letters to Washington mentions this particular source, even though Harrison did comment about other sources on the Final Solution.

The chief proponent of the Sommer-Salin-McKittrick connection was Dr. Haim Pazner (Posner), who had served as an assistant in the Jewish Agency for Palestine's office in Geneva during the war and who had once studied with Salin. Pazner also claimed that he too had been informed of the Final Solution by Salin. This thesis was mentioned in the preface to the Hebrew edition of Morse's book. It was interesting but wrong. Sommer was not the man behind the Riegner telegram, and even if he at one time or another told someone about the death camps, the information never reached Washington or London, or even Jewish circles in Switzerland.

In an article published in *Commentary* in March 1980 I wrote about my lengthy search for the industrialist's identity, my examining and discarding of various candidates. In one passage I noted that I had tried to imagine the kind of man who would accept the great risk of passing on such dangerous information in wartime.

> Obviously, he had to have been a man of firm beliefs, deeply convinced of the evil character of the Nazi regime, repelled by its inhuman policies. Would he have made a secret of his convictions? Possibly, but there was no certainty. I thought of him as a man who had seen a great deal of the world, and was in a position to compare, but also a person unlikely to attract attention, someone about whom even his closest collaborators, when faced with the evidence, would say: "Old S. could never have done it . . . True, he made a critical remark from time to time, but didn't we all?"

This was, as it later turned out, a fairly accurate description of Eduard Schulte.

The article produced more correspondence. It appeared that not a few German and Austrian industrialists had visited Switzerland during the war, passed on information about conditions in Germany, and might have warned the West about the Final Solution. Upon further examination, the candidates were all proved lacking in one respect or another.

In the summer of 1980, while visiting a friend in Zurich, I heard of Siegmund Hirsch, the former head of one of the largest metal enterprises in Germany specializing in copper. After emigrating from Germany, he had managed a much smaller firm in Egypt. Hirsch was then almost ninety-five years old, but in good spirit and full of stories. I chatted with him for a while and discussed various possibilities. Hirsch mentioned Dr. Messner of Zurich, a man of many parts: a professor of metallurgy of world renown, a widely respected consultant with many connections, a manager of a factory in Dornach. He had also served as a major in the Swiss Army during the war.

I made Messner's acquaintance and found him unfailingly helpful. In fact, Messner took a personal interest in the search. He had little doubt about the identity of the industrialist—it had to have been Schulte, managing director of Giesche in Breslau. He had not known Schulte very well, but he had heard much about him from one of Schulte's lieutenants, Arthur Burkhardt, who later became a major industrialist in his own right.

The name Schulte did not mean anything to me, although I had heard of Giesche's Heirs, one of the leading corporations in eastern Germany before the Second World War. In fact, on my way to school in Breslau I had to pass the Giesche offices every day. There had been a classmate of mine named Ruprecht Schulte whose father was an industrialist, but I recalled this only later.

When I received this information from Messner, my book *The Terrible Secret* was about to be published. There was just time to add a footnote in which Schulte and a few other names were mentioned as possibilities. But my search for the mysterious messenger had to end, for I had other commitments.

PART II by Richard Breitman

In the spring of 1980 I became fascinated by Walter Laqueur's article in *Commentary* about his search for the mysterious messenger. I had never met Laqueur, but as a specialist in German history, I knew of Laqueur's work in German and European history. It seemed a worthy challenge to pick up where Laqueur had left off.

I had already done some related research, for I was working with my colleague Alan Kraut on a study of American refugee policy and European Jewry during the Roosevelt years. I had previously read Arthur Morse's book and noted the role of the

German industrialist in getting news of the Final Solution to
Switzerland. Laqueur had added an additional clue—the letter
S—and had pointed the way to various research leads. Moreover, he had shown which avenues were not likely to produce
results too, which saved a lot of time for the next scholar.

For a study of American refugee policy it would have been
nice to fill in the name of the industialist, but Alan Kraut and I
had a great deal of research to do besides look for one man. We
made a couple of visits together to the National Archives in
search of the messenger without results.

Whether or not it was related to wartime American policies
toward European Jews, I also wanted to investigate ties maintained by anti-Nazi Germans with Allied intelligence. Perhaps
my research would produce a book about various Germans, the
mysterious messenger among them. My sabbatical in the fall of
1982 gave me enough time to do intensive research.

Laqueur had covered the German and Swiss possibilities as
well as anyone could. If the mystery could be solved, the key
lay in Washington, where I had the good fortune to live and
teach. I had checked Leland Harrison's papers in the Library
of Congress to make sure that Laqueur had not overlooked
anything. He had not, which took me back to the National Archives.

The main archives building is in downtown Washington
between Pennsylvania and Constitution avenues—a huge neo-
classical granite and limestone building, with giant Greco-
Roman columns on all four sides and an elaborate frieze on the
two sides with the largest bronze doors in the world. The National Archives building occupies a full block within view of
the Capitol, has twenty-one levels, three incompatible sets of
elevators, 196 stack areas, and a great deal of dust. One thing
that it is short of is windows; except for a fortunate few, most
employees and researchers do not see daylight. They are, in effect, miners burrowing into the past.

The key to the whole system are the archivists, usually
overworked and underpaid, but often with a feeling for history
and a great deal of experience with the records. If you show the
archivist that you are serious, persistent, and reasonable, you
will usually learn how to find what you want. But it takes time
and hard work poring through files sometimes untouched by
human hands for decades.

After some fruitless work in the diplomatic records, I re-
thought the problem. One thing that Laqueur had not men-

tioned in his article was the records of the American Legation
in Bern, which I knew to be stored at the Washington National
Records Center in Suitland, Maryland. If Riegner and Lichtheim had handed Leland Harrison a sealed envelope on October 22, 1942, with the messenger's name in it, the most logical
place for Harrison to keep it was not in his personal files, but in
his office files. It might have been removed later, withdrawn by
government classification experts, but it also might still be
there.

I found in the Bern files a great deal of fascinating information about Nazi Germany, the war, and American sources of
information in Switzerland, but I saw nothing about the October 22, 1942 meeting of Riegner and Lichtheim with Harrison.
In fact, there was very little about Nazi persecution of the Jews
in 1942 at all. I asked the archivist, David Pfeiffer, whether he
had given me all the boxes for Bern; he replied that he could
not even be certain of that. There was always a chance that he
would come across another box in a different storage area. But
he had given me everything that he knew of.

Reluctantly, I concluded that if there had been a special
Bern file on Nazi persecution of Jews in 1942, someone had
withdrawn it from the records, and that it now would be impossible to locate. The simplest, most direct way to solve the
mystery was blocked. I would have to think of something else.

From Suitland, I went back to the main archives building
downtown to check the OSS records and to consult with John
Taylor, the longtime archives expert on United States military
records. Taylor's disheveled desk was crowded with piles of
documents, and more piles of requests for documents and
scholars' inquiries. I quickly learned that this gruff but kindly
white-haired man had encyclopedic knowledge of the
sources—and not just those under his jurisdiction. His suggestions and advice were invaluable to me on numerous occasions.

Taylor confirmed that there were OSS secret intelligence
reports on information provided by anti-Nazi Germans, but I
would have two problems. First, OSS agents had virtually always removed the source names from their reports. And if they
failed, the declassifiers took the names out. Second, the OSS
file for Germany was immense, and the indexing system was
antiquated and inefficient.

I eventually found a couple of intelligence documents that
looked promising. Although they contained no names of informants, what was said about the sources matched what I al-

ready knew about the mysterious messenger. I put the documents into my own file marked "Mysterious Messenger." If all my assumptions about the new documents were correct, the messenger had a connection with Polish intelligence.

Perhaps Harrison had discussed the industrialist with other American Foreign Service officials in Switzerland, whose files were available at Suitland. I decided to go through all the records of the American consulates in Switzerland, to check out every possibility that the name had been mentioned to someone.

A month or so later I had worked my way to the Zurich records. I saw enough information there for several books, but nothing for the one I wanted to do. Wearily, I leafed through the 1945 records. This was almost three years after the industrialist's 1942 mission; there seemed to be virtually no chance of finding any related information here.

Suddenly, I came across a set of 1945 documents about an Eduard Schulte who had worked with Allied intelligence agencies during the war—the Poles, the French, the British, and the Americans. I had never heard the name before. The documents revealed that this man was a German who had been in touch with Dulles in Switzerland—and a great deal more. Schulte seemed to have been one of the major German informants for the Allies during the war, and he had fled from the Gestapo to Switzerland in December 1943. Dulles, it appeared, was recommending him for a job with the American military government in Berlin in 1945.

All of this was entirely new to me, and I immediately requested photocopies of the documents. I knew that I could use this information for a book on anti-Nazi Germans. But I did not yet know that Schulte was the mysterious messenger. In fact, nowhere in the file was there the slightest hint that Schulte was a German industrialist. His name began with *S*, but so did that of millions of other Germans. Still, the mysterious messenger was known to have provided intelligence on other occasions to the Allies, so Schulte was a possibility. I made a mental note to find out more about Eduard Schulte. Meanwhile, I went on looking for more direct clues.

I found names of German industrialists who had been in Switzerland during the war, some of whom had even passed information to the Allies. Each time I found a name that began with *S*, I came home in great excitement and announced to my wife that I had solved the mystery. Sometimes I told my col-

league Alan Kraut as well. Within a few days of each "discovery," following some more checking, my enthusiasm was damp-
ened—his firm was too small, he was not a top executive, he
had not been in Switzerland at the right time, etc.

Meanwhile, I tried to check out Eduard Schulte too, but I
ran into difficulties. He was not mentioned in any of the works
on wartime espionage. I consulted Laqueur's article in *Commentary,* which had mentioned a good many German industrialists,
but Schulte was not among them. I looked again at Laqueur's
book *The Terrible Secret,* which I had read previously. Schulte
was not mentioned in the text or listed in the index. I neglected
to check all the footnotes—an error that caused me a great deal
of additional work. I could have learned by reading the tiny
print at the bottom of page 100 that Eduard Schulte was an
important German industrialist.

Instead, I went back to the primary sources—works published in Nazi Germany. There was only one edition of *Wer
ist's?,* the German version of *Who's Who,* published during the
Nazi era. The copy in the Library of Congress was missing. I
went out to the University of Maryland library in College Park
to check out Schulte and several other candidates. Schulte's
name did not appear in the book. Either he was not very important or he was very shy of publicity.

Then I contacted Henry Turner at Yale, a specialist in
German business history, whom I had studied under as an un-
dergraduate. Turner told me that there was a directory of German business executives published in 1940–42. If Schulte was
an important German industrialist, he would certainly be listed
there. Again, the Library of Congress copy was missing; several
search requests produced no results. I put Schulte on hold.

In February 1983 Alan Kraut and I read in the *Washington
Post* that Gerhart Riegner was in the U.S. We wanted to interview him for our study on refugee policy and because of the
mysterious messenger. On February 10 we met Riegner in the
New York office of the World Jewish Congress. After we talked
about Riegner's wartime efforts to alert the world about Nazi
killings, we reached the subject of the messenger. Riegner said
that he was a tall man, a convinced democrat, and a "captain"
in the world of industry. Riegner confirmed the accuracy of
what Laqueur had written about the man—his name began
with *S,* his firm employed at least thirty thousand people, he
supplied information to the Allies. Today we would not recog-

nize the industrialist's name, Riegner said, but at the time the man was quite well known. He would not say more than that.

By this time I had crossed off all my S names but three—Schulte; Willy Schlossstein, an official of the Bosch electrical concern; and Hermann Schlosser, managing director of a German chemical firm. I was about to send off inquiries to Germany, and I was leaning toward Schlossstein. Impulsively, I told Riegner that I thought I knew who the man was. Somewhat taken aback, Riegner warned that others before me had claimed to have solved the mystery and had been wrong. We agreed to notify him before we published the man's identity.

Schlossstein turned out to be too junior an official to qualifiy as a "captain" of industry, which left only Schlosser and Schulte. In April I visited friends and relatives in the Boston area and conducted some research at Harvard University, where I had gone to graduate school. I knew that Harvard's Widener Library, a treasure-house for scholars, would certainly have the German business directory that had been missing from the Library of Congress. I was not disappointed. I opened the huge dusty red cover of the business directory to find that Eduard Schulte was the managing director of a large German corporation, and that he served on the board of trustees of seven other corporations. Truly, he was a captain of industry.

As I drove back from Cambridge to Washington on April 20, 1983, I weighed the merits of the two candidates. The odds now favored Schulte, because I had no proof that Schlosser had given important intelligence to the Allies, as Riegner's industrialist was known to have done. Subsequent investigation turned up the fact that Schulte's corporation, Georg von Giesche's Erben, had indeed employed some thirty thousand people. I made private inquiries about Schulte and obtained confirmation that Schulte was the mysterious messenger.

Alan Kraut and I wrote up what I had discovered about Schulte and Riegner's message to Stephen Wise and submitted the article to *Commentary,* the same magazine that had published Laqueur's article in 1980. The editors there would surely appreciate the significance of the discovery. *Commentary* first wanted substantial revisions in the article and then delayed publication until October. In the interim, I called Walter Laqueur's Washington office to notify him, as a courtesy, that I had learned the identity of the mysterious messenger. Laqueur, however, was in London, so I failed to make contact with him.

In August Monty Penkower, a professor at Touro College in New York, told the *Jewish Week* of New York that working in archives in London and Jerusalem (Yad Vashem) he had discovered the identity of the mysterious German industrialist who had warned of the Final Solution. His name was Eduard Schulte, and Penkower had first turned up his name in the records of the World Jewish Congress in London. Then in Jerusalem, in the diary of A. Leon Kubowitzki, a World Jewish Congress official, Penkower learned of a February 16, 1945, conversation between Kubowitzki and Riegner about Schulte. I was heartened to see additional evidence about Schulte's role, but unhappy to have been scooped—the result of the delay at *Commentary*.

Accompanied by feature articles in the *Washington Post* and United Press International, the *Commentary* article finally appeared in October. It revealed what was then known about Schulte, and created considerable public interest. Professor Penkower's *The Jews Were Expendable: Free World Diplomacy and the Holocaust* appeared in December 1983. Unfortunately, it played down the significance of Schulte's mission in July 1942, since the author was among those persuaded that Pazner (Posner) had received the earliest information about the Final Solution from Salin, who in turn had gotten it from Arthur Sommer. Penkower wrote that Schulte's message came just afterward. This version, accepted by some scholars for a while, has now been discarded. The documents indicate that Riegner's telegram was the first solid piece of evidence about the Final Solution, and that the information came from Eduard Schulte.

Walter Laqueur and I met in late 1983 and decided to find more information about Schulte. I went back to the archives at Suitland to look for more information about Eduard Schulte's connection with Allied intelligence. My faithful archivist David Pfeiffer brought me the records that I had asked for and told me that he had found another box of records from the American Legation in Bern. He had finally been able to reorganize the Bern files and had stumbled across the new box. He did not know whether there was anything for me there, but why not look? I had little expectation of finding anything there by then.

In the midst of the box was a 1942 folder marked "840.1 Jews." Instantly I remembered that much earlier I had tried and failed to find this folder. This was where the Riegner-

Lichtheim report to Harrison and the mysterious messenger's name should be. I raced through the file and located a Riegner-Lichtheim aide-mémoire, "Documents Submitted to His Excellency the Honorable Leland Harrison, Minister of the United States in Berne, October 22, 1942." At the end, there was a section on the sources of information used. The sealed envelope was gone, but there was a half sheet of paper there indicating that the source of the information about the Final Solution was "Managing Director Dr. Schulte, Mining Industry, in close or closest contact with prominent circles in the defense economy." My original notion of how to solve the mystery had been right after all, even if the discovery came with some delay.

But, as so often in research, one discovery led to a new and not less difficult search. Who was this elusive man who had taken such good care to cover his tracks? That is the question we set out to answer in this book.

Notes

INTRODUCTION

Pages 11–12, section ending with "the most feared."
Interview with Dr. Arthur Burkhardt, Stuttgart. Dr. Burkhardt's unpublished autobiography, "Lebenssinfonie in A-Dur." Otto Fitzner File, Berlin Document Center.

Pages 12–14, "for a purpose."
On Himmler, see Roger Manvell and Heinrich Fraenkel, *Himmler* (New York, 1965); Felix Kersten, *The Kersten Memoirs 1940–1945*, tr. Constantine FitzGibbon and James Oliver (New York, 1957); Helmut Heiber, ed., *Reichsführer: Briefe an und von Himmler* (Stuttgart, 1968). Himmler's schedule in Hauptarchiv, Collection Himmler, copy in United States National Archives (hereafter NA), Microfilm T-581, Roll 39A, 17 July 1942; Rudolf Hoess. *Commandant of Auschwitz: The Autobiography of Rudolf Hoess*, tr. Constantine FitzGibbon (New York 1961), 197–200. Report on Himmler's tour of I. G. Farben installations in NA Record Group (hereafter RG) 238, T-301, NI 14551. German railway official referred to in Walter Laqueur, *The Terrible Secret: Suppression of the Truth about Hitler's "Final Solution"* (Boston, 1980), 29, and Raul Hilberg, "German Railroads/Jewish Souls," *Society* 14 (1976): 71.

Pages 14–16, "others kept silent?"
Interviews with Dr. Albrecht Jung, Bad Homburg; Dr. Arthur Burkhardt, Stuttgart; and Dr. Walter Grünfeld, Zurich. Also Eduard Schulte's notarized affidavit in Zurich, 25 July 1945, NA RG #84, Zurich Confidential File 1945, Box 2386, 800. Hoess, *Autobiography*, 195–97.

CHAPTER ONE

Pages 17–23, "to acquire wealth."
There is a privately printed history of the Schulte family: Else Heintze, *Die Geschlechter Schulte-Hülsenbeck* (Hanover, 1937). The

details on Eduard Schulte's childhood and adolescence are based mostly on information from Oskar Schulte, Eduard's younger brother (interview in Arnsberg, West Germany), and Oskar Schulte's recollections (unpublished).

Pages 23–24, "vision and initiative."
F. Lau and O. Mist, *Geschichte der Stadt Düsseldorf* (Düsseldorf, 1921).

Pages 24–26, "Bütow in Pomerania."
See notes for pages 17–23.

Pages 26–27, "found himself unemployed."
On the Handelsgesellschaft, Hans Fürstenberg, *Carl Fürstenberg: Die Lebensgeschichte eines deutschen Bankiers, 1870–1914* (Berlin, 1931). On Jeidels, see Schulte to Jeidels, 28 November 1940, U.S. Department of Justice, Alien Property Custodian Records, Silesian-American Corporation Case File. Schulte's curriculum vitae, 16 July 1945, obtained from Ruprecht Schulte. Interview with Ruprecht Schulte.

Pages 27–28, "the bare essentials."
Interviews with Oskar and Ruprecht Schulte. Wilhelm Treue, *Georg von Giesche's Erben 1704–1964* (Hamburg, 1964), 92. This history of Giesche indicates that two officials of the Disconto-Gesellschaft recommended Schulte for the job at Giesche.

Page 28, "asylum in Switzerland."
"Huge Mine Property of Giesche's Heirs in American Hands," *New York Times,* 2 August 1926. Treue, *Giesche,* 81–93.

Pages 28–30, "at all bad."
A. Tauber, ed., *Geliebtes Breslau* (Munich, 1966); Niels von Holst, *Breslau, ein Buch der Erinnerung* (Hameln, 1950); Paul Driske, *Der Wirtschaftsorganismus Gross-Breslau; ein Beitrag zur Wirtschaftsgeographie einer Grossstadt* (Berlin, 1936).

Pages 30–35, "to be surprised."
Interviews with Ruprecht and Oskar Schulte. Clara Schulte, *Charlotte Brontë, Genie in Schatten* (Dresden, 1936), *Das Haus am Ring* (Berlin, 1941), *Der Ritter mit dem Drachen* (Berlin, 1943).

Pages 35–36, "two to one."
An American assessment of Schulte in 1945 was that his political views (then) corresponded to those of the liberal Democratic Party, presumably the Deutsche Demokratische Partei of the Weimar Republic. NA RG 260, OMGUS Transition Files, Box 10, Civilian Personnel October–December 1945. On Schulte's political views earlier, interviews with Ruprecht Schulte and Oskar Schulte.

Pages 36–37, "it would end."
On conditions in Silesia, see Richard Bessel, *Political Violence and the Rise of Nazism: The Storm Troopers in Eastern Germany 1925–1934*

(London, 1984), 80, 85–86, 89–92, 25; Paul Kluke, "Der Fall Potempa," *Vierteljahrshefte für Zeitgeschichte* 5 (1957): 279–97. Interviews with Dr. Albrecht Jung, Bad Homburg; Dr. Arthur Burkhardt, Stuttgart; and Ruprecht Schulte.

CHAPTER TWO

Pages 39–41, "a raving lunatic."

For Hitler's and Göring's speeches, see *Trial of the Major War Criminals before the International Military Tribunal* (hereafter *IMT*); (Nuremberg, 1947–49) Vol. 35, 42–48, document 203-D. On Schacht's role, see Edward Norman Peterson, *Hjalmar Schacht: For and Against Hitler; A Political-Economic Study of Germany 1923–1945* (Boston, 1954), especially 127; and Henry Ashby Turner, Jr., *German Big Business and the Rise of Hitler* (New York, 1985), 329–31; also interrogation of Georg von Schnitzler, NA RG 242, T-301, R 20/380-81. Schulte's presence on 20 February, Turner, *German Big Business,* 468n.81.

Pages 41–43, "refineries in Germany."

Wilhelm Treue, *George von Giesche's Erben 1704–1964* (Hamburg, 1964), 83–98. W. A. Harriman and Company to Anaconda Copper Mining Company, 30 July 1925, Anaconda–Silesian-American Corporation Records, Box 0110, Giesche Spolka 1927–1932, Atlantic Richfield Corporation Corporate Archive (hereafter ARCO). Estimate of value of German Giesche in Anaconda–Silesian-American Corporation Records, Box 0984, Chronological File 1925–1957. 10 July 1926, ARCO. "Ueberraschende Wendung bei Giesches Erben," *Berliner Tageblatt,* no. 525, 5 November 1925; "Zu dem Vertrage zwischen der Bergwerkgesellschaft von Giesches Erben und der Harriman-Gruppe," *Berliner Tageblatt,* no. 526, 6 November 1925; "Wendung bei Giesche," *Frankfurter Zeitung,* no. 320, 6 November 1925; "Anaconda—Giesche," *Frankfurter Zeitung,* no. 321, 7 November 1925; "Giesche und der preussische Staat," *Berliner Tageblatt,* no. 536, 12 November 1925. Interview Dr. O. H. C. Messner, Zurich.

Pages 43–44, "deal went through."

New York Times, 20 November 1925. Schacht was in the United States when the news of the Giesche sale first appeared, and he cabled his favorable view to Berlin. Later, he took part directly in the negotiations. Anaconda–Silesian-American Corporation Chronological File, Box 0984, 12 and 29 November 1925, ARCO. Interviews with Dr. Albrecht Jung, Bad Homburg; and Ruprecht Schulte.

Pages 44–45, "the political dangers."

Cornelius F. Kelley to John D. Ryan, 6 May 1926, Anaconda–Silesian-American Records, Box x-1028, Preliminary Negotiations May–July 1926. Agreement between the Polish Government and W. A. Harriman and Company [3 July 1926], and Kelley to Harriman, 26 August 1926, Montana Historical Society, Anaconda Copper Mining Collection, Folder 6.4dx, Contracts 1925–28. "Huge Mine Property of Giesche Heirs in American Hands," *New York Times,* 2 August 1926. Treue, *Giesche,* 91–93.

Page 45, "of the company."

Brooks to Laist, 17 August 1926, and Brooks to Kelley, 1 March 1927, Montana Historical Society, Anaconda Copper Mining Collection, Folder 6.4d, Government Relations 1926–28, and Folder 6.4dx, Contracts 1925–28. In April 1927 the president of Polish Giesche's executive committee wrote his Anaconda superior: "I think that you will discover on your visit over here that unless real pressure can be brought to bear upon Schulte [,] he is a very difficult man to bring round to any point of view favorable to the freedom of Spolka [Polish Giesche] to do business without his company's domination." Brooks to Kelley, 8 April 1927, Montana Historical Society, Anaconda Copper Mining Collection, Folder 6.4dx, Contracts 1925–28. Brooks to Kelley, 1 August 1927, and Kelley to Brooks, 25 November 1927, Montana Historical Society, Anaconda Copper Mining Collection, Folder 6.4d, Government Relations August–December 1927. On Schulte and Gaethke, interview with Ruprecht Schulte, San Diego. See also p. 204 in the text.

Pages 45–46, "Germany moving again."

Treue, *Giesche,* 99–100. Wilhelm Groener to Reich chancellor and Reich economics minister, 30 April 1932, NA RG 238, T-301, NI 577, 578. The Office of U.S. Chief of Counsel Staff Evidence Analysis states incorrectly that Groener wrote to Chancellor von Papen. On April 30 Brüning was still chancellor. By the time Papen was appointed, Groener was out of office. See also Otto Fischer to Chancellor Franz von Papen, 20 July 1932, NA RG 238, T-301, NI 576; I. G. Farben, Unterredung im Reichswehr-Ministerium, 29 July 1932, NA RG 238, T-301, NI 649; Das Magdeburger-Giesche Zinkelektrolyse Unternehmnen, 6 November 1932, NA RG 238, T-301, NI 564.

Pages 46–47, "troublesome, independent unions."

On the Nazis and big business, see the comprehensive study by Turner, *German Big Business,* especially 47–99.

Page 47, "the new regime."

On November 13, 1934, Hitler issued a decree authorizing his economic adviser Wilhelm Keppler to carry out needed measures to replace imported raw materials with domestically produced substitutes. See NA RG 238, T-301, NI 14648. This policy, however, began well before Keppler's appointment. I. G. Farben executives signed an agreement with the government on December 14, 1933, to expand synthetic oil production, and Hitler and high government officials had expressed interest in the I. G. Farben process months earlier. See Joseph Borkin, *The Crime and Punishment of I. G. Farben* (New York, 1979), 70–75. For later expressions of Hitler's views on autarky, see particularly Keppler to Bosch, 8 April 1935, NA RG 238, NI 15576. Statistics on zinc in "Statistische Zusammenstellungen über Aluminium, Blei, Kupfer, Zink, Zinn, Kadmium, Nickel, Quecksilber und Silber," Metallgeschaft Aktiengesellschaft, Nr. 231, copy in NA RG ‚T-84, R 51/1332539, and Treue, *Giesche*, 100–01. See also B. J. Aylett, *The Chemistry of Zinc, Cadmium, and Mercury* (Oxford, 1975), and H. J. Holtmeier, ed., *Zink, ein lebenswichtiges Mineral* (Stuttgart, 1976). Interview Dr. O. H. C. Messner, Zurich. Letter from Dr. Arthur Burkhardt.

Pages 48–49, "an overwhelming victory."
The actual results in the Reichstag elections of 1936 were 98.8 percent in favor of the Nazi list of candidates. On Hitler's rising popularity in this period, see, for example, Alan Bullock, *Hitler: A Study in Tyranny* (New York, 1961), 299–300.

Pages 49–53, "it would lose."
Interviews with Dr. Albrecht Jung, Ruprecht and Oskar Schulte.

Page 53, "copper sales company."
Interviews with Dr. Albrecht Jung, Bad Homburg; Dr. Alfred Schaefer, Zurich; and Dr. Hans La Roche, Basel. Treue, *Giesche*, 105.

Pages 53–56, "the following day."
This reconstruction of Schulte's conversation with Julius Schloss is based on an interview with a senior staff member of Brandeis Goldschmidt who worked with both men.

Page 56, " 'to do it?' "
On Hitler and *Kristallnacht*, see *IMT*, Vol. 12, 381: Fritz Herwerth testimony based on conversation with SA official Obernitz. Quote from unpublished ms. by Dr. Hans Buwert, Cologne, who met Schulte in Munich on 10 November 1938. Also interview Oskar Schulte.

CHAPTER THREE

Pages 57–58, "to attack Britain."
On Hitler's foreign policy in this period generally, see Gerhard Weinberg, *The Foreign Policy of Hitler's Germany: Starting World War II, 1937–1939* (Chicago, 1980), 313–627. Hitler quotation in Joachim Fest, *Hitler* tr. Richard and Clara Winston (New York, 1975), 571–72. On Hitler and Poland, in addition to Weinberg, see Telford Taylor, *Munich: The Price of Peace* (New York, 1980), 964–74.

Pages 58–59, "with this group."
Information on Schulte from Dr. Alfred Schaefer, Dr. Albrecht Jung, and Ruprecht Schulte. On the German military's attitude

toward Hitler in the 1930s, see Peter Hoffmann, *The History of the German Resistance, 1933–1945,* tr. Richard Barry (Cambridge, Mass., 1977), 36–46, 81–152; generally, Ger van Roon, *German Resistance to Hitler* tr. Peter Ludlow (New York, 1971), and Klaus-Jürgen Müller, *Das Heer und Hitler: Armee und nationalsozialistisches Regime 1933–1940* (Stuttgart, 1969).

Pages 59–60, "with some money."
Hitler's Reichstag speech is quoted in Lucy S. Dawidowicz, *The War Against the Jews* (New York, 1976), 142. On Schulte and Mannheim, see the affidavit given to American authorities by Schulte's colleague Lothar Siemon, 28 November 1946, Department of Justice, Silesian-American Corporation Case File. The same document indicated that there were other such cases. See also James M. Markham, "An Unsung Good German: Fame Comes at Last," *New York Times,* 9 November 1983.

Pages 60–61, "on deaf ears."
Quotation from unsigned Memorandum on the Silesian-American Corporation, NA RG 226, Entry 106, Box 12. This document was written by Schulte's business associate Jacques Rosenstein, who had come to the United States to try to bring about a Swiss purchase of Silesian-American. In it Rosenstein also mentioned that Schulte (whom he described only as a leading person of the Giesche concern) had helped to save Jewish lives and property.

Pages 61–62, "to his dilemma."
On Gaevernitz, see Fabian von Schlabrendorff, *Begegnungen in fünf Jahrzehnten* (Tübingen, 1979), 321–47. Also interviews with Professor Douglas Steere, Haverford, Pa., and Mrs. Cordelia Hood. Letters from Mrs. Marga Stinnes (Gaevernitz's sister). We inspected the Gaevernitz papers in the Bundesarchiv-Militärarchiv, Freiburg. There are others at the Hoover Library at Stanford. There is a short biography of Gerhart von Schulze-Gaevernitz by Kurt Zielenziger, *Gerhart von Schulze-Gaevernitz: Eine Darstellung seines Lebens und seiner Werke* (Berlin, 1926).

Pages 62–65, "war on Germany."
Information from Ruprecht Schulte and Günter Schwerin.

Pages 65–67, "was already decided."
Information from Ruprecht Schulte, Dr. Alfred Schaefer, and Dr. Hans La Roche.

Pages 67–68, "foreign exchange available."
Cornelius F. Kelley, President, Silesian-American Corporation, to Secretary of State Cordell Hull, 16 November 1939; Schulte to Kelley, 11 October 1939; Kelley to Dr. Heinrich F. Albert, 12 December 1939; and Albert to Kelley, 24 October 1939; all in Anaconda–Silesian-American Corporation File, Box 0984, Government of Poland Folder, Atlantic Richfield Corporation Archives, Los Angeles.

Pages 68–70, "Silesia in 1941."

Otto Fitzner File, Berlin Document Center. Dr. Arthur Burkhardt, "Lebenssinfonie in A-Dur" (unpublished memoirs). Interviews with Dr. Burkhardt and Dr. Albrecht Jung. Seev Goshen, "Eichmann und die Nisko-Aktion im Oktober 1939," *Vierteljahrshefte für Zeitgeschichte* 29 (1981): 85. In this article Fitzner's name is spelled incorrectly as Pfitzner.

Pages 70–71, "during the war."

Information from Ruprecht Schulte. On Chojnacki, see Studium Polski Podziemnej, File 5.2 Bern; oral and written information from Jan Nowak, Washington, D.C.; Cesare Szulczewski, Merano; Michael Rybikowski, Southampton, N.Y.; and Leon Sliwinski, St. Moritz. On the Poles and Enigma, see Witold Bieganski, *W. konspiracji i walce: z kart polskiego ruchu oporu we Francji* (Warsaw, 1979); Leszek Gondek, *Wywiad polski w Trzeciej Reszy 1933–1939* (Warsaw, 1974); Wladislaw Kozaczuk, *Bitwa o tajemnice* (Warsaw, 1967), and *Wojna w eterze* (Warsaw, 1977); M. Z. Rygor-Slowikowski, *W. tajnej sluzbie* (London, 1977); Ronald Lewin, *Ultra Goes to War: The First Account of World War II's Greatest Secret Based on Official Documents* (New York, 1980) 7–31.

We are grateful to the late Ronald Lewin, who shared with us the substance of his conversations with the late Colonel Mayer, head of Polish intelligence during the 1930s, Colonel Lisicki, and others.

Chojnacki's 19 July 1945 affidavit for Schulte indicates that the two men began their intelligence contacts in September 1939. See NA RG 84, Zurich Confidential File 1945, Box 2386, 800.

Pages 71–73, "during the war."

See Gaevernitz memorandum, 18 March 1940, Leland Harrison Papers, Box 29, R Folder, Library of Congress. This unsigned report is one of a series from Gaevernitz. See [Gaevernitz] Memorandum of 6 May 1940, ibid.; report of 12 November 1940 from Gaevernitz, NA RG 59, CDF 740.0011 E. W. 1939/6962. On Gaevernitz and Messersmith, see Gaevernitz to Stinnes, 10 July 1938, private possession; and Messersmith to Harrison, 31 May 1940, Harrison Papers, Box 29, Messersmith Folder, Library of Congress, and Messersmith to Bigelow, 10 December 1940, Messersmith Papers, Folder 1419, University of Delaware. Gaevernitz is the unnamed friend mentioned by Messersmith in both these letters—and *is* named in Harrison to Secretary of State, 12 November 1940 (NA RG 59 CDF 740. 0011 E. W. 1939/6962). Yet Harrison subsequently described his contacts with Gaevernitz as follows: ". . . he gave me an oral report containing his version of conditions in Germany, and subsequently handed me a memorandum on this subject. I think I saw Verne [Gaevernitz] once or twice thereafter when he called on me at the Legation for only a few minutes." [Harrison] Memorandum, 17 April 1943, NA RG 84, Bern Confidential File 1945, 820.02 von Gaevernitz, Gero.

On Case Weser Exercise, see H. R. Trevor-Roper, ed., *Blitzkrieg to Defeat: Hitler's War Directives 1939–1945* (New York, 1971), 22–25.

Pages 73–74, "in his criticism."
Information from Ruprecht Schulte, Dr. Arthur Burkhardt, and Dr. Alfred Schaefer.

CHAPTER FOUR

Pages 75–79, "was not reached."
On the Hitler-Molotov-Ribbentrop meeting, see *Documents on German Foreign Policy 1918–1945,* (Washington, D.C., 1960) Series D, Vol. 11, doc. nos. 325, 326, 328, 329, pp. 533–70. H. R. Trevor-Roper, ed., *Blitzkrieg to Defeat: Hitler's War Directives 1939–1945* (New York, 1971), 48–52. Barton Whaley, *Codeword Barbarossa* (Cambridge, Mass., 1973), passim.

Schulte's report on the Hitler-Molotov meeting became known to Sagalowitz and Riegner when they were checking out their industrialist's reliability in 1942. See Chapters Five and Six.

One of Schulte's sources about the invasion of Russia may have been Dr. Erwin Respondek, a former Reichstag deputy (Catholic Center Party) from Silesia, but this, for a variety of reasons, is now impossible to prove. Respondek, who was one of those in charge of manufacturing German currency for the occupied areas in Russia, was the first to pass on to the Americans, via Sam Woods, the detailed Barbarossa blueprint. In the United States former German chancellor Heinrich Brüning (who knew Respondek) vouched for the authenticity of the source. In his memoirs Secretary of State Cordell Hull referred to this episode.

In his *Codeword Barbarossa,* 38–39, Barton Whaley, on the basis of information received from Professor Harold C. Deutsch, mistakenly identified Sam Woods's main informant as Hans Herwarth von Bittenfeld, a young German officer and Foreign Ministry official. But Professor Deutsch was subsequently told by the former ambassador "Chip" Bohlen that Respondek and not Herwarth had been the source. 1982 affidavit by Professor Deutsch, and interview Hans Herwarth von Bittenfeld.

On intelligence reaching the British, see F. H. Hinsley et al., *British Intelligence in the Second World War: Its Influence on Strategy and Operations.* Vol. I (New York, 1979), 429–83; on the battle, Andreas Hillgruber, *Hitlers Strategie: Politik und Kriegsführung 1940–1941* (Frankfurt am Main, 1965), 536–63.

Pages 79–81, "included the Gestapo."
On Hermann Schulte, information from Ruprecht and Oskar Schulte. Hermann Schulte File, Berlin Document Center. On Department Z, see Erkennungsmarkenverzeichnis, Amt Ausland/Abwehr (Zentralabteilung), and Arbeitsplan Amt Ausland/Abwehr, R 5, S. 40 and RW 4 783, S. 54b–55, Bundesarchiv-Militärarchiv, Freiburg. Interrogation of Walter Huppenkothen. 3 December 1947, NA RG 238. Also Heinz Höhne, *Canaris* (New York, 1977), 383–84. On

Oster generally, see Romedio Galeazzo Graf von Thun-Hohenstein, *Der Verschwörer: General Oster und die Militäropposition* (West Berlin, 1982).

Pages 81–82, "of his office."

On the decline of the Abwehr generally, see especially Höhne, *Canaris*. On Allied perceptions of the Abwehr, see "The German Intelligence Services" [British Report], in NA RG 319, XE 003641. On Hermann Schulte, information from Ruprecht Schulte.

Pages 83–84, "the German command."

See the undated affidavit by senior Gestapo official Walter Huppenkothen on the Polish radio traffic between Bern and London, NA RG 238, Huppenkothen File.

Riegner and Sagalowitz learned of the report about changes in the German High Command during their 1942 investigation. On Germany's shortage of raw materials, see Georg Thomas, *Geschichte der deutschen Wehr- und Rüstungswirtschaft*, Schriften des Bundesarchivs, no. 14 (Boppard am Rhein, 1966). Albert Seaton, *The German Army 1933–1945* (London, 1983), 188.

The January 1942 report came from an Allied intelligence service to the Americans through the British. Although the name of the country of origin is twice deleted in the British telegram to Donovan (who was given the code designation "Q"), the size of the spaces in the telegram make it almost certain that the country was Poland (which had the most active intelligence service of the other Allied nations anyway). This Allied service was said to think very highly of the source who had supplied the information.

The document describes the source as follows: "He is stated—and we believe with justification—to be in touch with high German personalities. We have frequently quoted this sourse [sic] and our experience of him has on the whole been good. He accurately forecast the German attack on Russia." See NA RG 226, 12854, 12856. All of this fits Schulte perfectly.

Intelligence reports identify their sources by name only on rare occasions—and even if they do, government declassification experts usually delete names before such documents are made accessible to the public. Polish intelligence reports, which were passed both to the British and the Americans, were no exception. The British government has released neither its own World War II intelligence files nor the records of the Second Bureau of the Polish General Staff, which came into British custody after the war. Even the Freedom of Information Act in the United States allows the government to withhold the names of informants and agents.

When the Germans ultimately (mid-1943—see p. 174) cracked the codes used by the Poles in Switzerland and could read Polish radio messages from Switzerland to London, however, they learned a good deal about Chojnacki's Polish network and Schulte's role in it. Walter Huppenkothen, a senior Gestapo official, revealed some of these details in a postwar affidavit, and Schulte also commented on his intelligence work in certain postwar documents. What emerges from this evidence is that Schulte had access to information from the German General Staff and Hitler's headquarters. Knowing this, we were able to plow through hundreds of Polish intelligence reports that were passed to the Americans (and are found in the National Archives) and match the type of information that came from Schulte with a particular code designation used by the Polish military attaché.

In other cases, where decoded Polish transmissions were found in German or American files without code name or number, we found information that Schulte probably would have been in a position to know, and we made a tentative identification. Confirmation will not come until the British government releases its Polish intelligence records, which will not be for the rest of this century.

Pages 84–85, "generally quite good."

Polish Intelligence Report 241, 25 August 1942, NA RG 319, Box 957, Germany 9505; Polish Report 340/43, 29 January 1943, NA RG 165, Box 1431, Policy O/B Intelligence. We are grateful to Professor Gerhard Weinberg of the University of North Carolina who called the latter folder to our attention.

On the other German industrialist passing information, see "Information über Deutschland," 28 July 1942, copy in the possession of Gerhart Riegner.

Pages 85–86, "their German friends."

The files of the Schweizerisches Bundesarchiv (Bern) concerning Schulte are not yet open. We are grateful to the director of the archive and his deputy Dr. Christopher Graf for providing official summaries of Schulte's activities. Although more material may be made public in the not-too-distant future, it is unlikely to include operational files concerning information conveyed by Schulte to the Swiss. But Dr. Alfred Schaefer was most informative about Schulte.

We also owe a debt of gratitude to Professor H. R. Kurz, author of *Nachrichtenzentrum Schweiz: Die Schweiz im Nachrichtendienst des Zweiten Weltkrieges* (Frauenfeld, 1973), with whom we discussed some of the issues of this book. Another important source is Hans Rudolf Fuhrer, *Spionage gegen die Schweiz: Die geheimen deutschen Nachrichtendienste gegen die Schweiz im Zweiten Weltkrieges 1939–1945* (Frauenfeld, 1982). On Masson, see Schweizerisches Bundesarchiv, 10 019-10 040, 10 098, and much more. One of the best collections of the range of information reaching Swiss military intelligence is a journalistic account: K. Emmenegger, *"Q-n" wusste Bescheid* (Zurich, 1965).

On Swiss-German relations, see Edgar Bonjour, *Geschichte der schweizerischen Neutralität: Vier Jahrhunderte eidgenössischer Aussenpolitik, 1939–1945*, Vols. 4–8 (Basel, 1970–1975), especially 5: 47–67, 241–78.

On Waibel and Viking, see among others, Fuhrer, *Spionage*, 131; Jozef Garlinski, *The Swiss Corridor* (London, 1981), 110–11, 117–18; Nigel West, *Unreliable Witness: Espionage Myths of the Second World War* (London, 1984), 51–67.

Page 86 footnote:

"The O. K. W.'s Military Plans," 31 March 1943, NA RG 165, Box 1431, Polish O/B Intelligence.

Pages 86–87, "taking place there."

Joseph Goebbels, *Final Entries 1945: The Diaries of Joseph Goebbels* (New York, 1979), 51, 308. Michael H. Kater, *The Nazi Party: A Social Profile of Members and Leaders, 1919-1945* (Cambridge, Mass., 1983), 228, 382*n*.20. Hanke File, Berlin Document Center. See also Peter Hüttenberger, *Die Gauleiter: Studie zum Wandel des Machtgefüges in der NSDAP* (Stuttgart, 1969), 199. Although Hanke was not formally named Gauleiter until 1941, Hitler decided to reward him with a Gauleiter post as early as December 1939. See [Bormann] Aktenvermerk für Pg. Friedrichs, 7 December 1939, NA RG 242, T-580, R 80, no frame number. On Hanke and Goebbels, Albert Speer, *Inside the Third Reich*, tr. Richard and Clara Winston (New York, 1970), 204–5, 208; Viktor Reimann, *The Man Who Created Hitler: Joseph Goebbels*, tr. Stephen Wendt (London, 1977), 198, 229–30. On Hanke and the Night of the Long Knives, Friedrich-Christian, Prinz zu Schaumburg-Lippe, *Dr. G.: Ein Porträt des Propagandaministers* (Wiesbaden, 1972), 88–93. On Hanke and Auschwitz, Speer, *Inside*, 480–81.

Pages 87–89, "summer of 1942."

Information about Schulte from Dr. Arthur Burkhardt and Dr. Albrecht Jung. Werlin File, Berlin Document Center. For Werlin at Hitler's headquarters, see *Adolf Hitler: Monologe im Führerhauptquartier 1941-1944, Die Aufzeichnungen Heinrich Heims*, ed. Werner Jochmann (Hamburg, 1980), 194; and Confidential Intelligence Report No. 398, 28 March 1944, NA RG 84, Zurich Confidential File 1944, 800. In this report Werlin's name is misspelled Wernle.

CHAPTER FIVE

Pages 91–96, "very far off."

Details of the trip have been put together on the basis of Schulte's known habits as related by his associates and family. Hunting diary and information on Kleist from Ruprecht Schulte. On the Jews of Breslau as of 15 November 1941, see NA RG 242, T-81, R 676/5485696. Details at the Hotel Baur-au-Lac from the management of the hotel, to whom we are grateful.

Pages 96–101, "house of God."

On Schulte, Rosenstein, and Koppelmann, information from Hans La Roche, Basel, Dr. Jonathan Friedmann, Basel, and Dr. Alfred Schaefer, Zurich; on Rosenstein and Koppelmann, oral and written information from Dr. Gerhart Riegner. On Doris Kurz, information from Dr. Arthur Burkhardt. Information about Koppelmann and his sister from Dr. S. Scheps, Geneva. On Sagalowitz and his companion, information from Sagalowitz's sister-in-law, Mrs. Lucie Sagal, and his niece, Mrs. Nina Zafran-Sagalowitz, both of Zurich.

The chess tournament was covered in the Swiss newspapers, such as the *Neue Zürcher Zeitung* and the monthly *Schweizerische Schachzeitung*. We are indebted to Alois Nagler, who knew Sagalowitz and was in Lausanne during the competition; Dr. Alois Müller, deputy president of the Swiss chess federation; and Dr. Schudel, who won the Lausanne Hauptturnier in 1942.

Pages 101–05, "a simple ceremony."

Part of the Sagalowitz Papers are at Yad Vashem, Jerusalem, but most personal files remain in private hands in Zurich. Some biographical information is contained in a booklet published shortly after his death by his friends. Additional details from sources listed for Pages 96–101, and from Dr. J. Treitel, St. Gallen; Jules Passweg, Zurich; Dr. Gerhart Riegner; and several Zurich journalists.

On Steiger and Rothmund, see Alfred A. Häsler, *Das Boot is voll* (Zurich, 1967).

Pages 105–10, "agreed without hesitation."

On Sagalowitz, information from Mrs. Lucie Sagal and Mrs. Nina Zafran-Sagalowitz. Curt Riess, *Cafe Odeon: Unsere Zeit, ihre Hauptakteure und Betrachter* (Zurich, 1973). Winston Churchill's speech in "Botschaft Churchills an die amerikanischen Juden," *Neue Zürcher Zeitung*, 23 July 1942 (Morgenausgabe). Köcher's complaints and Goebbel's threats in Edgar Bonjour, *Geschichte der schweizerischen Neutralität*, Vol. V (Basel, 1970–75), 161–238, 243–46, 250–51, 260. On the Jewish organizations in Switzerland as well as on Sagalowitz and Riegner, letters and interviews with Dr. Riegner.

Pages 110–13, "the general picture?"

Letters and interviews with Dr. Riegner. Riegner's letter, "Zur Klarstellung," *Israelitisches Wochenblatt*, 1 June 1984.

Pages 113–15, "the deported Jews."

On the origins of the early Nazi killing in Poland, see Helmut Krausnick, "Hitler und die Morde in Poland," *Vierteljahrshefte für Zeitgeschichte* 11 (1963): 196–209. Hitler's relevant speeches are quoted in Lucy S. Dawidowicz, *The War Against the Jews* (New York, 1976), 147–48n. On the Wannsee Conference, see Raul Hilberg, *The Destruction of the European Jews* (Chicago, 1967), 262–64, and Hilberg, ed., *Documents of Destruction: Germany and Jewry 1933–1945* (London, 1972), 89–99. On the extent of contemporary knowledge of these events, Riegner, "Zur Klarstellung," *Israelitisches Wochenblatt*, 1 June 1984; letters and interviews with Riegner. On Lichtheim's knowledge and reports, see Walter Laqueur, *The Terrible Secret: Suppression of the Truth about Hitler's "Final Solution"* (Boston, 1980), 171–83 (quotes from 174 and 176), and Martin Gilbert, *Auschwitz and the Allies* (New York, 1981), 28–35.

Pages 115–17, "and half-deserted Geneva."

On the general disbelief of reports of mass killings, Laqueur, *Terrible Secret*, passim. On the thinking of Riegner and Sagalowitz in

July–August 1942, letters and interviews with Dr. Riegner. Riegner, "Zur Klarstellung," *Israelitisches Wochenblatt*, 1 June 1984.

CHAPTER SIX

Pages 119–23, "in Schulte's report."

Interview with Dr. Arthur Burkhardt. Letters and interviews with Dr. Riegner. Riegner, "Zur Klarstellung," *Israelitisches Wochenblatt*, 1 June 1984. Dr. Riegner's (unpublished) letter of 4 August 1942 to Guggenheim, which Dr. Riegner graciously made available to us. Guggenheim's 6 August 1942 letter of introduction for Dr. Riegner to Squire in NA RG 84, Geneva Confidential File 1942, 110.2. We must emphasize that Dr. Riegner himself still feels bound by his promise not to reveal the industrialist's name.

Pages 123–24, "was under way."

Interviews with Dr. Riegner. Riegner's letter of 8 August 1942 to Guggenheim. The fact that Squire was on vacation in Crans-sur-Sierre appears in Squire to Harrison, 8 August 1942, NA RG 84, Bern Confidential File 1942, 800-Germany. Interviews with Elting and Dr. Riegner.

Pages 124–25, "in New York."

Elting Memorandum, 8 August 1942, re conversation with Riegner, NA RG 84, Geneva Confidential File 1942, 110.2. Elting to Secretary of State, 10 August 1942, NA RG 59, CDF 862.4016/2234. Quotation from Harrison to Secretary of State, 11 August 1942, NA RG 59, CDF 862.4016/2234; also quoted by Saul S. Friedman, *No Haven for the Oppressed: United States Policy Toward Jewish Refugees, 1938–1945* (Detroit, 1973), 131. The State Department summary passed to OSS in NA RG 226, Entry 4, Box 1, Despatches from Neutral Posts, 11 August 1942.

Pages 125–26, "be dismissed unceremoniously."

On Wise generally, see Stephen Wise, *Challenging Years: The Autobiography of Stephen Wise* (New York, 1949), and Melvin I. Urofsky, *A Voice That Spoke for Justice: The Life and Times of Stephen S. Wise* (Albany, 1982). Quotation from Urofsky, 73. The present authors' evaluation of Wise is based on close reading of his private papers, located at the American Jewish Historical Society, Waltham, Mass. On State Department attitudes toward Wise in 1942, see for example, Eddy to Gordon, 7 December 1942, NA RG 59, CDF 862.4016/2251.

Pages 126–27, "under the circumstances."

NA RG 59, CDF 862.4016/2235 and 2233 Confidential File. Huddle to Elting, 21 August 1942, NA RG 84, Geneva Confidential File 1942, 110.2. Squire to Riegner 24 August 1942, NA RG 84, Geneva Confidential File 1942, 800. Riegner to Squire, 26 August 1942, Geneva Confidential File 1942, 800.

Page 127, "even been told."
Complete Presidential Press Conferences of Franklin D. Roosevelt,
(New York, 1972) Vols. 19–20, 21 August 1942.

Page 128, "three weeks earlier."
Interviews with Dr. Riegner. British official reaction to the
telegram is discussed extensively by Martin Gilbert, *Auschwitz and the
Allies* (New York, 1981), 59. The State Department received a copy of
Silverman's telegram to Wise, which can be found in NA RG 59, CDF
740.00116 E. W. 1939/553.

Pages 128–29, "bureaucracy would move."
Wise to Welles, 2 September 1942, NA RG 59, CDF 840.48
Refugees/3080. Wise to Frankfurter, 4 September 1942, reprinted in
Stephen S. Wise: Servant of the People: Selected Letters, ed. Carl Hermann
Voss (Philadelphia, 1969), 248–49. On Welles and Hull, see Robert
Dallek, *Franklin D. Roosevelt and American Foreign Policy, 1932–1945* (New
York, 1981), 149, 421. Also, interview with Elbridge Durbrow. On
Hull's attitude toward Jewish requests, see David S. Wyman, *The
Abandonment of the Jews, 1941–1945* (New York, 1984), 190. Atherton to
Welles, 3 September 1942, NA RG 59, CDF 840.48 Refugees/3080:
notation indicates that information was telephoned to Wise on 3 Sep-
tember. Wise to Frankfurter, 4 September 1942, in Voss, ed., *Stephen S.
Wise,* 248–49.

Pages 129–30, " 'regarding this prophecy.' "
A. Leon Kubowitzki Diary, 15 February 1945, World Jewish Congress, London. Letters and interviews with Dr. Riegner.
There were other Jews in Switzerland passing on information about the Nazi killings that was partly true, partly false. Wyman,
Abandonment, 45–47, has additional details of the reception of various
çables in New York. Hitler's speech on September 30 was monitored
and translated in the U.S. See NA RG 165, Box 1193, Germany 3700.
Excerpts are quoted by Arthur Morse, *While Six Million Died: A Chronicle
of American Apathy* (New York, 1967), 6–7.

Pages 130–31, " 'Bolsheviks' as well."
Wise to Frankfurter, 16 September 1942, reprinted in Voss,
ed., *Stephen S. Wise,* 250–51. Cox to Ciechanowski, 14 September 1942,
Oscar Cox Papers, Box 6, Franklin D. Roosevelt Library. Allen Dulles
liked this idea of a War Crimes Commission too. Allen Dulles to James
G. McDonald, 24 September 1942, McDonald Papers, Dulles Folder,
G-113, Columbia School of International Affairs. Taylor's general mis-
sion was to persuade the pope to exercise moral leadership and to re-
frain from any pressure for a compromise peace. See President's
Secretary's File, Box 71, Vatican: Myron Taylor, Franklin D. Roosevelt
Library. Copy of the Lichtheim-Welles despatch in NA RG 84, Bern
Confidential File 1942, 840.1 Jews. On this episode, see Gilbert, *Ausch-
witz,* 64–65, 71. On the request for the Vatican's confirmation of reports, see Wyman, *Abandonment,* 49; NA RG 84, Bern Confidential File

1942, 840.1 Jews. Memorandum of Conversation of 25 September 1942 ... PSF, Box 71, as cited above. Taylor to Maglione, 26 September 1942, and Welles to Taylor, 21 October 1942, Taylor Papers, Box 1, 1942, Library of Congress. Tittman Report of Audience with Pope, 5 January 1943, copy in William J. Donovan Papers, Box 102A, Vol. 5, U.S. Army Military History Institute, Carlisle, Pa.

Page 132, "cable to Wise."

Welles to Harrison, 5 October 1942, NA RG 84, Bern Confidential File 1942, 840.1 Jews, and RG 59, CDF 740.00116 E. W. 1939/600A. Harrison's life-style is revealed in his private papers, Library of Congress. Wise to Mack, 6 October 1942, Box 115, Wise Papers, American Jewish Historical Society. Harrison to Squire and Huddle to Squire, 6 October 1942, NA RG 84, Geneva Confidential File 1942, 800. Wise to Frankfurter, 9 October 1942, Wise Papers, Box 109.

Pages 132–35, "could be obtained."

White House press release in Official File 5152, Franklin D. Roosevelt Library. Letter and interviews Dr. Riegner. Documents submitted to His Excellency ... Leland Harrison, 22 October 1942, NA RG 84, Bern Confidential Correspondence 1942, 840.1 Jews. The name Eduard Schulte is found in a source appendix for the document about the Final Solution.

Squire to Harrison, 29 October 1942, NA RG 84, Bern Confidential File 1942, 800. Harrison to Welles, 24 October 1942, NA RG 84, Bern Confidential File, 840.1 Jews. Squire to Secretary of State, 29 October 1942, and Squire to Harrison, 29 October 1942, Geneva Confidential File 1942, 800. Harrison to Welles, 31 October 1942, NA RG 84, Bern Confidential File 1942, 840.1 Jews.

Pages 135–36, "Schulte's original report."

Biographical information about Burckhardt in Wilhelm Kosch, *Biographisches Staatshandbuch: Lexicon der Politik, Presse, und Publizistik* (Bern, 1963). Interview with Dr. Riegner. Hitler-Burckhardt meeting described by Burckhardt in *Mein Danziger Mission* (Zurich, 1960) 341–48. Squire to Harrison [7 November 1942], NA RG 84, Bern Confidential File 1942, 840.1 Jews; Squire to Harrison, 7 and 9 November 1942, NA RG 84 Geneva Confidential File 1942, 800.

Page 136, "anything generated previously."

Wise to Bakstansky, 29 September 1942, Wise Papers, Box 104. NA RG 59, CDF 740.00116 E. W. 1939/656. Wyman, *Abandonment*, 50–52.

Pages 136–37, "inquiries to Wise."

State Department report of 15 December 1942, cited in Memorandum on the Bermuda Conference, 22 February 1944, War Refugee Board Records, Box 3, FDR Library; Eddy to Gordon and attached, 7 December 1942, NA RG 59, CDF 862.4016/2251.

Pages 137–39, "Europe were dead."

Wertheim et al. to Mr. President, 8 December 1942, and attached, OF 76-C, FDR Library. Monty N. Penkower, *The Jews Were Expendable: Free World Diplomacy and the Holocaust* (Urbana, 1983), 85–86. On Frankfurter, see Walter Laqueur, *The Terrible Secret* (Boston, 1980), 3. On Roosevelt and the Third War Powers Bill, see Wyman, *Abandonment*, 56–58. On FDR's conference with Wallace and Rayburn, which is not mentioned in Wyman, see Wallace Diary, 26 November 1942, p. 1995, Columbia Oral History Collection, Columbia University, cited in Dallek, *Franklin D. Roosevelt*, 446. On the advice FDR was receiving on the Jewish problem around this time, see Richard Breitman, "The Allied War Effort and the Jews, 1942–43," *Journal of Contemporary History* (January 1985): 138–43. On Britain, Bernard Wasserstein, *Britain and the Jews of Europe 1939–1945* (Oxford, 1979), 171–74. State Department report of 15 December 1942 (cited for pp. 160–61). For the text of the United Nations joint statement and Wise's statement, *Bulletin of the World Jewish Congress* (January 1943): no. 4, 10–11.

CHAPTER SEVEN

Pages 141–42, "month or two."

Information from Dr. Alfred Schaefer, Dr. Arthur Burkhardt, and Ruprecht Schulte. On the frequency of Schulte's trips to Switzerland, official summaries, Schweizerisches Bundesarchiv, Bern.

Pages 142–43, "residence and office."

On the belated American decision to send a representative to Switzerland, see William J. Donovan's Memorandum to the President, 27 May 1942, President's Secretary's File, Box 166, OSS: Donovan Reports, FDR Library. On Dulles, see Allen Dulles, *Germany's Underground* (New York, 1947), 125–28; on Dulles's recruitment of and work with Gero von Gaevernitz, interviw with Mrs. Cordelia Hood. Also, but less reliable, Leonard Mosley: *Dulles: A Biography of Eleanor, Allen, and John Foster Dulles and Their Family Network* (New York, 1978), 126–32. Dulles quotation from Allen Dulles, *The Craft of Intelligence* (New York, 1963), 15.

Pages 143–44, "into new codes,"

Dulles's cook episode in Dulles, *The Craft of Intelligence*, 203–04, and Mosley, *Dulles*, 140. On the legation's security problems, see Dulles, *Germany's Underground*, 130–31, and NA RG 84, Bern Confidential File 1942, 820.02 Gero von Gaevernitz. Also interview with Mrs. Cordelia Hood. The Nazi spy's name was Jacob Fürst.

Pages 144–45, "were essentially correct."

On the German secret services in Switzerland, the most important studies are David Kahn, *Hitler's Spies* (New York, 1978); Heinz Höhne, *Canaris* (New York, 1977); Paul Leverkuehn, *German Military Intelligence* (London, 1954); and Wilhelm F. Flicke, "War Secrets in the

Ether," 2 vols., copy in Philip Strong Papers, Mudd Library, Princeton. On the importance of Gisevius as an intelligence source, see Dulles's comments in Warren M. Chase's Office Memorandum of 25 October 1945, NA RG 84, Bern Confidential Correspondence 1945, 800 Germany—Remnants of Subversive Movements. Gisevius's importance is confirmed by a reading of the cables (with identifying source numbers) that Dulles sent to Washington. See NA RG 226, Entry 134, Radio and Cables from Bern. Gisevius's papers, to the best of our knowledge, are still in private hands. But see Hans Bernd Gisevius, *To the Bitter End*, tr. Richard and Clara Winston (Boston, 1947), and *Wo ist Nebe: Erinnerungen an Hitlers Reichskriminaldirector* (Zurich, 1966), both of which contain autobiographical information. See also Mary Bancroft, *Autobiography of a Spy* (New York, 1983), 163–240. Gisevius quote from Klaus Urner, *Der Schweizer Hitler-Attentäter: Drei Studien zum Widerstand und seinen Grenzbereichen* (Frauenfeld, 1980), 19–20. Verification of Gisevius's role in saving Jews in Interrogation of Aloys Schreiber, 22 August 1946, NA RG 238, M-1270 R 27/0435-36.

Pages 145–46, "partner Anaconda Copper."

We are grateful to Dr. Eduard Waetjen for his recollections about Gisevius and Schulte. On the code episode, see notes for pages 167–68. On the background to Dulles's contact with Schulte, see pages 239–41. Confirmation of the contact in Dulles cable to Washington, 15 May 1943, NA RG 226, Entry 134, Box 307. On the prior meeting of Schulte and Dulles, information from Dr. Albrecht Jung and Ruprecht Schulte. Also James M. Markham, "An Unsung Good German: Fame Comes at Last," *New York Times,* 9 November 1983.

Pages 146–47, "on his list."

Dulles and Schulte met in May, July, September, and October 1943—they may have met more than once in some months. Initial Dulles reaction in CIA Schulte File. Other Dulles comments in Bern to OSS, 15 May 1943, NA RG 226, Entry 134, Box 307; 3 July 1943, ibid.; quotation from 29 October 1943, Box 171; 17 November 1943, Box 170. Also, information from Dr. Eduard Waetjen and Ruprecht Schulte. Washington's reaction to Schulte's memo in OSS to Bern, 13 December 1943, Box 341; Washington's instruction about Germans who could help the U.S. in OSS to Ustravic London, 30 October 1943, Box 340: all in NA RG 226, Entry 134.

Pages 147–49, "be quite accurate."

OSS query, 25 August 1943, Box 338; Dulles's answer with information from Schulte, 9 September 1943, Box 340; quotation based on Schulte's information on Hitler, 1 October 1943, Box 171: all in NA RG 226, Entry 134.

Pages 149–52, "had been feared."

On the Oslo Report, see F. H. Hinsley et al., *British Intelligence in the Second World War,* Vol. I (New York, 1979), 508–12; on the V-2 reports, Allied assessment of them, and the potential and actual damage, see ibid., Vol. I, 99; Vol. III, part 1, (New York, 1984), 357–

455. Also useful is R. V. Jones, *Most Secret War* (London, 1978), 523–84. Schulte's report on the V-2 is in Bern to OSS, 9 September 1943, NA RG 226, Entry 134, Box 340.

Somewhat later the V-2's accuracy was improved to about 150 yards. Walter Dornberger, *V2*, tr. James Cleugh and Geoffrey Halliday (New York, 1954), 167ff., 220. Gisevius's report in Bern to Secretary of State for OSS, 15 September 1943, NA RG 226, Entry 134, Box 340. Source "680" is mentioned in this same document. Dulles citation dated 18 July 1946, Dulles Papers, Box 19, Peenemünde Raid Folder, Mudd Library, Princeton University. Dulles's reservations about reports of secret weapons in Dulles to OSS, 28 May 1943, NA RG 226, Entry 134, Box 307.

Pages 152–53, "Waetjen and Gisevius."

Dwight D. Eisenhower, *Crusade in Europe* (New York, 1948), 260. Dornberger, *V2*, 169. In 1946 American intelligence official Peter M. F. Sichel wrote that the information Schulte had turned over on the German economy had been evaluated highly by the U.S. Army. Sichel to Sorter, 8 November 1946, Justice Department, Silesian-American Corporation Case File.

On Schulte's meeting with Waetjen, information from Dr. Eduard Waetjen.

CHAPTER EIGHT

Pages 155–60, "just been renewed."

Interview Dr. Albrecht Jung. Letter Günter von Poseck. Interview Dr. Eduard Waetjen. See also, Allen Dulles, *Germany's Underground* (New York, 1947), 134, where the incident is described briefly but without the use of Schulte's name. Interviews Ruprecht Schulte and Oskar Schulte. The passport was renewed in October 1943 in Breslau. See Chojnacki affidavit, 19 July 1945, NA RG 84, Zurich Confidential File 1945, 800.

Pages 160–63, "interest in him."

Wolfgang Schulte letter and Swiss border police document in possession of Ruprecht Schulte. Interviews Ruprecht and Oskar Schulte, Dr. Eduard Waetjen.

Pages 163–66, "administration of justice."

Interview and letters Dr. Eduard Waetjen. Much of the story is narrated in documents assembled by Schulte in November 1946. "Dr. Schulte's Pro-Allied Activities," NA RG 84, Zurich Confidential File 1945, 800. On Daufeldt, see Hans Daufeldt File, Berlin Document Center, and Eggen Bericht and postwar interrogation, Schweizerisches Bundesarchiv E 27 9846 and 12 3190.

Page 165, footnote.

Interview Dr. Eduard Waetjen, and Dulles, *Germany's Underground,* 134.

Page 166, "the time being."

On 22 September 1942 von Steiger told the Swiss Parliament that the government could not treat all refugees entering illegally as political refugees. The newcomers, he said, represented a danger to internal order, and legal measures permitting their expulsion had to be applied. Swiss border control would be tightened. The text of this speech is in NA RG 84, Bern Confidential File 1942, 800 Switzerland—Refugees. On Swiss refugee policy generally, Häsler, *Das Boot;* Bonjour, *Geschichte der schweizerischen Neutralität,* VI, 13–44; Interview Dr. Waetjen.

Pages 166–68, "to be involved."

Interview Dr. Eduard Waetjen. On Meisner, see Hans Rudolf Fuhrer, *Spionage gegen die Schweiz* (Frauenfeld, 1982), 110.

Page 167, footnote.

Dulles told Washington about his supposed economic assignment, which he used as a cover, in Bern to Washington, 12 June 1944, NA RG 226, Entry 134, Box 192.

Page 168, "nothing against him."

On Abwehr III, Heinz Höhne, *Canaris* (New York, 1977), 529, 557–58. Interview with Dr. Eduard Waetjen.

Pages 168–71, "to be regularized."

Interviews Ruprecht and Oskar Schulte. Medical certificate in possession of Ruprecht Schulte.

Pages 171–73, "rejoined his battalion,"

Interviews Dr. Alfred Schaefer, Dr. Albrecht Jung, Ruprecht and Oskar Schulte.

Page 173, "services were appreciated."

Interviews Ruprecht Schulte, Dr. Eduard Waetjen, Dr. Albrecht Jung. On the War Cross of Merit, which apparently was awarded in May 1944, see Stauffer to Political Adviser, 3 June 1946, State Department documents in Justice Department, Alien Property Custodian Documents, Silesian-American Corporation Case File.

Page 174, "code name was Jerzy."

On German signal intelligence and Bern, see Wilhelm F. Flicke, "War Secrets in the Ether," 2 vols., copy in Philip Strong Papers, Mudd Library, Princeton, Vol. II, 237–40, 245–49, 315–16, 396. On Firla, see NA RG 242 EAP 173-B-16-12, Himmler Collection, Box 26. On the repercussions of the Toulouse arrest(s), Huppenkothen's undated affidavit on the Polish radio network, NA RG 238, Huppenkothen File.

Pages 174–75, "to the search."

See notes for pages 208–09a. Also on the German decoding of Polish reports, decoded messages in NA RG 242, T-175, R 122/2647255-57; R 404/2926344-45; T-175, R404/2926312-14; R 488/9349114. On Kursk, see Wilhelm F. Flicke, *Agenten funken nach*

Moskau: Sendergruppe 'Rote Drei' (Kreuzlingen, 1954), 337–38. Quote from Flicke, "War Secrets," Vol. II, 316. Huppenkothen's undated affidavit, NA RG 238, Huppenkothen File.

Pages 175–76, "did not fit Schulte."
Huppenkothen's undated affidavit, NA RG 238, Huppenkothen File. Häusler, Heller, and Bruno Urbanski Files, Berlin Document Center. Geschäftsverteilungsplan des Amtes IV, NA RG 319, XE 002783. On Jerzy arrests, NA RG 242, T-175, R 485/9342513-20.

Pages 176–79, "of knowing this."
Bern to OSS, 9 September 1943, NA RG 226, Entry 134, Box 169. Schulte mentioned the September 1943 sending of his real name to London in his curriculum vitae, 25 March 1946, Justice Department Alien Property Custodian Records, Silesian-American Corporation Case File. Heller and Huppenkothen Files, Berlin Document Center. Dulles quote from Bern to OSS, 20 December 1943, NA RG 226, Entry 134, Box 170. The German Postal Censorship Watch List of 21 August 1944 lists Koppelmann as the main figure of Organization "Jersey" [Jerzy] and mentions Schulte and a number of others who were in contact with Koppelmann. See CIA Schulte File. That piece of evidence as well as Huppenkothen's postwar affidavit make it highly probable that the Gestapo had decided on Schulte's guilt by the summer of 1944.
Schulte's postwar account in curriculum vitae, 25 March 1946, United States Department of Justice, Alien Property Custodian Records, Silesian-American Corporation Case File.

CHAPTER NINE

Pages 181–83, "reason for concern."
Interviews Ruprecht Schulte, Dr. Albrecht Jung, Dr. Alfred Schaefer.

Pages 183–84, "an uncomfortable choice."
Set of memoranda on Sherman's Magdeburg project, NA, RG 226, Entry 106, Box 12. Telephone interview with Irving Sherman. It is unclear from the documents just what Schulte was expected to do. Sherman wrote that Schulte would be asked about the most effective way to destroy the refinery. In certain instances in France OSS agents went to the management and "requested" that the plant be put out of action; otherwise the plant would have to be bombed and would be entirely destroyed. The threat worked in some cases, sparing Allied aircraft, men, and materials. "Blackmail Scheme," NA RG 226, Entry 91, Secret Operations War Diary, Vol. 1, pp. 51–52.
It is also unclear whether the Joint Chiefs of Staff were ever formally asked to approve the project, or whether Sherman simply assumed that they would back the proposal. A search of the JCS records

produced nothing on this project, but not everything may be in the records.

Pages 184–88, "the sole author."

Eduard Schulte, "Gutachten betreffend die grundlegende Behandlung der deutschen wirtschaftlichen Nachkriegsprobleme einschliesslich konkreter Vorschläge zu den wichtigsten Wirtschafts-Komplexen," possession of Ruprecht Schulte. CIA Schulte File. On Andreae, interview with Dr. H. Rathenau, New York.

Pages 188–90, "Homer into German."

Interviews with Dr. Eduard Waetjen. CIA Waetjen File, courtesy of Dr. Klemens von Klemperer. On Waetjen supplying Dulles with information about the planned coup against the Nazi regime, see for example, Dulles to OSS, 6 April 1944, NA RG 226, Entry 134, Box 228, Breakers January–March 1944.

Page 190, "of the war."

Bern to OSS, 22 February 1944, NA RG 226, Entry 134, Box 169. The fact that Schulte was the unnamed industrialist who made the suggestions that Dulles endorsed and passed on to Washington is revealed in the CIA Schulte File. On Schulte's suggestion of an advisory personnel committee, see Bern to OSS, 14 August 1944, NA RG 226, Entry 134, Box 169, and CIA Schulte File.

Pages 190–91, "such as Schulte."

Bern to OSS, undated, no. 4498–4500 [approximately 15 August 1944], NA RG 226, Entry 134, Box 277; OSS Washington's response, 19 August 1944, ibid.

Pages 191–95, "to be frustrated."

On Schulte's illness, E. O. Sowerwine to Robert F. Kelley, 19 October 1945, SEC Exhibit 33, Proceedings for the Reorganization of the Silesian-American Corporation, United States Court of Appeals for the Second Circuit, 26 December 1950, copy in Anaconda Copper Mining Corporations Records, Atlantic Richfield Company Corporate Archives. Also interview Ruprecht Schulte.

Schulte and Riegner: Interview with Dr. Gerhart Riegner. End of the war and Giesche: interview with Dr. Albrecht Jung. The authors are grateful to Mrs. Cordelia Hood and Mrs. Charlotte Stone (Hasenclever), who worked with Emmy Rado, for the information about her. Her office in New York was at 270 Madison Avenue, and her activities were later reported in various sensationalized accounts, such as Elizabeth P. MacDonald. *Undercover Girl* (New York, 1947), 248–53. Freud once complimented Sandor Rado highly, but this did not prevent an estrangement between them in later years.

On Ruprecht Schulte, interviews with Ruprecht Schulte; also American Consulate General, Zurich to Visa Division, 22 July 1946: Visa Case of Ruprecht Franz Hubertus Schulte, NA RG 84, Zurich Confidential File 1946, 811.11.

Office of Strategic Services Mission for Germany, "German Government Personnel," 6 August 1945, NA RG 226, XL 22686.

CHAPTER TEN

Pages 197–203, "production to resume."
Information from Melvin Lasky and A. Hauschner. There is an excellent rendering of Berlin's atmosphere in Wolfgang Staudte's film *Die Mörder sind unter uns* (1946). For Schulte's attitudes, his 1944 manuscript and information from Ruprecht Schulte and Dr. Arthur Burkhardt.

Pages 203–04, "Allied Control Council."
Breakfast remark quoted by General Clay, according to John H. Backer, *Winds of History: The German Years of Lucius DuBignon Clay* (New York, 1983), 54. Details of Building C in RG 260, Economics Division, Box 21, Folder 17/8302 (28), 322-2. Listing of Schulte as a consultant in NA RG 260, Economics Division, Box 20, Folder 17/8302 (15), 320.4 (1945). Schulte's 1944 treatise given to Colonel Boyd and Major Demuth, Schulte's curriculum vitae, 25 March 1946, Justice Department, Alien Property Custodian Records, Silesian-American Corporation Case File. See Schulte's April 1946 memorandum, in NA RG 260, Economics Division, Box 134, 3/134-1, 32-2. Gaethke's recommendation to Legal Advisers, Industry Branch, 31 January 1946, Justice Department, Alien Property Custodian Records, Silesian-American Corporation Case File.

Schulte's nomination in Colonel James Boyd to Director, Economics Division, 26 October 1945, NA RG 260, Transition Files, Box 10, Folder Civilian Personnel October-December 1945.

Page 204, "the American zone."
Thilo Vogelsang, "Die Bemühungen um eine deutsche Zentralverwaltung 1945/46," *Vierteljahrshefte für Zeitgeschichte* 18 (1970): 512–17.

Pages 204–05, "the truthful ones."
Backer, *Winds of History,* 63. Conrad F. Latour and Thilo Vogelsang, *Okkupation und Wiederaufbau: Die Tätigkeit der Militärregierung in der amerikanischen Besatzungszone Deutschlands 1944–1947* (Stuttgart, 1973), 134–35.

Page 206, "to suspect everybody."
Special Branch Subsection of Public Safety: Proposed Organization and Procedure, undated, NA RG 260, Civil Administration Division, Public Safety Branch, Folder 15/108-2/1. Statistics in NA RG 260, Civil Administration Division, Box 429, Public Safety Branch Folder 15/120-3/4, 100.

Pages 206–07, "two unfavorable categories."

Latour and Vogelsang, *Okkupation,* 134–35. See for example, Statistical Report on the Results of Implementation of Control Council Directive No. 24 in the Four Zones of Occupation of Germany and in the Sectors of the City of Berlin, 1 January–30 June 1946, NA RG 260, Civil Administration Division, Box 429, Folder 15/120-3/4, 100. Special Branch Subsection of Public Safety: Proposed Organization and Procedure, undated, NA RG 260, Civil Administration Division, Public Safety Branch, Folder 15/108-2/1.

Pages 207–08, "three occupying powers."

7 July 1945 order in Dulles to Lt. Col. Howard Jones, 30 Sept. 1945, NA RG 84, Zurich Confidential File 1945, 800. Dulles to American Consulate Zurich, 5 July 1946 [should read 5 July 1945], NA RG 84, American Consulate Zurich 1946, Box 2397, 811.11-867.7. Information on Darling from Ruprecht Schulte. The fact that Schulte's employment was limited to the Industry Branch is indicated by Boyd to Director, Economics Division, 26 October 1945, NA RG 260, OMGUS Transition Files, Box 10, Civilian Personnel October-December 1945. We were unable to locate Schulte's Fragebogen Action Sheet, but the fact that on 3 November 1945 Public Safety gave him a designation of "No Evidence of Nazi Activity" is stated in Major Haakon Limdjord's Memorandum for File, 9 June 1947, Army Intelligence Investigative Records, Ft. Meade, Md., NA RG 319, indexed under Schulte, Eduard. That the nominees needed spotless records is explained in Thomas B. Stauffer to Colonel Durand, 3 June 1946, Justice Department, Alien Property Custodian Records, Silesian-American Corporation Case File.

Pages 208–09, "undergo minute examination."

Major R. H. Demuth to Working Committee of Denazification Policy Board, 17 December 1945, NA RG 260, Civil Administration Division, Box 307, Folder 15/124-3/16, 102. For the incorrect date on Schulte's appointment, see Colonel H. G. Sheen to A. C. of S., G-2, 21 February 1946, NA RG 319, Schulte, Eduard (Fort Meade Index). For the actual date of Schulte's appointment as *Wehrwirtschaftsführer,* see Schulte file, Berlin Document Center. On the Nazi take-over of the nominations, see Partei-Kanzlei Rundschreiben Nr. 110/42, 23 July 1942, NA RG 242, T-81, R-1/11952. For the American attitude toward industrialists, NA RG 260, Box 377, Folder 11/17-3/13, Industrialists. General Clay's desire to punish industrialists in C. R. Coleman to Ambassador Murphy and Mr. Steere, 1 April 1946, NA RG 260, Box 673, F. Lists—Personalities, Firms 17/250-1/31. Quote from Gantt to Lyon, Heath, and Sprecher, 9 December 1946, NA RG 238, Entry 203, Box 34, item 6.

Pages 209–11, " 'an active Nazi.' "

Eisenhower/Clay story in letters from Stauffer. Stauffer's view of the Schulte situation especially in Stauffer to Colonel Durand, 3 June 1946, Justice Department, Silesian-American Corporation Case

File. Biographical information and account of meeting with Schulte from letters from Stauffer.

Page 211, "necessary at all."

Curriculum vitae of 25 March 1946, Justice Department, Alien Property Custodian Records, Silesian-American Corporation Case File. Citations and certificates in NA RG 84, Zurich Confidential File 1945, 800. Schulte to Fritts and Schulte to Wilkinson, 16 September 1946; Wilkinson to Schulte, 30 September 1946; Schulte to Urbig, 7 September 1946; copies of all in Justice Department, Alien Property Custodian Records, Silesian-American Corporation Case File.

Pages 211–12, "to be embittered."

Schulte's collection of documents in NA RG 84, Zurich Confidential File 1945, 800. Schulte to Siemon, 6 January 1947, SEC Exhibit 8-H, Reorganization of the Silesian-American Corporation, United States Court of Appeals for the Second Circuit, 26 December 1950, copy in Atlantic Richfield Company Corporate Archive. Dulles to Helms, 15 July 1946, quoted in Helms to Cushing, 10 February 1947, CIA Schulte File.

Pages 212–15, "to the Allies."

See Gaevernitz to Dulles, 22 October 1945, N 524/v. 6, Bundesarchiv-Militärarchiv, Freiburg. Chase Office Memorandum, 25 October 1945, NA RG 84, Bern Confidential File 1945, 800 Germany—Activities of Remnants of Subversive Movement. On Gisevius, interview Dr. Eduard Waetjen, and Klaus Urner, *Der Schweizer Hitler-Attentäter* (Frauenfeld, 1980), 20ff.

Pages 215–17, "Hermann Göring Werke."

On the Russian dismantling of Giesche's Magdeburg plant, see *The Metal Bulletin*, 26 September 1947. The Polish nationalization of Giesche, regarded as German property, occurred in January 1946. See Brief for J. Howard McGrath, Attorney General, Appellant, in the Matter of Silesian-American Corporation, in the United States Court of Appeals for the Second Circuit (case decided 26 December 1950), copy in Justice Department. Alien Property Custodian Records, Silesian-American Corporation Case File, p. 2. (This document, hereafter referred to as Brief, is a relatively good guide through the labyrinth of events, even though it completely misconstrues Schulte's motives.)

The Trading with the Enemy Act allowed the President, through executive order, to regulate foreign exchange transactions and all transactions in the United States involving foreign-owned property. This led to a series of executive orders requiring Treasury Department licenses for certain types of transactions, and the Treasury Department denied a license for the Silesian-American deal three times (July and October 1941, January 1942). Brief, pp. 7–10. Silesian-American Corporation went into receivership.

But Schulte, determined to go ahead, struck the secret deal with the Swiss banks. Empowered with a broad power of attorney, Schulte did not even inform Giesche's *Repräsentanten-Kollegium* (board).

The United States Justice Department later had the gall to contend that this agreement with the Swiss banks was not legal because it was not licensed by the Nazi government, which surely would have executed Schulte if it learned what he was doing!

For the text of the agreement, see Trustee's Exhibit 27, Witness Exhibit 4, Schulte Deposition, Agreement between La Roche and Giesche, 21 August 1942, Proceedings for the Reorganization of the Silesian-American Corporation, United States Court of Appeals for the Second Circuit, 26 December 1950, copy in Atlantic Richfield Company Corporate Archive, Anaconda-SICO Records (hereafter referred to as Court Proceedings). For Schulte's explanation, see Statement of Dr. Eduard Schulte to Lawyers of the Alien Property Custodian, 5 September 1947, Anaconda-SICO Records, Box X-1028, Schulte Folder.

On Schulte and the Göring Werke, see Schulte's affidavit of 25 July 1945 in NA RG 84, Zurich Confidential File 1945, 800. Also interview with Dr. Albrecht Jung; Wilhelm Treue, *Georg von Giesche's Erben 1704–1964* (Hamburg, 1964), 106–08.

Page 217, "the Swiss investors."
I. F. Stone, "When's a German Firm Not German," *P.M.,* 15 November 1946.

Pages 217–19, "on the visa."
Marcel Maliga to Secretary of State, 16 April 1946, NA RG 59, CDF 860C.63 Silesian-American Corporation/4-1646; Acheson to American Legation, Bern, 14 June 1946, copy in Justice Department, Alien Property Custodian Records, Silesian-American Corporation Case File; Consulate General Zurich, Secret memorandum, 27 November 1946, NA RG 84, Zurich Confidential File 1946, 811.11; Hamilton Robinson, State Department, Office of Economic Security Policy, to Donald Cook, Office of Alien Property, Justice Department, 6 December 1946, copy in NA RG 84, Zurich Confidential File 1945, 811.11.

On the visa application, see Woods to Secretary of State, 21 November 1946; Consulate General Zurich, Secret memorandum, 27 November 1946; Legge to Woods, 18 November 1946 regarding Paul Blum's view; all in NA RG 84, Zurich Confidential File 1946, 811.11. Stauffer to the Office of the Director of Political Affairs, 21 November 1946; Office of the Political Adviser to American Legation, Bern, 24 December 1946; American Legation Bern to Office of the Political Adviser, Berlin, 21 January 1947; all in Justice Department, Alien Property Custodian Records, Silesian-American Corporation Case File.

Page 219, "given much weight."
Report Dr. Lothar Siemon to Audits and Investigations Branch, Finance Division, OMGUS, 28 November 1946; Hella Jerchel Affirmation, 28 November 1946; Günther von Poseck Affidavit, 29 November 1946; all in Justice Department, Alien Property Custodian Records, Silesian-American Corporation Case File.

Pages 219–20, "in his resignation."
Dulles to Clayton, 3 December 1946, Allen Dulles Papers, Box 26, Schulte File, Mudd Library, Princeton University. Clayton to Dulles, 9 December 1946, Clayton Papers, Dulles Folder, Harry S. Truman Library. The State Department 22 January 1947 response is missing, but Dulles quotes from State's 7 January 1947 letter to him in his letter of 8 July 1947 to Robert Alexander of the Visa Division, Box 32, Schulte File, Dulles Papers, Mudd Library, Princeton. See also Consulate General Zurich to Secretary of State, 7 February 1947, Zurich Confidential File 1946, 811.11. Schulte to Wilkinson, 24 January 1947, Justice Department, Alien Property Custodian Records, Silesian-American Corporation Case File.

That Schulte was complaining of his treatment is mentioned in Consulate General Zurich to Secretary of State, 7 February 1947, Zurich Confidential File 1946, 811.11.

Pages 220–21, "wanted to hear."
McGrath to Sonnet, 20 February 1947, Justice Department, Alien Property Custodian Records, Silesian-American Corporation Case File. Dr. Arthur Burkhardt letter and interview about the Justice Department's interrogation of Dr. Wolf, which is also mentioned in McGrath to Sonnet, 26 February 1947; McGrath radiogram, 25 February 1947; Connor to Searls, 28 February 1947; Jones to McGrath, 3 April 1947; Abramson to George Searls, 23 July 1947, relaying the State Department's approval of the visa and the new Justice strategies: all in Justice Department, Alien Property Custodian Records, Silesian-American Corporation Case File.

Hughes Memorandum, 15 May 1947, NA RG 260, Office of Director for Intelligence, 004 (1). Hess Memorandum, 15 May 1947, NA RG 260, Box 3, General Correspondence. Schepsis Memorandum to Commanding Officer, 970th Counter Intelligence Corps, 20 May 1947; Deputy Commander Harold Marr, Jr.'s Memorandum of 23 May 1947; NA RG 260, Box 3, General Correspondence. McGrath to Harry LeRoy Jones, 12 August 1947, Justice Department, Alien Property Custodian Records, Silesian-American Corporation Case File.

Statement of Dr. Eduard Schulte to Lawyers of the Alien Property Custodian, 5 September 1947, copy in Anaconda–Silesian-American Records, Box X-1028, Schulte Folder, Atlantic Richfield Corporate Archives. Schulte to Siemon, 4 September 1947, SEC Exhibit 8L, Court Proceedings. McGrath to Harry LeRoy Jones, 13 September 1947, Justice Department, Silesian-American Corporation Case File. For the continuing quest for damaging evidence on Schulte, see Harrison, Litigation Branch, to McGrath, 19 March 1948; Hosiosky to Judge Dougherty, 24 May 1948; Justice Department, Alien Property Custodian Records, Silesian-American Corporation Case File.

Pages 221–22, "generous gesture."
Schulte to Stauffer, 16 and 22 June 1951, in possession of Stauffer. Letters from Thomas B. Stauffer.

Page 222, "a runaway bureaucracy."
"Poland Will Pay $40,000,000 to U.S. to Settle Claims,"
New York Times, 17 July 1960.

Chapter Eleven

Page 223, "gradually disengage himself."
Interviews Dr. Arthur Burkhardt, Dr. O. H. C. Messner,
Günter Schwerin, Dr. Alfred Schaefer, Ruprecht Schulte. Also Eduard
Schulte's letters to Ruprecht Schulte.

Pages 223–27, "he had done."
Information from Ruprecht Schulte. E. Gagliardi, *Alfred
Escher* (Frauenfeld, 1919). Announcement of death in *Neue Zürcher Zei-
tung,* 7 January 1966. Dr. Gerhart Riegner's letter to Mrs. D. Schulte,
Geneva, 10 January 1966.

Pages 231–33, "a bad cause."
Court documents in the possession of Ruprecht Schulte.
Deutsche Juristenzeitung, 20 November 1952.

Archival Sources

RECORDS OF THE AMERICAN GOVERNMENT

United States National Archives

Washington, D.C. Area
Record Group 59, General Records of the Department of State, Central Decimal File.
Record Group 84, Records of the Foreign Service Posts of the Department of State (at Washington National Records Center, Suitland, Maryland).
Record Group 165, Records of the War Department General and Special Staffs (at Wshington National Records Center, Suitland, Maryland), Military Intelligence.
Record Group 226, Office of Strategic Services,
Plain Number Files, L and XL Files
Entry 4, Security Classified Dispatches from Neutral Posts.
Entry 91, London Branch, War Diaries.
Entry 106, Secret Intelligence.
Entry 134, Radio and Cables.
Record Group 238, National Archives Collection of World War II War Crimes Records, Records of the United States Chief of Counsel for War Crimes, Nuremberg, Military Tribunals Relating to German Industrialists.
Record Group 243, Records of the U.S. Strategic Bombing Survey.
Record Group 260, Office of Military Government United States (OMGUS) (at Washington National Records Center, Suitland, Maryland).
Record Group 319, Records of the Army Staff. Includes U.S. Army Intelligence Investigative Records, Fort Meade, Maryland.

Presidential Records at Franklin D. Roosevelt Presidential Library (FDRL), Hyde Park, New York.
Official File
President's Secretary's File
Oscar Cox Papers, at FDRL.
Henry Morgenthau, Jr., Presidential Diaries at FDRL.
War Refugee Board Records, FDRL.

Presidential Records at Harry S. Truman Presidential Library, Independence, Missouri.
Will Clayton Papers at Truman Library.

OTHER AMERICAN GOVERNMENT RECORDS

United States Central Intelligence Agency Records.
United States Department of Justice, Federal Bureau of Investigation Records.
United States Department of Justice, Office of Alien Property Custodian, Silesian-American Corporation Case File.

PRIVATE COLLECTIONS IN THE UNITED STATES

American Jewish Committee Archives, New York City.
Anaconda Copper Mining Corporation Records, Atlantic Richfield Company Corporate Archives, Los Angeles, California.
Anaconda Copper Mining Corporation Records, Montana Historical Society, Helena, Montana.
William J. Donovan Papers at U.S. Army Military History Institute, Carlisle, Pennsylvania.
Allen W. Dulles Papers, Seeley G. Mudd Library, Princeton University, Princeton, New Jersey.
Leland Harrison Papers, Library of Congress.
James G. McDonald Papers, Columbia University School of International Affairs, New York.
George S. Messersmith Papers, University of Delaware.
Philip G. Strong Papers, Seeley G. Mudd Library, Princeton University, Princeton, New Jersey.
Henry A. Wallace Collection, Columbia University Oral History Collection, New York City.
Stephen S. Wise Papers, American Jewish Historical Society, Waltham, Massachusetts.

RECORDS OF NAZI GERMANY

Biographical Records of the Nazi Party, Berlin Document Center.
Miscellaneous Non-Biographic Material (Schumacher Material), Berlin Document Center and United States National Archives, Record Group 242, Microfilm T-580.
Records of the Reich Ministry for Public Enlightenment and Propaganda, copies in United States National Archives, Record Group 242 (hereafter NA RG 242), Microfilm T-70.
Records of Headquarters, German Armed Forces High Command, NA RG 242, T-77.
Record of Headquarters, German Army High Command, NA RG 242, T-78.
Miscellaneous German Records Collection, NA RG 242, T-84.
Records of the German Foreign Ministry and Reich Chancellery, NA RG 242, T-120.
Records of the Reich Leader of the SS and Chief of the German Police, NA RG 242, T-175.
Himmler Collection, NA RG 242, EAP 173-B-16-12/Boxes 1-4.
Amt Ausland/Abwehr, Bundesarchiv-Militärarchiv, Freiburg, Federal Republic of Germany.
Gero von Gaevernitz Papers, Bundesarchiv-Militärarchiv, Freiburg, Federal Republic of Germany.

SWISS GOVERNMENT RECORDS

Intelligence Records and Official Summaries of Records, Schweizerisches Bundesarchiv, Bern.

POLISH GOVERNMENT RECORDS

Studium Polski Podziemnej, London.

JEWISH RECORDS OUTSIDE THE U.S.

A. Leon Kubowitzki Diary, World Jewish Congress Records, London.

Benjamin Sagalowitz Papers, Yad Vashem, Jerusalem.

INTERVIEWS AND CORRESPONDENCE

Dr. Hermann Abs
Nicholas Baer
Mary Bancroft
Mrs. Gerda Bassenge
Dr. Arthur Burkhardt
Dr. Hans Buwert
Dr. Paul Carter
Dr. Gerhard Charig
Degussa A. G.
Dr. Harold Deutsch
Joseph H. Domberger
Wolf von Eckhart
Dr. Lutz Ehrlich
Howard Elting, Jr.
Charles Fenyvesi
Dr. Jonathan Friedmann
Dr. Eugen Gerstenmaier
Dr. Walter Grünfeld
Dr. Katja Guth
W. Averell Harriman
A. Hauschner
Hans Heilsohn
Dr. Thomas Helde
Hans Herwarth von Bittenfeld
Siegmund Hirsch
Mrs. Cordelia Hood
Dr. Albrecht Jung
Dr. Benjamin M. Kahn
David Kahn
Andrew King
Dr. Klemens von Klemperer
Dr. H. R. Kurz
Hans La Roche
Fred Lessing
Ronald Lewin
James M. Markham
Dr. O. H. C. Messner
Ms. Sophia M. Miskiewicz
Dr. Alois Müller

Alois Nagler
Jan Nowak
Dr. Dietrich Orlow
Jules Passweg
The Polish Government-in-Exile
Günter von Poseck
Dr. H. Rathenau
Patrick Reid
Dr. Gerhart M. Riegner
Peter Rosenstein
Michael Rybikowski
Mrs. Lucie Sagal
Mrs. Nina Zafran-Sagalowitz
Dr. Alfred Schaefer
Dr. S. Scheps
Dr. Schudel
Oskar Schulte
Ruprecht Schulte
Günter Schwerin
Irving Sherman
Peter M. F. Sichel
Herman Simon
Leon Sliwinski
Thomas B. Stauffer
Dr. Douglas Steere
Mrs. Marga Stinnes
Mrs. Charlotte Stone
Shepard Stone
Cesare Szulczewski
Dr. J. Treitel
Dr. Wilhelm Treue
Thomas Troy
Dr. Henry Turner
Dr. Hans Tütsch
Dr. K. Urner
Dr. Eduard Waetjen
Dr. Gerhard Weinberg
Mrs. C. Wichmann

Acknowledgments

Many individuals whom we approached went beyond the call of duty to help us search for, and gain access to, documents for this study. John Taylor of the Modern Military Branch in the National Archives provided critical and constant assistance with regard to the OSS records and other relevant holdings; and Lawrence McDonald guided us most efficiently through some recently declassified OSS records. Also in the Modern Military Branch, Director Robert Wolfe, John Mendelsohn, and George Wagner frequently helped us track down relevant material in the captured German records and Nuremberg documents. Sally Marks ably assisted us in the Diplomatic Branch, and David Pfeiffer and Fred Pernell patiently handled our many requests at the Washington National Records Center. It was David Pfeiffer's initiative that turned up a key document for us. Thomas F. Conley, Chief of the Freedom of Information Office at Fort Meade, promptly gave us information from the Army Intelligence files. Director William R. Emerson of the Franklin D. Roosevelt Library provided expert advice on documents, and his staff was of great assistance to us. Dennis Bilger of the Harry S. Truman Library and Gary Cohen of the Manuscript Division of the Library of Congress volunteered their help as well.

Sandra Rozenblad of the Freedom of Information Act Office, Civil Division, Department of Justice, helped us to obtain essential American government records and made her office facilities available. Her assistance was invaluable. Daniel P. Simon, Director of the Berlin Document Center, gave us countless files on individuals connected with Eduard Schulte.

One of the most important collections for us surprisingly turned out to be the Anaconda Copper Mining Corporation Records, now part of the Atlantic Richfield Company Corporate Archives, where Roxanne Burg was unfailingly helpful and made facilities available to us. Also of great value was the Anaconda Collection at the Montana Historical Society, where Ellen H. Arguimbau picked out relevant documents for us. Dr. Richard J. Sommer of the U.S. Army Military History Institute, Carlisle Barracks, Pennsylvania, and Mrs. J. Holliday of the Seeley G. Mudd Manuscript Library, Princeton University, guided us through the important William J. Donovan and Allen W. Dulles collections. Dr. O. Gauye and Dr. Christopher Graf of the Schweizerisches Bundesarchiv, Bern, provided us with official summaries of certain relevant records. Professor Klemens von Klemperer of Smith College made available documents that he had obtained in his own research. Thomas B. Stauffer supplied us with documents and personal information. Sean Moran tracked down some leads for us.

We are also grateful to the director and staff of the Bundesarchiv-Militärarchiv, Freiburg; the Studium Polski Podziemnej, London; the World Jewish Congress, London; Yad Vashem, Jerusalem; the American Jewish Historical Society, Waltham, Massachusetts; and the Manuscript Division, University of Delaware Library.

The number of those who corresponded with us or were interviewed in the course of our research is so great that it is unfortunately impossible to list all of them. A partial list appears at the end of our Archival Sources. Foremost among them is Ruprecht Schulte, without whose constant assistance this book would not have been written. Oskar Schulte, Eduard's younger brother, was equally helpful, and so was Dr. Eduard Waetjen, who at one stage played a crucial role in our story. Dr. Gerhart Riegner's lips are still sealed about the mysterious messenger's identity, but he could not have been more helpful in discussing other aspects of this case.

We had the good luck of having Bob Bender at Simon and Schuster as our editor. His good advice helped us to eliminate many weaknesses in this book. Carol Breitman was an effective critic, rapid typist, and source of moral support in the days when the mysterious messenger's identity was unknown. Julie Moran also served as typist. The American University, Wash-

ington, D.C., provided support for research. The unique materials kept at the Wiener Library, London, were of enormous
help and our thanks are due in particular to Mrs. C. Wichmann, the chief librarian, for having helped us to complete this
book. We are grateful to Adolf Wood who helped us edit the
manuscript.

Index